Arm Assembly Language Programming for Cortex-M3 and Cortex-M4

Using Keil

First Edition

Muhammad Ali Mazidi

Sepehr Naimi

Sarmad Naimi

Naimi & Mazidi books

Copyright © 2019-2022

To contact authors, use the following email addresses:

Sepehr.Naimi@gmail.com

mazidibooks@gmail.com

Visit our websites at

https://NicerLand.com

https://MicroDigitalEd.com

ISBN-13: 978-1-970054-13-2

ISBN-10: 1-970054-13-1

"Regard man as a mine rich in gems of inestimable value. Education can, alone, cause it to reveal its treasures, and enable mankind to benefit therefrom."

Baha'u'llah

Dedication

To the faculty, staff, and students of BIHE university for their dedication and steadfastness.

Table of Contents

Preface

The Arm processor is becoming the dominant CPU architecture in the computer industry. It is already the leading architecture in cell phones and tablet computers. With such a large number of companies producing Arm chips, it is certain that the architecture will move to the laptop, desktop and high-performance computers presently dominated by x86 architecture from Intel and AMD. Currently the PIC and AVR microcontrollers dominate the 8-bit microcontroller market. The Arm architecture will have a major impact in this area too as designers become more familiar with its architecture. This book is intended as an introduction to Arm Assembly programming. To write programs for Arm microcontrollers, you need to know both Assembly and C languages. So, the book covers the Arm Assembly language. However, Chapter 6 contains more advanced topics and you can skip it if you like.

Prerequisites

We assume no prior background in assembly language programming with other CPUs. But we urge you to study Chapter 0 covering the fundamentals of digital systems such as hexadecimal numbers, various types of memory, memory and I/O interfacing, bus designing, and memory address decoding. Chapter 0 is available free of charge on our website (www.NicerLand.com).

Keil tutorials

We have used the Keil Compiler for the programs throughout this book. See our website (www.NicerLand.com and www.MicroDigitalEd.com) for the Keil step-by-step tutorial. You can freely download the Keil IDE and use it for programs which are less than 32KB.

Power Point, Source codes, and other materials

The source codes, lab manuals, and Power points of the book are available on the websites (www.NicerLand.com and www.MicroDigitalEd.com). If you are a professor using this book for a university course you can contact us to receive the solutions to the end-of-chapter problems.

Chapter 1: The History of Arm and Microcontrollers

In Section 1.1 we look at the history of microcontrollers then we introduce some of the available microcontrollers. The history of Arm is provided in Section 1.2.

Section 1.1: Introduction to Microcontrollers

The evolution of Microprocessors and Microcontrollers

In early computers, CPUs were designed using a number of vacuum tubes. The vacuum tube was bulky and consumed a lot of electricity. The invention of transistors, followed by the IC (Integrated Circuit), provided the means to put a CPU on printed circuit boards. The advances in IC technology allowed putting the entire CPU on a single IC chip. This IC was called a *microprocessor*. Some of the microprocessors are the x86 family of Intel used widely in desktop computers, and the 68000 of Motorola. The microprocessors do not contain RAM, ROM, or I/O peripherals. As a result, they must be connected externally to RAM, ROM and I/O, as shown in Figure 1-1.

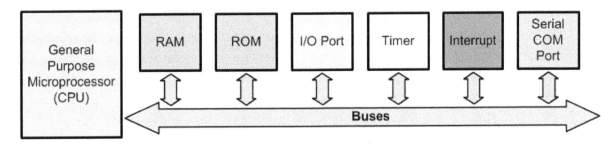

Figure 1-1: A Computer Made by General Purpose Microprocessor

In the next step, the different parts of a system, including CPU, RAM, ROM, and I/Os, were put together on a single IC chip and it was called *microcontroller*. MCU (Micro Controller Unit) is another name used to refer to microcontrollers. Figure 1-2 shows the simplified view of the internal parts of microcontrollers.

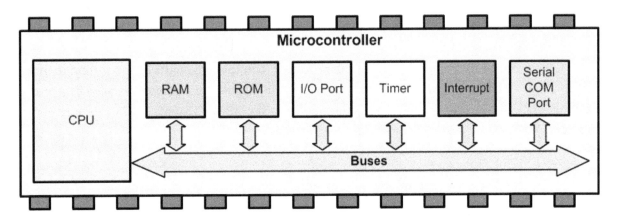

Figure 1-2: Simplified View of the Internal Parts of Microcontrollers (SOC)

Since the microcontrollers are cheap and small, they are widely used in many devices.

Types of Computers

Typically, computers are categorized into 3 groups: desktop computers, servers, and embedded systems.

Desktop computers, including PCs, tablets, and laptops, are general purpose computers. They can be used to play games, read and edit articles, and do any other task just by running the proper application programs. The desktop computers use microprocessors.

In contrast, embedded systems are special-purpose computers. In embedded system devices, the software application and hardware are embedded together and are designed to do a specific task. For example, digital camera, vacuum cleaner, mp3 player, mouse, keyboard, and printer, are some examples of embedded systems. It is interesting to note that embedded systems are the largest class of computers though they are not normally considered as computers by the general public. In most cases embedded systems run a fixed program and contain a microcontroller. But sometimes microcontrollers are inadequate for a task. For this reason, sometimes general-purpose microprocessors are used to design embedded systems. In recent years many manufacturers of general-purpose microprocessors such as Intel, NXP (formerly Motorola), and AMD (Advanced Micro Devices, Inc.) have targeted their microprocessors for the high end of the embedded market. Currently, because of Linux and Windows standardization, in these embedded systems Linux and Windows operating systems are widely used. In many cases, using the operating systems shortens development time because a vast library of software already exists for the Linux and Windows platforms. The fact that Windows and Linux are widely used and well-understood platforms means that developing a Windows-based or Linux-based embedded product reduces the cost and shortens the development time considerably.

Servers are the fast computers which might be used as web hosts, database servers, and in any application in which we need to process a huge amount of data such as weather forecasting. Similar to desktop computers, servers are made of microprocessors but, multiple processors are usually used in each server. Both servers and desktop computers are connected to a number of embedded system devices such as mouse, keyboard, disk controller, Flash stick memory and so on.

Making computers using SoCs

It is becoming common to integrate the processor with the most parts of the system to make a single chip. Such a chip is called an SoC (System on Chip). In recent years, companies have begun to sell Field-Programmable Gate Array (FPGA) and Application-Specific Integrated Circuit (ASIC) libraries for their processors. This makes the production of the new chips easier.

A Brief History of the Processors

In the late 1970s the first processor chips were introduced. In the beginning years of 1980s IBM used the x86 (8088/86, 80286, 80386, 80486, and Pentium) to make their Personal Computers and Apple used the 68xxx (68000, 68010, 68020, etc.) to make their Macintosh PC. Consequently, Intel and Motorola became the dominated the field of microprocessors and also microcontrollers in the 1980s and 1990s. Many embedded systems used Intel's 32-bit chips of x86 (386, 486, Pentium) and Motorola's 32-bit 68xxx for high-end embedded products such as routers. For example, Cisco routers used 68xxx for the CPU. At the low end, the 8051 from Intel and 68HC11 from Motorola were the dominant 8-bit microcontrollers. With the introduction of PIC from Microchip and AVR from Atmel, they became major players in the 8-bit market for microcontroller. At the time of this writing, PIC and AVR are the leaders in terms of volume for 8-bit microcontrollers. In the late 1990s, the Arm microcontroller started to challenge the dominance of Intel and Motorola in the 32-bit market. Although both Intel and Motorola used RISC features to enhance the performance of their microprocessors, due to the need to maintain compatibility with legacy software, they could not make a clean break and start over. Intel used massive amounts of gates to keep up the performance of x86 architecture and that in turn increased the power consumption of the x86 to a level unacceptable for battery-powered embedded products. Meanwhile Motorola streamlined the instructions of the 68xxx CPU and created a new line of microprocessors called ColdFire, while at the same time worked with IBM to design a new RISC processor called PowerPC. While both PowerPC and Coldfire are still alive and being used in the 32-bit market, it is Arm which has become the leading microcontroller in the 32-bit market.

Introduction to some 32-bit microprocessors and microcontrollers

x86: The x86 and Pentium processors are based on the 32-bit architecture of the 386. Although both Intel and AMD are pushing the x86 into the embedded market, due to the high power consumption of these chips, the embedded market has not embraced the x86. Intel is working hard to make a low-power version of the 386 called Atom available for the embedded market.

PIC32: It is based on the MIPS architecture and is getting some attention due to the fact it shares some of the peripherals with the PIC24/PIC18 chips and also using the MPLAB for IDE. Microchip hopes the free MPLAB IDE and engineers' knowledge of the 8-bit PIC will attract embedded developers to the PIC32 as they move to 32-bit systems for their high end embedded products.

ColdFire: The NXP (formerly Freescale, Motorola) is based on the venerable 680x0 (68000, 68010) popular in the 1980s and 1990s. They streamlined the 68000 instructions to make it more RISC-type architecture and is the top seller of 32-bit processors from the Freescale. In recent years Freescale revamped and redesigned the 8-bit HCS08 (from the 6808) to share some of the peripherals with ColdFire and are pushing them under the name Flexis. They hope engineers use the HCS08 at the low-end and move to Coldfire for high-end of the embedded products with minimum learning curve.

PowerPC: This was developed jointly by IBM and Motorola. It was used in the Apple Mac for a few years. Then Apple switched to x86 for a while and currently is using Arm in all their products. Nowadays, both Freescale and IBM market the PowerPC for the high-end of the embedded systems.

How to choose a microcontroller
The following two factors can be important in choosing a microcontroller:

- ***Chip characteristics:*** Some of the factors in choosing a microcontroller chip are clock speed, power consumption, price, and on-chip memories and peripherals.
- ***Available resources:*** Other factors in choosing a microcontroller include the IDE compiler, legacy software, and multiple sources of production.

Review Questions

1. True or false. Microcontrollers are normally less expensive than microprocessors.
2. When comparing a system board based on a microcontroller and a general- purpose microprocessor, which one is cheaper?
3. A microcontroller normally has which of the following devices on-chip?
    (a) RAM   (b) ROM   (c) I/O   (d) all of the above
4. A general-purpose microprocessor normally needs which of the following devices to be attached to it?
    (a) RAM   (b) ROM   (c) I/O   (d) all of the above
5. An embedded system is also called a dedicated system. Why?
6. What does the term "embedded system" mean?
7. Why does having multiple sources of a given product matter?

Section 1.2: The Arm Family History

In this section, we look at the Arm and its history.

A brief history of the Arm

The Arm came out of a company called Acorn Computers in United Kingdom in the 1980s. Professor Steve Furber of Manchester University worked with Sophie Wilson to define the Arm architecture and instructions. The VLSI Technology Corp. produced the first Arm chip in 1985 for Acorn Computers and was designated as Acorn RISC Machine (Arm). Unable to compete with x86 (8088, 80286, 80386, ...) PCs from IBM and other personal computer makers, the Acorn was forced to push the Arm chip into the single-chip microcontroller market for embedded products. That is when Apple Corp. got interested in using the Arm chip for the PDA (personal digital assistants) products. This renewed interest in the chip led to the creation of a new company called Arm (Advanced RISC Machine). This new company bet its entire fortune on selling the rights to this new CPU to other silicon manufacturers and design houses. Since the early 1990s, an ever increasing number of companies have licensed the right to make the Arm chip. See Table 1-1 for the major milestones of the Arm.

Table 1-1: Arm Company milestones (www.Arm.com)
1982
■ Acorn produced a computer for BBC named BBC micro. Good sales of the computer motivated Acorn to decide to make its own microprocessor.
1983
■ Acorn and VLSI began designing the Arm microprocessor.
1985
■ Acorn Computer Group developed the world's first commercial RISC processor. The ARMv1 had 25,000 transistors, and worked with a frequency of 4MHz.

1987

- Acorn's Arm processor debuts as the first RISC processor for low-cost PCs

1989

- Acorn introduced ARMv3 with a frequency of 25MHz. It had a 4KB cache as well.

1990

- Advanced RISC Machines (Arm) spins out of Acorn and Apple Computer's collaboration efforts with a charter to create a new microprocessor standard. VLSI Technology becomes an investor and the first licensee.

1991

- Arm introduced its first embeddable RISC core, the ARM6 solution using ARMv3 architecture.

1992

- GEC Plessey and Sharp licensed Arm technology

1993

- Texas Instruments licensed Arm technology
- Arm introduced the ARM7 core.

1995

- Arm announced the Thumb architecture extension, which gives 32-bit RISC performance at 16-bit system cost and offers industry-leading code density
- Arm launched Software Development Toolkit

1996

- Arm and VLSI Technology introduced the ARM810 microprocessor
- Arm and Microsoft worked together to extend Windows CE to the Arm architecture

1997

- Hyundai, Lucent, Philips, Rockwell and Sony licensed Arm technology

- ARM9TDMI family announced

1998

- HP, IBM, Matsushita, Seiko Epson and Qualcomm licensed Arm technology
- Arm developed synthesizable version of the ARM7TDMI core
- Arm Partners shipped more than 50 million Arm-powered products

1999

- LSI Logic, STMicroelectronics and Fujitsu licensed Arm technology
- Arm announced synthesizable ARM9E processor with enhanced signal processing

2000

- Agilent, Altera, Micronas, Mitsubishi, Motorola, Sanyo, Triscend and ZTEIC licensed Arm technology
- Arm launched SecurCore family for smartcards
- TSMC and UMC became members of Arm Foundry Program

2001

- Arm's share of the 32-bit embedded RISC microprocessor market grew to 76.8 per cent
- Arm announced new ARMv6 architecture
- Fujitsu, Global UniChip, Samsung and Zeevo licensed Arm technology
- Arm acquired key technologies and an embedded debug design team from Noral Micrologics Ltd

2002

- Arm announced that it had shipped over one billion of its microprocessor cores to date
- Arm technology licensed to Seagate, Broadcom, Philips, Matsushita, Micrel, eSilicon, Chip Express and ITRI
- Arm launched the ARM11 micro-architecture
- Arm launches its RealView family of development tools
- Flextronics became the first Arm Licensing Partner program member, allowing it to sub-license Arm technology to its own customers

2004

- The Arm Cortex family of processors, based on the ARMv7 architecture, is announced. The Arm Cortex-M3 is announced in conjunction, as the first of the new family of processors
- Arm Cortex-M3 processor announced, the first of a new Cortex family of processor cores
- MPCore multiprocessor launched, the first integrated multiprocessor
- OptimoDE technology launched, the groundbreaking embedded signal processing core

2005

- Arm acquired Keil Software
- Arm Cortex-A8 processor announced

2007

- Five billionth Arm Powered processor shipped to the mobile device market
- Arm Cortex-M1 processor launched – the first Arm processor designed specifically for implementation on FPGAs
- RealView Profiler for Embedded Software Analysis introduced
- Arm unveils Cortex-A9 processors for scalable performance and low-power designs

2008

- Arm announces 10 billionth processors shipment
- Arm Mali-200 GPU Worlds First to achieve Khronos Open GL ES 2.0 conformance at 1080p HDTV resolution

2009

- Arm announces 2GHz capable Cortex-A9 dual core processor implementation
- Arm launches its smallest, lowest power, most energy efficient processor, Cortex-M0

2010

- Arm launches Cortex-M4 processor for high performance digital signal control
- Arm together with key Partners form Linaro to speed rollout of Linux-based devices
- Microsoft becomes an Arm Architecture Licensee
- Arm & TSMC sign long-term agreement to achieve optimized Systems-on-Chip based on Arm processors, extending down to 20nm
- Arm extends performance range of processor offering with the Cortex-A15 MPCore processor
- Arm Mali becomes the most widely licensed embedded GPU architecture
- Arm Mali-T604 Graphics Processing Unit introduced providing industry-leading graphics performance with an energy-efficient profile

2011

- Microsoft unveils Windows on Arm at CES 2011
- IBM and Arm collaborate to provide comprehensive design platforms down to 14nm
- Arm and UMC extend partnership into 28nm
- Cortex-A7 processor launched
- Big-Little processing announced, linking Cortex-A15 and Cortex-A7 processors
- ARMv8 architecture unveiled at TechCon
- AMP announce license and plans for first ARMv8-based processor
- Arm Mali-T658 GPU launched

- Arm expands R&D presence in Taiwan with Hsinchu Design Center
- Arm and Avnet launch Embedded Software Store (ESS)
- Arm, Cadence and TSMC tape out first 20nm Cortex-A15 multicore processor

2012

- Arm, Gemalto and G&D form joint venture to deliver next-generation mobile security
- First Windows RT (Windows on Arm) devices revealed
- Arm, AMD, Imagination, MediaTek and Texas Instruments founding members of Heterogeneous System Architecture (HAS) Foundation
- Arm and TSMC work together on FinFET process technology for next-generation 64-bit Arm processors
- Arm forms first UK forum to create technology blueprint "Internet of Things" devices
- Arm named one of Britain's Top Employers
- MIT Technology Review named Arm in its list of 50 Most Innovative Companies

Currently the Arm Corp. receives its entire revenue from licensing the Arm to other companies since it does not own state of the art chip fabrication facility. This business model of making money from selling IP (intellectual property) has made Arm one of the most widely used CPU architectures in the world. Unlike Intel or Freescale who define the architecture and fabricate the chip, hundreds of companies who have licensed the Arm IP feel a level playing field when it comes to competing with the originator of the chip.

Arm and Apple

When Steve Jobs came back to run the Apple in 1996, the company was in decline. It had lost the personal computer race that had started 20 years earlier. The introduction of iPod in 2001 changed the fortune of that company more than anything else. Apple had tried to sell a PDA called Newton in the 1990s but was not successful. The Newton was using the Arm processor and it was too early for its time. The iPod used an enhanced version of Arm called ARM7 and became an instant success. iPod brought the attention to the Arm chip that it deserved. Since then Apple has been using the Arm chip in iPhones and iPads. Today, the Arm microcontroller is the CPU of choice for designing cell phone and other hand-held devices. In the future, Arm will make further in-roads into the tablet and laptop PC market now that Microsoft Corp has introduced the Arm version of its Windows operating system.

Arm family variations

Although the ARM7 family is the most widely used version, Arm is determined to push the architecture into the low end of the microcontroller market where 8- and 16-bit microcontrollers have been traditionally dominating. For this reason, they have come up with a microcontroller version of Arm called Cortex. As we will see in future chapters, the Cortex family of Arm microcontrollers maintains compatibility with the ARM7 without sacrificing performance. The Arm architecture is also being pushed into high-performance systems where multicore chips such as Intel Xeon dominate.

Figure 1-3 shows some of the most widely used Arm processors. It should be emphasized that we cannot use the terms Arm family and Arm architecture interchangeably. For example, ARM11 family is based on ARMv6 architecture and ARMv7A is the architecture of Cortex-A family.

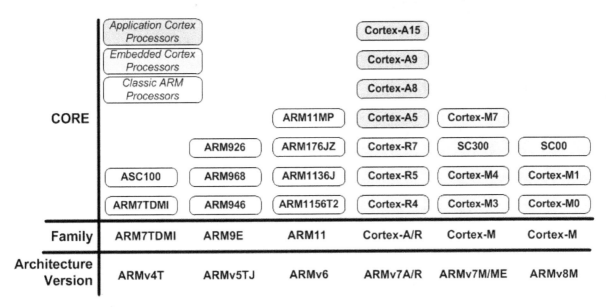

Figure 1-3: Arm Family and Architecture

One CPU, many peripherals

Arm has defined the details of architecture, registers, instruction set, memory map, and timing of the Arm CPU and holds the copyright to it. The various design houses and semiconductor manufacturers license the IP (intellectual property) for the CPU and can add their own peripherals as they please. It is up to the licensee (design houses and semiconductor manufactures) to define the details of peripherals such as I/O ports, serial port UART, timer, ADC, SPI, DAC, I2C, and so on. As a result, while the CPU instructions and architecture are the same across all the Arm chips made by different vendors, their peripherals are not compatible. That means if you write a program for the serial port of an Arm chip made by TI (Texas Instrument), the program might not necessarily run on an Arm chip sold by NXP. This is the only drawback of the Arm microcontroller. The good news is that the manufacturers do provide peripheral libraries or tools for their chips and make the job of programming the peripherals much easier. For example, ST Micro has the Cube, TI has the TivaWare for Tiva series devices, and Freescale (now part of NXP) has Processor Expert,. Figure 1-4 shows the Arm simplified block diagram and Table 1-2 provides a list of some Arm vendors.

Actel	Analog Devices	Atmel (now Microchip)
Broadcom	Cypress	Ember
Dust Networks	Energy	Freescale
Fujitso	Nuvoton	NXP
Renesas	Samsung	ST
Toshiba	Texas Instruments	Triad Semiconductor

Table 1-2: Arm Vendors

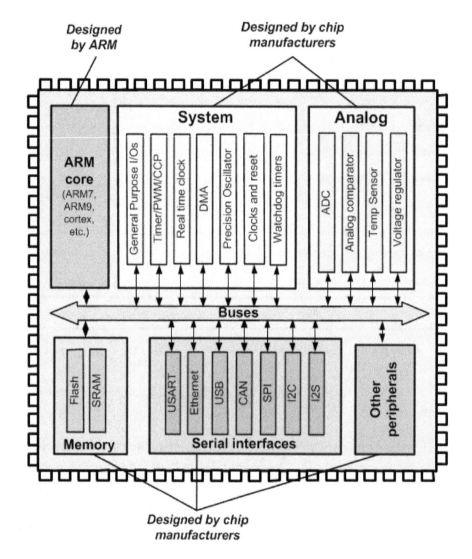

Figure 1-4: Arm Simplified Block Diagram

Review Questions

1. True or false. The Arm CPU instructions are universal regardless of who makes the chip.
2. True or false. The peripherals of Arm microcontroller are standardized regardless of who makes the chip.
3. An Arm microcontroller normally has which of the following devices on-chip?
   (a) RAM   (b) Timer   (c) I/O   (d) all of the above

4. For which of the followings, Arm has defined standard?
   (a) RAM size   (b) ROM size   (c) instruction set   (d) all of the above

Problems

Section 1.1: Introduction to Microcontrollers

1. True or False. A general-purpose microprocessor has on-chip ROM.
2. True or False. Generally, a microcontroller has on-chip ROM.
3. True or False. A microcontroller has on-chip I/O ports.
4. True or False. A microcontroller has a fixed amount of RAM on the chip.
5. What components are usually put together with the microcontroller onto a single chip?
6. List three embedded products attached to a PC.
7. Give the name and the manufacturer of some of the most widely used 8-bit microcontrollers.
8. In Question 7, which of them sell most?
9. Name some 32-bit microcontrollers.
10. In a battery-based embedded product, what is the most important factor in choosing a microcontroller?
11. In an embedded controller with on-chip ROM, why does the size of the ROM matter?

Section 1.2: The Arm Family History

12. What does Arm stand for?
13. True or false. In Arm, architectures have the same names as families.
14. True or false. In 1990s, Arm was widely used in microprocessor world.
15. True or false. Arm is widely used in Apple products, like iPhone and iPod.
16. True or false. All Arm chips have standard instructions.
17. True or false. All Arm chips have the same peripherals
18. True or false. The Arm corp. also manufactures the Arm chip.
19. True or false. The Arm IP must be licensed from Arm corp.
20. True or false. A given serial communication program is written for TI Arm chip. It should work without any modification on NXP Arm chip
21. True or false. At the present time, Arm has just one manufacturer.
22. What is the difference between the Arm products of different manufacturers?

Answers to Review Questions

Section 1.1

1. True
2. A microcontroller-based system
3. d
4. d
5. It is dedicated because it does only one type of job.
6. Embedded system means that the application (software) and the processor (hardware such as CPU and memory) are embedded together into a single system.
7. Having multiple sources for a given part means you are not hostage to one supplier. More importantly, competition among suppliers brings about lower cost for that product.

Section 1.2

1. True
2. False
3. d
4. c

Chapter 2: Arm Architecture and Assembly Language Programming

CPUs use registers to store data temporarily and most of the operations involve the registers. To program in assembly language, we must understand the registers of a given CPU and the role they play in processing data. In Section 2.1 we look at the registers of the Arm CPU. We demonstrate the use of registers with simple instructions such as MOV and ADD. Memory map and memory access of the Arm are discussed in Sections 2.2 and 2.3, respectively. In Section 2.4 we discuss the status register's flag bits and how they are affected by arithmetic instructions. In Section 2.5 we look at some widely used assembly language directives, pseudo-instruction, and data types related to the Arm. Section 2.6 discusses the memory allocation. In Section 2.7 we examine assembly language and machine language programming. The process of assembling and creating a ready-to-run program for the Arm is discussed in Section 2.8. Step-by-step execution of an Arm program and the role of the program counter are examined in Section 2.9. Section 2.10 examines some Arm addressing modes. The Pipeline and RISC architecture are examined in Sections 2.11 and 2.12.

Section 2.1: The General-Purpose Registers in the Arm

In the CPU, registers are used to store information temporarily. That information could be a piece of data to be processed, or an address pointing to the data to be fetched. Arm microcontrollers have 16 registers for arithmetic and logic operations. See Figure 2-2. All of the registers are 32-bit wide. The 32 bits of a register are shown in Figure 2-1. These range from the MSB (most-significant bit) D31 to the LSB (least-significant bit) D0. With a 32-bit data type, any data larger than 32 bits must be broken into 32-bit chunks before it is processed. Although the Arm default data size is 32-bit, some instructions also support the single bit, 8-bit, and 16-bit data types, as we will see in future chapters. In Arm, the 32-bit data size is often referred as "word" and the 16-bit data is referred to as half-word. Therefore, Arm supports byte, half-word (two bytes), and word (four bytes) data types.

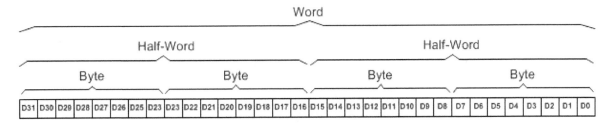

Figure 2-1: Arm Registers Data Size

To understand the use of the registers, we will show it in the context of some simple instructions.

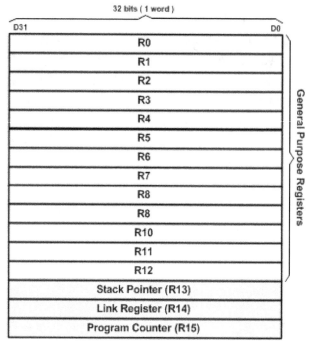

Figure 2-2: Arm Registers

MOV instruction

Simply stated, the MOV instruction copies data into register from register to register or from an immediate value. It has the following formats:

```
MOV      Rn, Op2      ; load Rn register with Op2 (Operand2)
                      ; Op2 can be an immediate value
```

Op2 can be a register Rm. Rn or Rm are any of the registers R0 to R15. Op2 can also be an immediate value.

Immediate value is a literal constant encoded in the instruction. In the Arm data processing instructions, the immediate value is an 8-bit value that can be 0–255 in decimal, (00–FF in hex). An immediate value is preceded by a '#' in the instruction.

The following instruction loads R5 with the value of R7.

```
MOV R5, R7           ; copy contents of R7 into R5 (R5 = R7)
```

The following instruction loads the R2 register with a value of 25 (decimal).

```
MOV R2, #25          ; load R2 with 25 (R2 = 25)
```

The following instruction loads the R1 register with the value 0x87 (87 in hex).

```
MOV R1, #0x87        ; copy 0x87 into R1 (R1 = 0x87)
```

Notice the order of the source and destination operands. As you can see, the MOV loads the right operand into the left operand. In other words, the destination register is written first in the instruction.

To write a comment in assembly language we use '; '. It is similar to the use of '//' in C language, which causes the remainder of the line to be ignored by the assembler. For instance, in the above examples the words after '; ' were written to explain the functionality of the instructions to the human reader, and do not have any effects on the execution of the instructions.

When programming the registers of the Arm microcontroller with an immediate value, the following points should be noted:

1. A '#' sign is written in front of an immediate value.
2. If we want to specify an immediate number in hexadecimal, a '0x' is put between '#' and the number, otherwise the number is treated as decimal. For example, in "MOV R1, #50", R1 is loaded with 50 in decimal, whereas in "MOV R1, #0x50", R1 is loaded with 50 in hex (80 in decimal).
3. Eight bits are moved into a 32-bit register, and the remaining 24 bits are loaded with all zeros. For example, in "MOV R1, #0xA5" the result will be R1 = 0x000000A5; that is, R1 = 00000000000000000000000010100101 in binary.
4. If an immediate value cannot be represented by an 8-bit value with even number bits of right rotate, the assembler will flag it as a syntax error.

LDR pseudo-instruction

We stated loading a register with MOV immediate value is limited to an 8-bit value. So the valid immediate values are limited. What do we do if we need to load a value that is not a legal immediate value of the MOV instruction? The Arm assembler provides us a pseudo-instruction of "LDR Rd, =32-bit_immediate_value" to load any 32-bit value into a register. We will examine how this pseudo-instruction works in Chapter 6. For now, just notice the '=' sign used in the syntax. The following pseudo-instruction loads R7 with 0x11223344.

```
LDR    R7, =0x11223344
```

We will use this pseudo-instruction to load 32-bit value into register extensively throughout the book. Some assembler such as Keil Arm Assembler, will replace the LDR pseudo-instruction with a MOV instruction if the immediate value fits a MOV instruction.

ADD instruction

The ADD instruction has the following format:

```
ADD    Rd, Rn, Op2 ; ADD Op2 to Rn and store the result in Rd
                    ; Op2 can be immediate value or Register Rm
```

The ADD instruction tells the CPU to add the value of Op2 to Rn and put the result into the Rd (destination) register. As we mentioned before, Op2 can be an immediate value or a register Rm. To add two numbers such as 0x25 and 0x34, one can do any of the following:

```
MOV    R1, #0x25    ; copy 0x25 into R1 (R1 = 0x25)
MOV    R7, #0x34    ; copy 0x34 into R1 (R7 = 0x34)
ADD    R5, R1, R7   ; add value R7 to R1 and put it in R5
                    ; (R5 = R1 + R7)
```

or

```
MOV    R1, #0x25        ; load (copy) 0x25 into R1 (R1 = 0x25)
ADD    R5, R1, #0x34    ; add 0x34 to R1 and put it in R5
                        ; (R5 = R1 + 0x34)
```

Executing the above lines results in R5 = 0x59 (0x59 = 0x25 + 0x34).

Figure 2-3 shows the general purpose registers (GPRs) and the ALU in Arm. The effect of arithmetic and logic operations on the status register will be discussed in Section 2.4. In Table 2-1 you see some of the Arm ALU instructions.

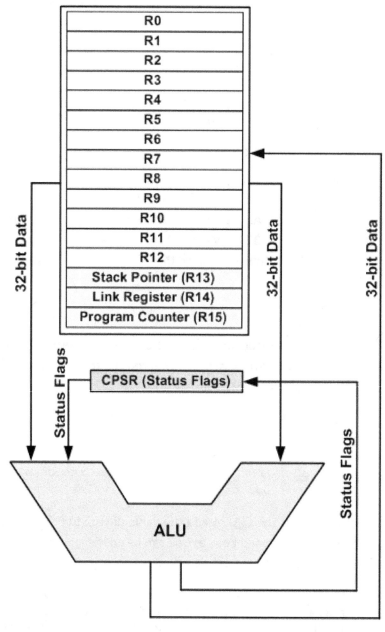

Figure 2-3: Arm Registers and ALU

Instruction		Description
ADD	Rd, Rn,Op2*	ADD Rn to Op2 and place the result in Rd
ADC	Rd, Rn,Op2	ADD Rn to Op2 with Carry and place the result in Rd
AND	Rd, Rn,Op2	AND Rn with Op2 and place the result in Rd
BIC	Rd, Rn,Op2	AND Rn with NOT of Op2 and place the result in Rd
CMP	Rn,Op2	Compare Rn with Op2 and set the status bits of CPSR**
CMN	Rn,Op2	Compare Rn with negative of Op2 and set the status bits
EOR	Rd, Rn,Op2	Exclusive OR Rn with Op2 and place the result in Rd
MVN	Rd,Op2	Store the negative of Op2 in Rd
MOV	Rd,Op2	Move (Copy) Op2 to Rd
ORR	Rd, Rn,Op2	OR Rn with Op2 and place the result in Rd
RSB	Rd, Rn,Op2	Subtract Rn from Op2 and place the result in Rd
RSC	Rd, Rn,Op2	Subtract Rn from Op2 with carry and place the result in Rd
SBC	Rd, Rn,Op2	Subtract Op2 from Rn with carry and place the result in Rd
SUB	Rd, Rn,Op2	Subtract Op2 from Rn and place the result in Rd
TEQ	Rn,Op2	Exclusive-OR Rn with Op2 and set the status bits of CPSR
TST	Rn,Op2	AND Rn with Op2 and set the status bits of CPSR
*	*Op2 can be an immediate 8-bit value #K which can be 0–255 in decimal, (00–FF in hex). Op2 can also be a register Rm. Rd, Rn and Rm are any of the general purpose registers*	
**	*CPSR is discussed later in this chapter*	
***	*The instructions are discussed in detail in the next chapters*	

Table 2-1: ALU Instructions Using GPRs

SUB instruction

The SUB instruction is like ADD instruction format. It subtracts Op2 from Rn and put the result in Rd (destination).

```
SUB    Rd, Rn, Op2      ; Rd = Rn - Op2
```

To subtract two numbers such as 0x34 and 0x25, one can do the following:

```
MOV    R1, #0x34       ; load 0x34 into R1 (R1 = 0x34)
SUB    R5, R1, #0x25   ; R5 = R1 - 0x25 (R5 = 0x34 - 0x25)
```

The Special Function Registers in Arm

In Arm the R13, R14, R15, and CPSR (current program status register) registers are called *SFRs (special function registers)* since each one is dedicated to a specific function. The function of each SFR is fixed by the CPU designer at the time of design because it is used for control of the microcontroller or keeping track of specific CPU status. The four SFRs of R13, R14, R15, and CPSR play extremely important roles in the systems with Arm CPU. The R13 is set aside for stack pointer. The R14 is designated as link register which holds the return address when the CPU calls a subroutine and the R15 is the program counter (PC). The CPSR (current program status register) is used for keeping condition flags among other things, as we will see in Section 2.4. In contrast to SFRs, the General-Purpose Registers (R0-R12) do not have any specific function and are used for storing data or as a pointer to the memory.

Program Counter in the Arm

One of the most important register in the Arm CPU is the PC (program counter). As we mentioned earlier, the R15 is the program counter. The program counter is used by the CPU to point to the address of the next instruction to be executed. As the CPU fetches the opcode from the program memory, the program counter is incremented automatically to point to the next instruction. The more bits the program counter has, the more memory locations a CPU can access. A 32-bit program counter can access a maximum of 4 gigabytes (2^{32} = 4G) of program memory locations.

Review Questions

1. Write instructions to move the value 0x34 into the R2 register.
2. Write instructions to add the values 0x16 and 0xCD. Place the result in the R1 register.
3. True or false. No value can be moved directly into the GPRs.
4. The GPR registers in Arm are _____-bit.
5. The R13-R15 registers are called _____.
6. The SFR registers in Arm are _____ -bit.

Section 2.2: The Arm Memory Map

In this section we discuss the memory map for Arm family members.

Memory mapped I/O in the Arm

Some of the CPU designs have two distinct spaces: the I/O space and memory space. In the Arm CPU we have only one space and it is memory space and it can be as high as 4 gigabytes. The Arm uses these 4 gigabytes for both memory and I/O space. This mapping of the I/O ports to memory space is called memory mapped I/O and was discussed in Chapter 0 on the website. This 4 gigabytes of memory space can be allocated to on-chip or off-chip memory.

Memory space allocation in Arm Microcontrollers

See Figure 2-4; the memory space of most Arm microcontrollers have 3 on-chip sections:

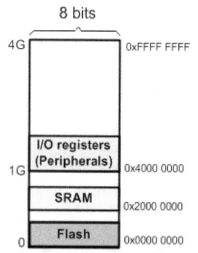

Figure 2-4: Memory Map in most Arm Microcontrollers

26

1. **I/O registers (Peripherals):** This area is dedicated to registers of peripherals such as timers, serial communication, ADC, and so on. The function and address location of each register is fixed by the chip vendor at the time of design. The number of locations set aside for registers depend on the pin numbers and peripheral functions supported by that chip. That number can vary from chip to chip even among members of the same family from the same vendor. Due to the fact that Arm does not define the type and number of I/O peripherals one must not expect to have same address locations for the peripheral registers among various devices.

2. **On-chip SRAM:** The SRAM space is used for data variables and stack and is accessed by the microcontroller instructions. The Arm microcontrollers' SRAM size ranges from 2K bytes to several thousand kilobytes depending on the chip. Even within the same family, the size of the SRAM space varies from chip to chip. Although in many of the Arm microcontrollers embedded systems the SRAM is used only for data; one can also design an Arm-based system in which the RAM is used for both data and program codes.

3. **On-chip Flash ROM:** A block of memory from a few kilobytes to megabytes is set aside for flash ROM. The flash ROM is used to store the program code. The memory can also be used for storage of static data such as text strings and look-up tables. The amount and the location of the Flash ROM space vary from chip to chip in the Arm products. See Table 2-2 and Examples 2-1 and 2-2.

Company	Device	Flash (K Bytes)	RAM (K Bytes)
Atmel	AT91SAM7X512	512	128
ST	STM32F103RB	128	20
TI	MSP432P401RIPZ	256	64
NXP (Freescale)	KL25Z128VLK4	128	16

Table 2-2: On-chip Memory Size for some Arm Chips

Arm-based Motherboards (Case Study)

In Arm systems for Microsoft Windows, Unix, and Android operating systems the Arm motherboards use DRAM for the RAM memory, just like the x86 and Pentium PCs. As the Arm CPU is pushed into the laptop, desktop, and tablets PCs, and the high end of embedded systems products such as routers, we will see the use of DRAM as primary memory to store both the operating systems and the applications. In such systems, the Flash memory will be holding the POST (power on self-test), BIOS (basic Input/output systems) and boot programs. Just like x86 system, such systems have both on-chip and off-chip high speed SRAM for cache. Currently, there are Arm chips on the market with some on-chip Flash ROM, SRAM, and memory decoding circuitry for connection to external (off-chip) memory. This off-chip memory can be SRAM, Flash, or DRAM. The datasheet for such Arm chips provide the details of memory map for both on-chip and off-chip memories. Next, we examine the Arm buses and memory access.

Example 2-1

A given Arm chip has the following address assignments. Calculate the space and the amount of memory given to each section.

(a) Address range of 0x20000000 – 0x20007FFF for SRAM

(b) Address range of 0x00000000 – 0x0007FFFF for Flash

(c) Address range of 0xFFFC0000 – 0xFFFFFFFF for peripherals

Solution:

(a) With address space of 0x20000000 to 0x20007FFF, we have 40007FFF – 40000000 + 1 = 8000 bytes. Converting 8000 hex to decimal, we get 32,768, which is equal to 32K bytes.

(b) With address space of 0x00000000 to 0x0007FFFF, we have 7FFFF – 0 + 1= 80000 bytes. Converting 80000 hex to decimal, we get 524,288, which is equal to 512K bytes.

(c) With address space of 0xFFFC0000 to 0xFFFFFFFF, we have FFFFFFFF–FFFC0000 + 1 = 40000 bytes. Converting 40000 hex to decimal, we get 262,144, which is equal to 256K bytes.

Example 2-2

Find the address space range of each of the following memory of an Arm chip:
(a) 2 KB of peripherals starting at address 0x50000000
(b) 16 KB of SRAM starting at address 0x20000000
(c) 64 KB of Flash ROM starting at address 0x00000000

Solution:

(a) With 2K bytes of peripheral memory, we have 2048 bytes (2 × 1024 = 2048). This maps to address locations of 0x50000000 to 0x500007FF.
(b) With 16K bytes of on-chip SRAM memory, we have 16,384 bytes (16 × 1024 = 16,384), and 16,384 locations gives 0x20000000–0x20003FFF.
(c) With 64K we have 65,536 bytes (64 × 1024 = 65,536), therefore, the memory space is 0x00000000 to 0x0000FFFF.

Review Questions
1. True or false. I/O registers are located in memory space in Arm microcontrollers.
2. What is the use of Flash memory in Arm microcontrollers?

Section 2.3: Load and Store Instructions in Arm

The instructions we have used so far worked with the immediate value and the content of registers. They also used the registers as their destination. We saw simple examples of using MOV, ADD, and SUB earlier in Section 2.1. This section discusses the instructions for accessing the data memory. Since these instructions either load the register with data from memory or store the data in the register to the memory, they are called the load/store instructions.

LDR Rd, [Rx] instruction

```
LDR    Rd,[Rx]        ; load Rd with the contents of location pointed
                      ; to by Rx register. Rx contains an address between
                      ; 0x00000000 to 0xFFFFFFFF
```

The LDR instruction tells the CPU to load (read in) one word (32-bit or 4 bytes) of data from a memory location pointed to by Rx to the register Rd. Since each memory location can hold only one byte (Arm is a byte addressable CPU), and the CPU registers are 32-bit wide, the LDR will bring in 4 bytes of data from 4 consecutive memory locations. The locations can be in the SRAM, a Flash memory or I/O registers. For example, the "LDR R2, [R5]" instruction copies the contents of memory locations pointed to by R5 into register R2. Since the R2 register is 32-bit wide, it expects a 32-bit operand in the range of 0x00000000 to 0xFFFFFFFF. That means the R5 register gives the base address of the memory in which it holds the data. Therefore, if R5=0x80000, the CPU will fetch into register R2 the contents of memory locations 0x80000, 0x80001,0x80002, and 0x80003.

The following instructions loads R7 with the contents of location 0x20000200. See Figure 2-5.

```
LDR    R5,=0x40000200    ; R5 = 0x40000200
LDR    R7, [R5]          ; load R7 with the contents of memory locations
                         ; 0x20000200-0x20000203
```

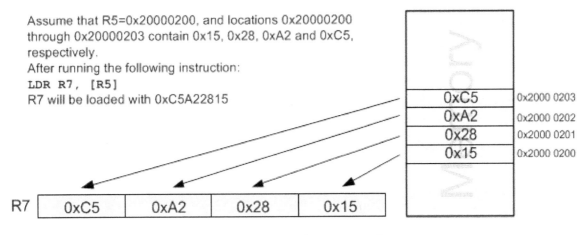

Figure 2-5: Executing the LDR Instruction

```
STR    Rx,[Rd]        ; store register Rx into locations pointed to by Rd
```

The STR instruction tells the CPU to store (copy) the contents of a CPU register to a memory location pointed to by the Rd register. Notice that the source register of STR instruction is placed before the destination register. Obviously since CPU registers are 32-bit wide (4-byte) we need four consecutive memory locations to store the contents of the register. The memory locations must be writable such as SRAM or I/O registers. See Figure 2-6. The "STR R3, [R6]" instruction will copy the contents of R3 into locations pointed to by R6, the locations 0x20000200 through 0x20000203 in the SRAM memory.

The following instruction stores the contents of R5 into locations pointed to by R1. Assume 0x40000340 is held by register R1.

```
                         ; assume R1 = 0x40000340
    STR    R5, [R1]      ; store R5 into locations pointed to by R1.
```

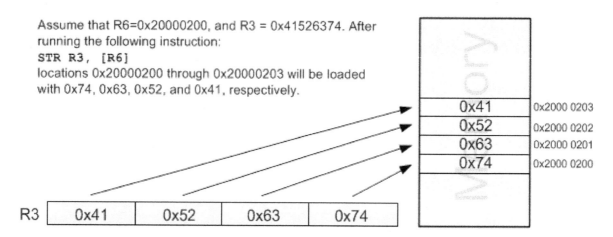

Assume that R6=0x20000200, and R3 = 0x41526374. After
running the following instruction:
STR R3, [R6]
locations 0x20000200 through 0x20000203 will be loaded
with 0x74, 0x63, 0x52, and 0x41, respectively.

Figure 2-6: Executing the STR Instruction

LDRB Rd, [Rx] instruction

The load/store instructions can also operate on smaller data sizes by appending 'B' or 'H' to the opcode.

```
    LDRB   Rd, [Rx]      ; load Rd with the contents of the location
                         ; pointed to by Rx register.
```

The LDRB instruction tells the CPU to load (copy) one byte from a memory location pointed to by Rx into the least significant byte of Rd. After this instruction is executed, the least significant byte of Rd will have the same value as the memory location pointed to by Rx. It must be noted that the unused portion (the upper 24 bits) of the Rd register will be filled by all zeros, as shown in Figure 2-7.

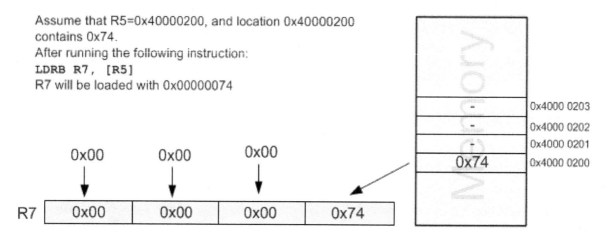

Assume that R5=0x40000200, and location 0x40000200
contains 0x74.
After running the following instruction:
LDRB R7, [R5]
R7 will be loaded with 0x00000074

Figure 2-7: Executing the LDRB Instruction

30

LDR vs. LDRB

As we mentioned earlier, we can use the LDR instruction to copy the contents of four consecutive memory locations into a 32-bit register. There are situations that we do not need to bring in all 4 bytes of data. A UART register is such a case. The UART registers are generally 8-bit and take only one memory space location (memory mapped I/O). Using LDRB, we can bring into CPU register a single byte of data from UART registers. This is a widely used instruction for accessing the 8-bit peripheral ports.

STRB Rx, [Rd] instruction

```
STRB   Rx, [Rd]       ; store the byte in register Rx into
                      ; memory location pointed to by Rd
```

The STRB instruction tells the CPU to store (copy) the least significant byte of Rx to a memory location pointed to by the Rd register. After this instruction is executed, the memory locations pointed to by the Rd will have the same byte as the lower byte of the Rx, as shown in Figure 2-8.

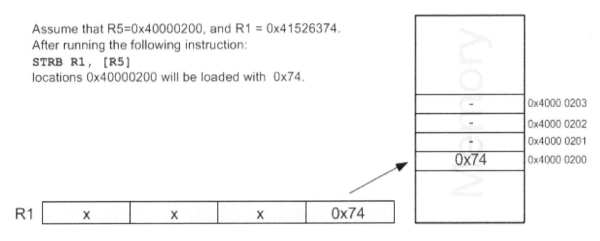

Figure 2-8: Executing the STRB Instruction

The following program first loads the R1 register with value 0x55, then stores this value into location 0x40000100:

```
LDR    R5, =0x40000100    ; R5 = 0x40000100
MOV    R1, #0x55     ; R1 = 0x55 (in hex)
STRB   R1, [R5]      ; copy R1 to location pointed to by R5
```

Example 2-3

State the contents of RAM locations 0x20000092 to 0x20000096 after the following program is executed:

```
LDR    R6, =0x20000092    ; R6 = 0x20000092
MOV    R1, #0x99     ; R1 = 0x99
STRB   R1, [R6]      ; store R1 into location pointed to by R6
                     ; (location 0x20000092)
ADD    R6, R6, #1    ; R6 = R6 + 1
MOV    R1, #0x85     ; R1 = 0x85
STRB   R1, [R6]      ; store R1 into location pointed to by R6
```

31

```
                         ; (location 0x20000093)
    ADD    R6, R6, #1    ; R6 = R6 + 1
    MOV    R1, #0x3F     ; R1 = 0x3F
    STRB   R1, [R6]      ; store R1 into location pointed to by R6

    ADD    R6, R6, #1    ; R6 = R6 + 1
    MOV    R1, #0x63     ; R1 = 0x63
    STRB   R1, [R6]      ; store R1 into location pointed to by R6

    ADD    R6, R6, #1    ; R6 = R6 + 1
    MOV    R1, #0x12     ; R1 = 0x12
    STRB   R1, [R6]
```

Solution:

After the execution of STRB R1, [R6] data memory location 0x20000092 has value 0x99.

After the execution of STRB R1, [R6] data memory location 0x20000093 has value 0x85.

After the execution of STRB R1, [R6] data memory location 0x20000094 has value 0x3F; and so on, as shown in the chart.

Address	Data
0x20000092	0x99
0x20000093	0x85
0x20000094	0x3F
0x20000095	0x63
0x20000096	0x12

Example 2-4

State the contents of R2, R1, and memory location 0x20000020 after the following program:

```
    MOV    R2, #0x5       ; load R2 with 5   (R2 = 0x05)
    MOV    R1, #0x2       ; load R1 with 2 (R1 = 0x02)
    ADD    R2, R1, R2     ; R2 = R1 + R2
    ADD    R2, R1, R2     ; R2 = R1 + R2
    LDR    R5, =0x20000020   ; R5 = 0x20000020
    STRB   R2, [R5]       ; store R2 into location pointed to by R5
```

Solution:

The program loads R2 with value 5. Then it loads R1 with value 2. Then it adds the R1 register to R2 twice. At the end, it stores the result in location 0x20000020 of memory.

After MOV R2, #0x05

Location	Data
R2	5
R1	
0x20000020	

After MOV R1, #0x02

Location	Data
R2	5
R1	2
0x20000020	

After ADD R2, R1, R2

Location	Data
R2	7
R1	2
0x20000020	

After ADD R2, R1, R2

Location	Data
R2	9
R1	2
0x20000020	

After STRB [R5], R2

Location	Data
R2	9
R1	2
0x20000020	9

STR vs. STRB

As we mentioned earlier, we can use the STR instruction to copy the content of a 32-bit register into four consecutive memory locations. Some of the peripheral registers are 8-bit and take only one memory space location (memory mapped I/O). Using STRB, we can send a byte of data from register to memory location such as a peripheral register.

LDRH Rd, [Rx] instruction

```
LDRH   Rd, [Rx]      ; load Rd with the half-word pointed
                     ; to by Rx register
```

The LDRH instruction tells the CPU to load (copy) half-word (16-bit or 2 bytes) from a memory location pointed to by Rx into the lower 16-bits of Rd Register. After this instruction is executed, the lower 16-bit of Rd will have the same value as two consecutive locations in the memory pointed to by base address of Rx. It must be noted that the unused portion (the upper 16 bits) of the Rd register will be filled with all zeros, as shown in Figure 2-9.

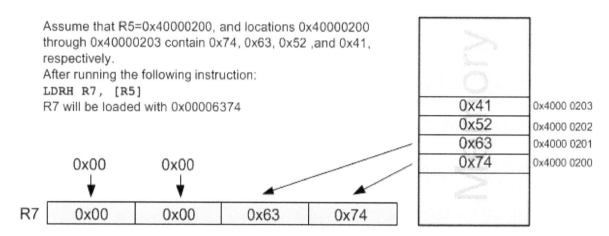

Figure 2-9: Executing the LDRH Instruction

Table 2-3 compares LDRB, LDRH, and LDR.

Data Size	Bits	Decimal	Hexadecimal	Load instruction used
Byte	8	0 – 255	0 - 0xFF	LDRB
Half-word	16	0 – 65535	0 - 0xFFFF	LDRH
Word	32	$0 - 2^{32}-1$	0 - 0xFFFFFFFF	LDR

Table 2-3: Unsigned Data Range in Arm and associated Load Instructions

STRH Rx,[Rd] instruction

```
STRH   Rx, [Rd]      ; store half-word (2-byte) in register Rx
                     ; into locations pointed to by Rd
```

The STRH instruction tells the CPU to store (copy) the lower 16-bit contents of the Rx to an address location pointed to by the Rd register. After this instruction is executed, the memory locations pointed to by the Rd will have the same value as the lower 16-bit of Rx Register. The locations are part of the data read/write memory space such as on-chip SRAM. For example, the "STRH R3,[R6]" instruction will copy the 16-bit lower contents of R3 into two consecutive locations pointed to by R6. As you can see in Figure 2-10, locations 0x20002000 and 0x20002001 of the SRAM memory will have the contents of the lower half word of R3 since R6 = 0x20002000.

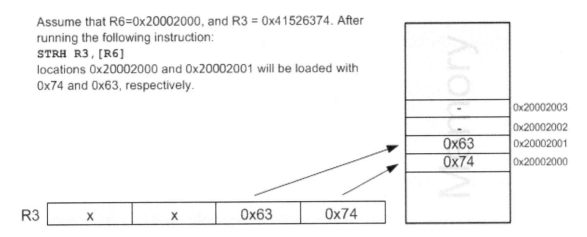

Assume that R6=0x20002000, and R3 = 0x41526374. After running the following instruction:
`STRH R3, [R6]`
locations 0x20002000 and 0x20002001 will be loaded with 0x74 and 0x63, respectively.

Figure 2-10: Executing the STRH Instruction

In Table 2-4 you see a comparison between STRB, STRH, and STR.

Data Size	Bits	Decimal	Hexadecimal	Load instruction used
Byte	8	$0 - 255$	0 - 0xFF	STRB
Half-word	16	$0 - 65535$	0 - 0xFFFF	STRH
Word	32	$0 - 2^{32}-1$	0 - 0xFFFFFFFF	STR

Table 2-4: Unsigned Data Range in Arm and associated Store Instructions

Review Questions

1. True or false. You can't store an immediate value directly into a memory location.
2. Write instructions to store byte value 0x95 into memory location with address 0x20.
3. Write instructions to store the content of R2 to memory location pointed to by R8.
4. Write instructions to load values from memory locations 0x20–0x23 into R4 register.
5. What is the largest hex value that can be stored in a single byte location in the data memory? What is the decimal equivalent of this value?
6. "LDR R6, [R3]" puts the result in _____.
7. What does "STRB R1, [R2]" do?
8. What is the largest hex value that can be moved into four consecutive locations in the data memory? What is the decimal equivalent of this value?

Section 2.4: Arm CPSR (Current Program Status Register)

Like all other microprocessors, the Arm has a flag register to indicate arithmetic conditions such as the carry bit. The flag register in the Arm is called the *current program status register (CPSR)*. In this section, we discuss various bits of this register and provide some examples of how it is altered. Chapters 3 and 4 show how the flag bits of the status register are used.

Arm current program status register

The status register is a 32-bit register. See Figure 2-11 for the bits of the status register. The bits N, Z, C, and V are called conditional flags, meaning that they indicate some conditions that resulted after an instruction is executed. Each of the conditional flags or the combinations of them can be used to perform a conditional execution, as we will see in Chapter 4.

31	30	29	28	27	26	25	24		19	16	15	10	9	8	7	6	5	4	3	2	1	0
N	Z	C	V	Q	IT1	IT0	J	Reser.	GE[3:0]		IT[7:2]		E	A	I	F	T	M4	M3	M2	M1	M0

Figure 2-11: CPSR (Current Program Status Register)

The following is a brief explanation of the flag bits of the current program status register (CPSR). The impact of instructions on this register is then discussed.

N, the negative flag

Binary representation of signed numbers uses D31 as the sign bit. The negative flag reflects the result of an arithmetic operation. If the D31 bit of the result is zero, then N = 0 and the result is positive. If the D31 bit is one, then N = 1 and the result is negative. The negative and V flag bits are used for the signed number arithmetic operations and are discussed in Chapter 5.

Z, the zero flag

The zero flag reflects the result of an arithmetic or logic operation. If the result is zero, then Z = 1. Therefore, Z = 0 if the result is not zero. See Chapter 4 to see how we use the Z flag for looping.

C, the carry flag

This flag is set whenever there is a carry out from the D31 bit. This flag bit is affected after a 32-bit addition or subtraction. Chapter 4 shows how the carry flag is used.

V, the overflow flag

This flag is set whenever the result of a signed number operation is too large, causing the high-order bit to overflow into the sign bit. In general, the carry flag is used to detect errors in unsigned arithmetic operations while the overflow flag is used to detect errors in signed arithmetic operations. The C and V flag bits are used for signed number arithmetic operations and are discussed in Chapter 5.

The T flag bit is used to indicate the Arm is in Thumb state. The I and F flags are used to enable or disable the interrupt.

S suffix and the status register

Most of Arm data processing instructions generate the status flags according to the result. But by default, the status flags of CPSR are not updated. If we need an instruction to update the value of status bits in CPSR, we have to put the 'S' suffix at the end of the opcode. That means, for example, ADDS instead of ADD is used.

ADD instruction and the status register

Next we examine the impact of the SUBS and ADDS instructions on the flag bits C and Z of the status register. Some examples should clarify their meanings. Although all the flag bits C, Z, V, and N are affected by the ADDS and SUBS instruction, we will focus on flags C and Z for now. The other flag bits are discussed in Chapter 5, because they relate only to signed number operations. Examine Example 2-5 to see the impact of the ADDS instruction on selected flag bits. See also Example 2-6 to see the impact of the SUBS instruction on selected flag bits.

Example 2-5

Show the status of the C and Z flags after the addition of

a) 0x0000009C and 0xFFFFFF64 in the following instruction:

```
; assume R1 = 0x0000009C and R2 = 0xFFFFFF64
ADDS   R2, R1, R2     ; add R1 to R2 and place the result in R2
```

b) 0x0000009C and 0xFFFFFF69 in the following instruction:

```
; assume R1 = 0x0000009C and R2 = 0xFFFFFF69
ADDS   R2, R1, R2     ; add R1 to R2 and place the result in R2
```

Solution:

a)

```
    0x0000009C          0000 0000 0000 0000 0000 0000 1001 1100
+   0xFFFFFF64      +   1111 1111 1111 1111 1111 1111 0110 0100
    0x100000000       1 0000 0000 0000 0000 0000 0000 0000 0000
```

C = 1 because there is a carry beyond the D31 bit.

Z = 1 because the R2 (the result) has value 0 in it after the addition.

b)

```
    0x0000009C    0000 0000 0000 0000 0000 0000 1001 1100
+   0xFFFFFF69    + 1111 1111 1111 1111 1111 1111 0110 1001
    0x100000005     1 0000 0000 0000 0000 0000 0000 0000 0101
```

C = 1 because there is a carry beyond the D31 bit.

Z = 0 because the R2 (the result) does not have value 0 in it after the addition. (R2=0x00000005)

Example 2-6

Show the status of the Z flag during the execution of the following program:

```
MOV    R2, #4          ; R2 = 4
MOV    R3, #2          ; R3 = 2
MOV    R4, #4          ; R4 = 4
SUBS   R5, R2, R3      ; R5 = R2 - R3 (R5 = 4 - 2 = 2)
SUBS   R5, R2, R4      ; R5 = R2 - R4 (R5 = 4 - 4 = 0)
```

Solution:

The Z flag is raised when the result is zero. Otherwise, it is cleared (zero). Thus:

After	Value of R5	Z flag
SUBS R5,R2,R3	2	0
SUBS R5,R2,R4	0	1

Not all instructions affect the flags

Some instructions affect all the four flag bits C, Z, V, and N (e.g. ADDS). But some instructions affect no flag bits at all. The branch instructions are in this category. Some instructions affect only some of the flag bits. The logic instructions (e.g. ANDS) are in this category. In general, only data processing instructions affect the status flags.

Table 2-5 shows some instructions and the flag bits affected by them. Appendix A provides a complete list of all the instructions and their associated flag bits.

Instruction	Flags Affected
ANDS	C, Z, N
ORRS	C, Z, N
MOVS	C, Z, N
ADDS	C, Z, N, V
SUBS	C, Z, N, V
B	No flags
Note that we cannot put S after B instruction.	

Table 2-5: Flag Bits Affected by Different Instructions

Flag bits and decision making

There are instructions that will make a conditional jump (branch) based on the status of the flag bits. Table 2-6 provides some of these instructions. Chapter 4 discusses the conditional branch instructions and how they are used.

Instruction	Flags Affecting the branch
BCS	Branch if C = 1
BCC	Branch if C = 0
BEQ	Branch if Z = 1
BNE	Branch if Z = 0
BMI	Branch if N = 1
BPL	Branch if N = 0
BVS	Branch if V = 1
BVC	Branch if V = 0

Table 2-6: Arm Branch (Jump) Instructions Using Flag Bits

Review Questions

1. The register holding the status flags in the Arm CPU is called the _____.

2. What is the size of the status register in the Arm?

3. Find the C and Z flag bits for the following code:

```
; assume R2 = 0xFFFFFF9F
; assume R1 = 0x00000061
ADDS  R2, R1, R2
```

4. Find the Z flag bit for the following code:

```
; assume R7 = 0x22
; assume R3 = 0x22
ADDS  R7, R3, R7
```

5. Find the C and Z flag bits for the following code:

```
; assume R2 = 0x67
; assume R1 = 0x99
ADDS  R2, R1, R2
```

Section 2.5: Arm Data Formats and Assembler Directives

In this section we look at some commonly used data formats and directives supported by the Arm assembler.

Data format representation

There are several ways to represent literal data in the Arm assembly source code. The numbers can be in hex, binary, decimal, ASCII or other formats. The following are examples of how each works using Keil Arm Assembler.

Hexadecimal numbers

To represent Hex numbers in Keil Arm assembler we put 0x (or 0X) in front of the number like this:

```
MOV   R1, #0x99
```

Here are a few lines of code that use the hex format:

```
MOV   R2, #0x75        ; R2 = 0x75
ADD   R1, R2, #0x11    ; R2 = R2 + 0x11
```

Decimal numbers

To indicate decimal numbers in some Arm assemblers such as Keil we simply use the decimal (e.g., 12) and nothing before or after it. Here are some examples of how to use it:

```
MOV   R7, #12     ; R7 = 00001100 or 0C in hex
MOV   R1, #32     ; R1 = 32 = 0x20
```

Binary numbers

To represent binary numbers in Keil Arm Assembler we put 2_ in front of the number. It is as follows:

```
MOV    R6, #2_10011001  ; R6 = 10011001 in binary or 99 in hex
```

Numbers in any base between 2 and 9

To indicate a number in any base n between 2 and 9 in Keil Arm Assembler we simply use the n_ in front of it. Here are some examples of how to use it:

```
MOV    R7, #8_33  ; R7 = 33 in base 8 or 011011 in binary format
MOV    R6, #2_10011001  ; R6 = 10011001 in base 2 or 99 in hex
```

ASCII characters

To represent ASCII data in Keil Arm Assembler we use single quotes as follows:

```
MOV    R3, #'2'   ; R3 = 00110010 or 32 in hex (See Appendix F)
```

This is the same as other assemblers such as the 8051 and x86. Here is another example:

```
MOV    R2, #'9'   ; R2 = 0x39, which is hex number for ASCII '9'
```

To represent a string, double quotes are used; and for defining ASCII strings (more than one character), we use the DCB directive which will be discussed next.

Assembler directives

In this section we look at some commonly used assembler directives supported by the Arm assembler. While instructions tell the CPU what to do, directives give directions to the assembler. For example, the MOV and ADD instructions are commands to the CPU, but EQU, END, and ENTRY are directives to the assembler. Table 2-7 shows some assembler directives.

Directive	Description
AREA	Instructs the assembler to assemble a new code or data section
END	Informs the assembler that it has reached the end of a source code.
EQU	Associate a symbolic name to a numeric constant.
INCLUDE	It adds the contents of a file to the current program.

Table 2-7: Some Widely Used Arm Directive

Note

Traditionally, pseudo-instruction and directive are treated as synonyms. But with Arm, the pseudo-instructions are translated to real instructions for CPU while directives are not.

AREA

The AREA directive tells the assembler to define a new section of memory. The memory can be code (instructions) or data and can have attributes such as READONLY, READWRITE, and so on. This is used to define one or more blocks of indivisible memory for code or data to be used by the linker. Every assembly language program has at least one AREA. The following is the format:

```
AREA            sectionname, attribute, attribute, ...
```

The following line defines a new area named MY_ASM_PROG1 which has CODE and READONLY attributes:

```
AREA  MY_ASM_PROG1, CODE, READONLY
```

Among commonly used attributes are CODE, DATA, READONLY, READWRITE, and ALIGN. The following paragraphs describe them in more details.

READONLY is an attribute given to an area of memory which can only be read from. Since it is READONLY section of the program it is by default for CODE. In Arm assembly language we use this area to write our instructions for machine code execution. All the READONLY sections of the same program are put next to each other in the flash memory by the linker.

READWRITE is an attribute given to an area of memory which can be read from and written to. Since it is READWRITE section of the program it is by default for DATA. In Arm assembly language we use this area to set aside SRAM memory for variables and stack. The linker puts all the READWRITE sections of the same program next to each other in the SRAM memory.

Note

In Keil, the memory space of **READONLY** and **READWRITE** are defined in the *Target* tabs of the **Project-Options**. Keil project wizard sets the default values according to the memory map of the chosen device.

CODE is an attribute given to an area of memory used for executable machine instructions. Since it is used for code section of the program it is by default READONLY memory. In Arm assembly language we use this area to write our instructions. The following line defines a new area for writing programs:

```
AREA  OUR_ASM_PROG, CODE, READONLY
```

DATA is an attribute given to an area of memory used for data and no instructions (machine instructions) can be placed in this area. Since it is used for data section of the program it is by default a READWRITE memory. In Arm assembly language we use this area to set aside SRAM memory for variables and stack. The following line defines a new area for defining variables:

```
AREA  OUR_VARIABLES, DATA, READWRITE
```

To define constant values in the flash memory we write the following:

```
AREA  OUR_CONSTS, DATA, READONLY
```

ALIGN is another attribute given to an area of memory to indicate how memory should be allocated according to the addresses. The ALIGN attribute of AREA has a number after like ALIGN=3 which indicates the information should be placed in memory with addresses of 2^3, that is 0x50000, 0x50008, 0x50010, 0x50018, and so on. The usage and importance of ALIGN attribute is discussed in Chapter 6.

EXPORT and IMPORT

To inform the assembler that a name or symbol will be referenced by other modules (in other files), it is marked by the **EXPORT** directive. If a module is referencing a name outside itself, that name must be declared as **IMPORT**. Correspondingly, in the module where the variable is defined, that variable must be declared as **EXPORT** in order to allow it to be referenced by other modules. The following example shows how the IMPORT and EXPORT directives are used:

```
; File1.s
; from the main program:
IMPORT MY_FUNC
...
BL     MY_FUNC        ;call MY_FUNC function
...


; File2.s (a different file)
AREA   OUR_EXAMPLE,CODE,READONLY
EXPORT MY_FUNC
IMPORT DATA1
MY_FUNC
LDR    R1,=DATA1
...
...
```

Notice that the *IMPORT* directive is used in the main procedure to show that *MY_FUNC* is defined in another module. This is needed because *MY_FUNC* is not defined in that module. Correspondingly, *MY_FUNC* is defined as *EXPORT* in the module where it is defined. *IMPORT* is used in the *MY_FUNC* module to declare that operand DATA1 has been defined in another module. Correspondingly, DATA1 is declared as EXPORT in the calling module.

END

Another pseudocode is the END directive. This indicates to the assembler the end of the source file. The END directive is the last line of the Arm assembly program, meaning that anything after the END directive in the source file is ignored by the assembler. Program 2-1 shows how the AREA and END directives are used.

Program 2-1

```
; Arm Assembly language program to add some data and store the SUM in R3.

      EXPORT  __main
      AREA    PROG_2_1, CODE, READONLY
__main
      MOV    R1, #0x25    ; R1 = 0x25
      MOV    R2, #0x34    ; R2 = 0x34
      ADD    R3, R2, R1   ; R3 = R2 + R1
HERE  B      HERE         ; stay here forever
      END
```

EQU (equate)

This is used to define a constant value or a fixed address by a name to make the program easier to read. The EQU directive does not set aside storage for a data item in the program, it merely associates an identifier with the constant value. The following code uses EQU for the counter constant, and then the constant is used to load the R2 register:

```
COUNT       EQU    0x25
...         ...    ....
    MOV    R2, #COUNT   ; R2 = 0x25
```

The assembler remembers the association between the word "COUNT" and the value 0x25 when it encounters the line with EQU. When it assembles the line with #COUNT, it replaces COUNT by the value 0x25. So the instruction "MOV R2, #COUNT" is converted to "MOV R2, #0x25". When executing the above instruction "MOV R2, #COUNT", the register R2 will be loaded with the value 0x25.

What are the advantages of using EQU? First, it enhances the readability. The meaning is more obvious in the word "COUNT" than the value "0x25." Furthermore, if a constant is used multiple times throughout the program, and the programmer wants to change its value everywhere. By the use of EQU, the programmer can change it once and the assembler will change all of its occurrences in the program. This allows the programmer to avoid searching the entire program trying to find and change every occurrence which is tedious and error prong.

Using EQU for special register address assignment

EQU is used to assign special function register (including peripheral registers) addresses to more readable names. This is so widely used, many manufacturers supply files with all the registers defined for the devices they make.

Examine the following code:

```
FIO2SET0    EQU    0x3FFFC058   ; PORT2 output set register 0 address
    MOV    R6, #0x01            ; R6 = 0x01
    LDR    R2, =FIO2SET0        ; R2 = 0x3FFFC058
    STRB   R6, [R2]             ; Write 0x01 to FIO2SET0
```

Each identifier may only be used by EQU once. If you try to use EQU to assign a name with a new value, an assembler error occurs.

Review Questions

1. Give an example of hex data representation in the Arm assembler.

2. Show how to represent decimal 20 in formats of (a) hex, (b) decimal, and (c) binary in the Arm assembler.

3. What is the advantage in using the EQU directive to define a constant value?

4. Show the hexadecimal value of the numbers used by the following directives:

   (a) ASC_DATA EQU '4'   (b) MY_DATA EQU 2_00011111

5. Give the value in R2 after the execution of the following instruction:

```
MYCOUNT        EQU     15
               MOV     R2, #MYCOUNT
```

6. Give the value in memory location 0x200000 after the execution of the following instructions:
```
MYCOUNT        EQU     0x95
MYMEM          EQU     0x200000
               MOV     R0, #MYCOUNT
               LDR     R2, =MYMEM
               STRB    R0, [R2]
```

7. Give the value in data memory 0x630000 after the execution of the following instructions:
```
MYDATA         EQU     12
MYMEM          EQU     0x00630000
FACTOR         EQU     0x10
               MOV     R1, #MYDATA
               MOV     R2, #FACTOR
               LDR     R3, =MYMEM
               ADD     R1 R2, R1
               STRB    R1, [R3]
```

8. Write an Arm assembly program that loads R2 and R3 with 22 and 33, respectively. Then, adds R2 to R3.

Section 2-6: Assembler data allocation directives

In most assembly languages there are some directives to allocate memory and initialize its value. In Arm assembly language DCB, DCD, and DCW allocate memory and initialize them. The SPACE directive allocates memory without initializing it.

DCB directive (define constant byte)

The DCB directive allocates a byte size memory and initializes their values.

```
MYVALUE        DCB     5                  ; MYVALUE = 5
MYMSAGE        DCB     "HELLO WORLD"      ; ASCII string
```

Each alphanumeric letter in a string is converted to its ASCII encoding value.

DCW directive (define constant half-word)

The DCW directive allocates a half-word size memory and initializes the values.

```
MYDATA         DCW     0x20, 0xF230, 5000, 0x9CD7
```

DCD directive (define constant word)

The DCD directive allocates a word size memory and initializes the values.

```
MYDATA         DCD     0x200000, 0x30F5, 5000000, 0xFFFF9CD7
```

See Tables 2-8 and 2-9.

Directive	Description
DCB	Allocates one or more bytes of memory, and defines the initial runtime contents of the memory
DCW	Allocates one or more halfwords of memory, aligned on two-byte boundaries, and defines the initial runtime contents of the memory.
DCWU	Allocates one or more halfwords of memory, and defines the initial runtime contents of the memory. The data is not aligned.
DCD	Allocates one or more words of memory, aligned on four-byte boundaries, and defines the initial runtime contents of the memory.
DCDU	Allocates one or more words of memory and defines the initial runtime contents of the memory. The data is not aligned.

Table 2-8: Some Widely Used Arm Memory Allocation Directives

Data Size	Bits	Decimal	Hexadecimal	Directive	Instruction
Byte	8	$0 - 255$	0 - 0xFF	DCB	STRB/LDRB
Half-word	16	$0 - 65535$	0 - 0xFFFF	DCW	STRH/LDRH
Word	32	$0 - 2^{32}-1$	0 - 0xFFFFFFFF	DCD	STR/LDR

Table 2-9: Unsigned Data Range in Arm and associated Instructions

In Program 2-2 you see an example of storing constant values in the program memory using the directives. Figure 2-12 shows how the data is stored in memory. In the example, the program goes from location 0x00 to 0x0F. The DCB directive stores data in addresses 0x10–0x17. As you see one byte is allocated for each data. The DCD allocates 4 bytes for each data. As a result, the lowest byte of 0x23222120 (which is 0x20) is stored in location 0x18 and the next bytes are stored in the next locations. In this order, the least significant byte of the word is stored at the lowest address and the most significant byte of the word is stored at the highest address. The ordering of bytes in a word is called "endian" and we will discuss it in more details Chapter 6.

Program 2-2: Sample of Storing Fixed Data in Program Memory

```
        EXPORT  __main
        AREA   PROG2_2, CODE, READONLY
__main
        LDR   R2, =OUR_FIXED_DATA     ; point to OUR_FIXED_DATA
        LDRB  R0, [R2]    ; load R0 with the contents
                          ; of memory pointed to by R2
                          ; Now, R0 contains 0x55
        ADD   R1, R1, R0  ; add R0 to R1
HERE    B     HERE        ; stay here forever
        AREA   LOOKUP_EXAMPLE, DATA, READONLY
OUR_FIXED_DATA
        DCB   0x55, 0x33, 1, 2, 3, 4, 5, 6
        DCD   0x23222120, 0x30
        DCW   0x4540, 0x50
        END
```

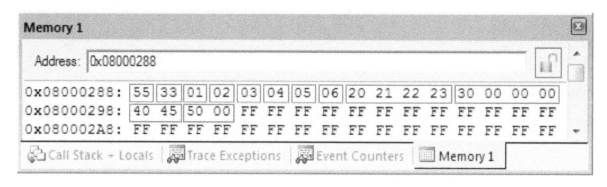

Figure 2-12: Memory Dump for Program 2-2

The DCW directive allocates 2 bytes for each data. For example, the low byte of 0x4540 is located in address 0x20 and the high byte of it goes to address 0x21. Similarly, the low byte of 0x50 is located in address 0x22 and the high byte of it in address 0x23.

In the program, to access the data, first the R2 register is loaded with the address of OUR_FIXED_DATA. In this example, OUR_FIXED_DATA has address 0x10. So, R2 is loaded with 0x10. Then, the contents of location 0x10 is loaded into register R0, using the LDRB instruction.

Notice that the ADR pseudo-instruction can also be used to load addresses into registers. For example, in Program 2-2 we can load R2 with the address of OUR_FIXED_DATA using the following pseudo-instruction:

```
ADR    R2, OUR_FIXED_DATA        ;point to OUR_FIXED_DATA
```

Strings

You can use DCB together with double quotations to store strings. The following snippet of code, stores "Hello World!" in the flash memory:

```
       AREA MY_STRINGS, CODE, READONLY
MY_MSG DCB   "Hello World!"
```

SPACE directive

Using the SPACE directive, we can allocate memory for variables without initial values. The following lines allocate 4 and 2 bytes of memory and name them as LONG_VAR and OUR_ALFA:

```
LONG_VAR    SPACE     4     ; Allocate 4 bytes
OUR_ALFA    SPACE     2     ; Allocate 2 bytes
```

The following snippet of code allocates 400 bytes of memory. Since the AREA is defined as READWRITE, the space is located in SRAM:

```
       AREA MYSTACK, DATA, READWRITE
       SPACE 400
```

46

In the following program, three variables are defined: A, B, and C. A and B are initialized with values 5 and 4, respectively. In the next step A and B are added together and the result is stored in C:

```
        EXPORT  __main
        AREA OUR_PROG, CODE, READONLY
__main
        ; A = 5
        LDR   R0, =A        ; R0 = Addr. of A
        MOV   R1, #5        ; R1 = 5
        STR   R1, [R0]      ; init. A with 5


        ; B = 4
        LDR   R0, =B        ; R0 = Addr. of B
        MOV   R1, #4        ; R1 = 4
        STR   R1, [R0]      ; init. B with 4


        ; R1 = A
        LDR   R0, =A        ; R0 = Addr. of A
        LDR   R1, [R0]      ; R1 = value of A


        ; R2 = B
        LDR   R0, =B        ; R0 = Addr. of A
        LDR   R2, [R0]      ; R2 = value of A


        ; C = R1 + R2 (C = A + B)
        ADD   R3, R1, R2  ; R3 = A + B
        LDR   R0, =C        ; R0 = Addr. of C
        STR   R3, [R0]      ; C = R3


        loop  B   loop


        AREA  OUR_DATA, DATA, READWRITE
        ; Allocates the followings in SRAM memory
A       SPACE 4
B       SPACE 4
C       SPACE 4
        END
```

ALIGN

This is used to make sure data is aligned on the 32-bit word or 16-bit half word address boundary. The following uses ALIGN to make the data 32-bit word aligned:

```
        ALIGN 4     ; the next instruction is word (4 bytes) aligned
        ...
        ALIGN 2     ; the next instruction is half-word (2 bytes) aligned
        ...
```

Example 2-7 shows the result of using the ALIGN directive.

Example 2-7

Compare the result of using ALIGN in the following programs:

a)

```
        AREA   E2_7A, READONLY, CODE
__main
        ADR    R2, DTA
        LDRB   R0, [R2]
        ADD    R1, R1, R0
H1      B      H1

DTA     DCB    0x55
        DCB    0x22
        END
```

b)

```
        AREA   E2_7B, READONLY, CODE
__main
        ADR    R2, DTA
        LDRB   R0, [R2]
        ADD    R1, R1, R0
H1      B      H1

DTA     DCB    0x55
        ALIGN 2
        DCB    0x22
        END
```

c)

```
        AREA   E2_7C, READONLY, CODE
__main
        ADR    R2, DTA
        LDRB   R0, [R2]
        ADD    R1, R1, R0
H1      B      H1

DTA     DCB    0x55
        ALIGN 4
        DCB    0x22
        END
```

Solution:

a) When there is no ALIGN directive the DCB directive allocates the first empty location for its data. In this example, address 0x10 is allocated for 0x55. So 0x22 goes to address 0x11.

48

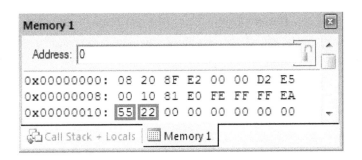

b) In the example the ALIGN is set to 2 which means the data should be put in a location with even address. The 0x55 goes to the first empty location which is 0x10. The next empty location is 0x11 which is not a multiple of 2. So, it is filled with 0 and the next data goes to location 0x12.

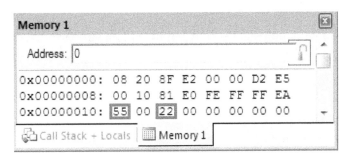

c) In the example the ALIGN is set to 4 which means the data should go to locations whose address is multiple of 4. The 0x55 goes to the first empty location which is 0x10. The next empty locations are 0x11, 0x12, and 0x13 which are not a multiple of 4. So, they are filled with 0s and the next data goes to location 0x14.

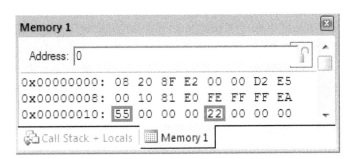

Rules for labels in assembly language

By choosing label names that are meaningful, a programmer can make a program much easier to read and maintain. There are several rules that label names must follow. First, each label name must be unique in the file. The names used for labels in assembly language programming consist of alphabetic letters in both uppercase and lowercase, the digits 0 through 9, and the special character underscore '_'. The first character of the label must be an alphabetical letter or underscore and cannot be a numeral. Every assembler has some reserved words that must not be used as labels in the program. Foremost among the reserved words are the mnemonics for the instruction opcodes and the directives. For example, "MOV" and "ADD" are reserved because they are instruction mnemonics. Check your assembler manual for the list of reserved words.

Review Questions
1. True or false. DCB allocates a byte of memory.
2. True or false. DCB cannot initialize memory.
3. True or false. SPACE allocates memory.

Section 2.7: Introduction to Arm Assembly Programming

In this section we discuss assembly language format and define some widely used terminology associated with assembly language programming.

While the CPU can work only in binary, it can do so at a very high speed. It is quite tedious and slow for humans, however, to deal with 0s and 1s in order to program the computer. A program that consists of 0s and 1s is called machine language. In the early days of the computer, programmers coded programs in machine language. Although the octal or hexadecimal system was used as a more efficient way to represent binary numbers, the process of working in machine code was still cumbersome for humans. Eventually, assembly languages were developed, which provided mnemonics for the machine code instructions, plus other features that made programming easier and less prone to error. The term mnemonic is frequently used in computer science and engineering literature to refer to codes and abbreviations that are relatively easy to remember. Assembly language programs must be translated into machine code by a program called assembler. Assembly language is referred to as a low-level language because it deals directly with the internal structure of the CPU. To program in assembly language, the programmer must know all the registers of the CPU and the size of each, as well as other details.

Today, one can use many different programming languages, such as C, C++, Java, Python, and numerous others. These languages are called *high-level* languages because the programmer does not have to be concerned with the internal details of the CPU. Whereas an assembler is used to translate an assembly language program into machine code, high-level languages are translated into machine code by a program called a compiler. For instance, to write a program in C, one must use a C compiler to translate the program into machine language.

Next we look at the Arm assembly language format.

Structure of assembly language

An assembly language program consists of, among other things, a series of lines of assembly language instructions. An assembly language instruction consists of a mnemonic of opcode, optionally followed by one, two or three operands. The operands are the data items being manipulated, and the opcodes are the commands to the CPU, telling it what to do with the operands. See Program 2-4.

Program 2-4: Sample of an Arm Assembly Language Program

```
; Arm Assembly language program to add some data and store the SUM in R3.
```

```
        EXPORT  __main
        AREA    PROG_2_4, CODE, READONLY
__main
        MOV     R1, #0x25   ; R1 = 0x25
        MOV     R2, #0x34   ; R2 = 0x34
        ADD     R3, R2, R1  ; R3 = R2 + R1
HERE    B       HERE        ; stay here forever
        END
```

In addition to the instructions, an assembly language program contains directives. While instructions tell the CPU what to do, directives give directions to the assembler. For example, in Program 2-4, the MOV and ADD instructions are commands to the CPU, AREA and END are directives to the assembler.

An assembly language instruction consists of four fields:

```
[label]   opcode   [operands]   [; comment]
```

Brackets indicate that a field is optional and not all lines have them. Brackets should not be typed in. Regarding the above format, the following points should be noted:

1. The label field allows the program to refer to the address of a line of code by name.

2. The assembly language opcode and operand(s) fields together perform the real work of the program and accomplish the tasks for which the program was written for. In assembly language statements such as

```
        MOV     R3, #0x55
        MOV     R2, #0x67
        ADD     R2, R2, R3  ; R2 = R2 + R3
```

ADD and MOV are the mnemonics of the opcodes; the "0x55" and "0x67" are the operands.

3. Instead of instructions, the program may contain directives. The following line is an assembly directive that tells the assembler that the following lines are for program instructions.

```
        AREA        PROG_2_4, CODE, READONLY
```

4. The comment field begins with a semicolon comment indicator "; ". Comments may be at the end of a line or on a line by themselves. The assembler ignores comments, but they are indispensable to programmers. Although comments are optional, it is recommended that they be used to describe the program in a way that makes it easier for someone else to read and understand.

5. Notice the label "HERE" in the label field in Program 2-4. In the B (Branch) statement the Arm is told to stay in this loop indefinitely.

Review Questions

1. What is the purpose of assembler directives?
2. _____ are translated by the assembler into machine code, whereas _____ are not.
3. True or false. Assembly language is a high-level language.
4. Which of the following instructions produces machine code? List all that do.
    (a) MOV R6, #0x25 (b) ADD R2, R1, R3 (c) END (d) HERE B HERE
5. True or false. Assembler directives are not used by the CPU itself. They are simply a guide to the assembler.
6. In Question 4, which one is an assembler directive?

Section 2.8: Creating an Arm Assembly Program

Now that the basic form of an Assembly language program has been given, the next question is: How it is created, assembled, and made ready to run? The steps to create an executable assembly language program (Figure 2-13) are outlined as follows:

1. First we use a text editor to type in a program similar to Program 2-4. In the case of Arm, we can use the Keil IDE, which has a text editor, assembler, simulator, debugger, and much more all in one software package. It is an excellent development software that supports all the Arm chips. A free version with 32k byte limit is available at www.keil.com. Many editors or word processors also can be used to create or edit the program. A widely used editor is the Notepad in Windows, which comes with all Microsoft operating systems. Notice that the editor must be able to produce an ASCII file. For assemblers, the file names follow the usual DOS conventions, but the source file should have the extension ".s", ".a" or ".asm". The ".asm" extension for the source file is used by an assembler in the next step.

2. The ".asm" source file containing the program code created in step 1 is fed to the Arm assembler. The assembler produces an object file, and a listing file. The object file has the extension ".o", and the listing file has ".lst" extension.

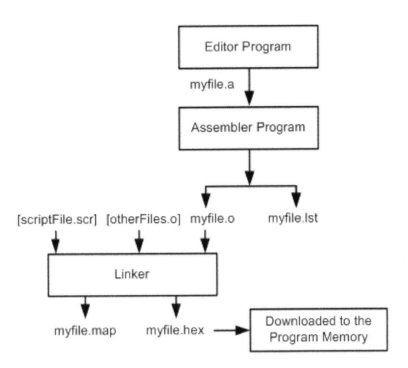

Figure 2-13: Steps to Create a Program

3. The object file plus a linker script file are used by the linker to produce the map file and the memory image files. The map file has the extension ".map"

4. The memory image file contains the binary code that can be downloaded to the target device or the simulator for execution. By default, Keil IDE produces a ".axf" file that contains the binary code and the symbols for debugger. Optionally, an Intel hex format file may be produced. The hex file has ".hex" extension. The linker script file (or scatter file in Keil) is optional and can be replaced by some command line options. After a successful link, the hex file is ready to be burned into the Arm processor's program FLASH memory and is downloaded into the Arm chip.

More about asm and object files

The assembler converts the assembler source file's assembly language instructions into machine code and provides the ".o" (object) file. The object file, as mentioned earlier, has a ".o" as its extension. The object file is used as input to the linker.

Before we can assemble a program to create a ready-to-run program, we must make sure that it is free of syntax errors. The Keil uVision IDE provides us error messages and we examine them to see the location and nature of the syntax error. The assembler will not assemble the program until all the syntax errors are fixed. A sample of an error message is shown in Figure 2-14.

```
Build target 'Target 1'
assembling a1.asm...a1.asm(7): error: A1163E: Unknown opcode MOVE, expecting opcode or Macro
Target not created
```

Figure 2-14: Sample of an Error Message

"lst" and "map" files

The map file shows the labels defined in the program together with their values. Examine Figure 2-15. It shows the Map file of Program 2-4.

The lst (listing) file shows the source code and the machine code; it also shows which instructions are used in the source code, and the amount of memory the program uses. See Figure 2-16.

These files can be accessed by a text editor such as Notepad and displayed on the monitor, or sent to the printer to get a hard copy. The programmer uses the listing and map files to help debugging the program.

There are many different Arm assemblers available for evaluation nowadays. If you use the Windows operating system, IAR IDE and Keil uVision can be used. They have great features and nice environments. GNU assembler is popular because it if free and open source. It is also generic and can be used for most of the processors in the market. The drawbacks of GNU assembler are that its syntax is slightly different from the other Arm assembler and it takes some effort to set up the toolchain.

```
Memory Map of the image

  Image Entry point : 0x080000ed

  Load Region LR_1 (Base: 0x08000000, Size: 0x0000028c, Max: 0xffffffff, ABSOLUTE)

    Execution Region ER_RO (Exec base: 0x08000000, Load base: 0x08000000, Size: 0x0000028c,
Max: 0xffffffff, ABSOLUTE)

    Exec Addr    Load Addr    Size        Type    Attr    Idx  E Section Name      Object

    0x08000000   0x08000000   0x000000ec  Data    RO      8      RESET    startup_stm32f10x_md.o
    0x080000ec   0x080000ec   0x00000040  Code    RO      9    * .text    startup_stm32f10x_md.o
    0x08000134   0x08000134   0x0000000e  Code    RO      1      PROG_2_4           main.o

    Execution Region ER_RW (Exec base: 0x20000000, Load base: 0x0800028c, Size: 0x00000000,
Max: 0xffffffff, ABSOLUTE)

    **** No section assigned to this execution region ****


    Execution Region ER_ZI (Exec base: 0x20000000, Load base: 0x0800028c, Size: 0x00000600,
Max: 0xffffffff, ABSOLUTE)

    Exec Addr    Load Addr    Size        Type    Attr    Idx  E Section Name      Object

    0x20000000    -           0x00000200  Zero    RW      7      HEAP     startup_stm32f10x_md.o
    0x20000200    -           0x00000400  Zero    RW      6      STACK    startup_stm32f10x_md.o

==============================================================================================
```

Figure 2-15: Sample of a Map File

```
Arm Macro Assembler       Page 1
1  00000000               ; Arm Assembly language program to add some data and store the SUM in
                          R3.
2  00000000
3  00000000                       EXPORT  __main
4  00000000                       AREA    PROG_2_4, CODE, READONLY
5  00000000               __main
6  00000000  F04F 0125            MOV     R1, #0x25       ; R1 = 0x25
7  00000004  F04F 0234            MOV     R2, #0x34       ; R2 = 0x34
8  00000008  EB02 0301            ADD     R3, R2,R1       ; R3 = R2 + R1
9  0000000C  E7FE        HERE     B       HERE            ; stay here forever
10 0000000E                       END
```

Figure 2-16: Sample of a List File for Arm

Review Questions

1. True or false. The editor of Keil IDE and Windows Notepad text editor both produce an ASCII file.

2. True or false. The extension for the assembly program source file may be ".a".

3. Which of the following files is usually produced by a text editor?

    (a) myprog.asm (b) myprog.obj (c) myprog.hex (d) myprog.lst

4. Which of the following files is produced by an assembler?

    (a) myprog.asm (b) myprog.obj (c) myprog.hex (d) myprog.lst

Section 2.9: The Program Counter and Program Memory Space in the Arm

In this section we discuss the role of the program counter (PC) in executing a program and show how the code is fetched from ROM and executed. We will also discuss the program (code) memory space for various Arm family members.

Program counter in the Arm

The most important register in Arm is the PC (program counter). As we mentioned earlier, register R15 is the program counter in Arm CPU. The program counter is used by the CPU to point to the address of the next instruction to be executed. As the CPU fetches the opcode from the program memory, the program counter is incremented automatically to point to the next instruction.

The program counter in the Arm family is 32 bits wide. This means that the Arm family can access addresses 00000000 to 0xFFFFFFFF, a total of 4 gigabytes of memory space locations.

Power up location for Arm

One question that we must ask about any microcontroller (or microprocessor) is: "at what address does the CPU wake up to when power is applied or when the CPU is reset?" Each microprocessor is different. In the case of the Cortex-M microcontrollers, when the CPU is powered up or reset, the PC (program counter) is loaded with the contents of memory location 0x00000004. For this reason, the address of the first instruction must be burned into memory location 0x00000004 of program ROM. As, we will see in Chapter 4, in the startup file, the location 4 is loaded with the address of a subroutine (named Reset_Handler) which initializes the Arm CPU and then branches to __main. Next, we discuss the step-by-step action of the program counter in fetching and executing a sample program.

Placing code in program ROM

To get a better understanding of the role of the program counter in fetching and executing a program, we examine the action of the program counter as each instruction is fetched and executed. First, we examine once more the listing file of the sample program and show how the code is placed into the Flash ROM of the Arm chip. As we can see in Figure 2-16, the machine code for each instruction is listed in the third column of the listing file and the address offset of each instruction is in the second column. The address offsets are given based on the __main label. For example, the listing shows that address offset 0x00000000 contains "F04F 0125", which is the machine code for moving an immediate value (in this case 0x25) into a register (in this case R1). Therefore, the instruction "MOV R1, #0x25" has a machine code of "F04F 0125". See Figure 2-16. Similarly, the machine code "F04F 0234" is located in location 0x00000004 and represents the opcode and the operands for the instruction "MOV R2, #0x34". In the same way, machine code "EB02 0301" is located in address offset 0x00000008 and represents the opcode and the operand for the instruction "ADD R3, R1, R2". The opcode for "B HERE" and its target address offset are located in location 0x0000000C.

Executing a program instruction by instruction

Assuming that the above program is burned into the ROM of an Arm chip, the following is a step-by-step description of the action of the Arm upon applying power to it:

1. When the Arm is powered up, the CPU reads the contents of locations 0x000000004 to 0x00007 and loads to the PC (program counter). So, the PC is loaded with the address of the subroutine which is in the startup file and the CPU executes the subroutine and then there is a branch to __main and the PC is loaded with the address of __main and the CPU starts to fetch the first instruction from location __main of the program ROM. In the case of the above program, the first machine code in the __main routine is "F04F 0125", which is the code for moving operand 0x25 to R1. Upon executing the code, the CPU places the value of 25 in R1. Now one instruction is finished. The program counter is already incremented by 0x00000004, which contains code "F04F 0234", the machine code for the instruction "MOV R2, #0x34".

2. Upon executing the machine code "F04F 0234", the value 0x34 is loaded to R2. The program counter is incremented by 0x00000004.

3. The next location has the machine code for instruction "ADD R3, R2, R1". This instruction is executed and the PC is incremented by 4.

4. PC points to the next instruction, which is "HERE B HERE". After the execution of this instruction, although the PC is incremented by 2 (the branch instruction is 2-byte long), the execution of the instruction loads PC with the address of the B instruction and the B instruction is executed infinitely. This keeps the program in an infinite loop. More on branch instructions will be in Chapter 4.

The actual steps of running a code in Arm is slightly different from what mentioned above because of the use of pipeline in Arm architecture. We will examine pipelines later in Section 2-11.

Review Questions

1. In the Arm, the program counter is _____ bits wide.
2. True or false. Every member of the Arm family wakes up at memory 0x00000008 when it is powered up.
3. At what ROM location do we store the address of the first opcode of a Cortex-M program?

Section 2.10: Some Arm Addressing Modes

The various ways operands are specified in the instruction are called addressing modes. In the narrower definition, it is the way CPU generates address from instruction to read/write the operands in the memory. But the term addressing mode is used to cover a broader definition including the operands that are not in the memory. With the RISC architecture, the destinations of all Arm instructions are always a register except the "store" instructions, which is a mirror of "load."

Using advanced addressing modes to access different data types and data structures (e.g. arrays, pointers) are discussed in Chapter 6. Some of the simple Arm addressing modes are:

1. register
2. immediate
3. register indirect (indexed addressing mode)

Register addressing mode

The register addressing mode involves the use of registers to hold the data to be manipulated. Memory is not accessed when this addressing mode is executed; therefore, it is relatively fast. See Figure 2-17.

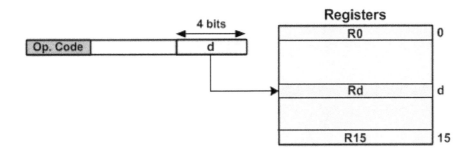

Figure 2-17: Register Addressing Mode

Examples of register addressing mode are as follow:

```
MOV    R6, R2        ; copy the contents of R2 into R6
ADD    R1, R1, R3    ; add the contents of R3 to contents of R1
SUB    R7, R7, R2    ; subtract R2 from R7
```

Immediate addressing mode

In the immediate addressing mode, the source operand is a literal constant. In immediate addressing mode, as the name implies, when the instruction is assembled, the operand comes immediately after the opcode in the encoding of the instruction. For this reason, this addressing mode executes quickly. See Figure 2-18. Examples:

```
MOV   R9, #0x25        ; move 0x25 into R9
MOV   R3, #62          ; load the decimal value 62 into R3
ADD   R6, R6, #0x40    ; add 0x40 to R6
```

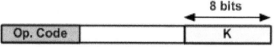

Figure 2-18: Immediate Addressing Mode

In the first two addressing modes, the operands are either inside the CPU or tagged along with the instruction, which is fetched into the CPU before the instruction is executed. In most programs, the data to be processed are originally in some memory location outside the CPU. There are many ways of accessing the data in the memory space. The following describes one of the methods. We will discuss more ways of accessing data memory in Chapter 6.

Register Indirect Addressing Mode (Indexed addressing mode)

In the register indirect addressing mode, the address of the memory location where the operand resides is held by a register. See Figure 2-19. For example:

```
STR   R5, [R6]     ; write the content of R5 into the memory location
                   ; pointed to by R6
LDR   R10, [R3]    ; load into R10 the content of the
                   ; memory location pointed to by R3.
```

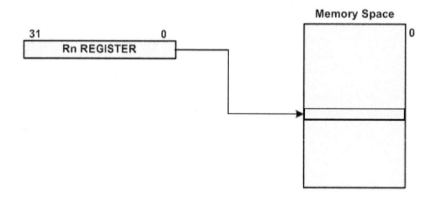

Figure 2-19: Register Indirect Addressing Mode

Using register indirect addressing mode, we can implement the different pointers. Since the registers are 32-bit they can address the entire memory space. Here you see a simple code in C and its equivalent in Assembly:

C Language:

```
char *ourPointer;
ourPointer = (char*) 0x12456; //Point to location 12456
*ourPointer = 25;   //store 25 in location 0x12456
ourPointer ++;     //point to next location
```

Assembly Language:
```
LDR    R2, =0x12456  ; point to location 0x12456
MOV    R0, #25    ; R0 = 25
STRB   R0, [R2]   ; store R0 in location 0x12456
ADD    R2, R2, #1  ; increment R2 to point to next location
```

Depending on the data type that the pointer points to, STR/LDR, STRH/LDRH, or STRB/LDRB might be used. In the above example, since it points to char (which is 8-bit) STRB is used.

Review Questions

1. Can the Arm programmer make up new addressing modes?
2. Which registers can be used for the register indirect addressing mode?
3. Where is the data located in immediate addressing mode?

Section 2.11: Pipelining and Harvard Architecture in Arm

There are three ways available to microprocessor designers to increase the processing power of the CPU:

1. Increase the clock frequency of the chip: Some drawbacks of this method are that the higher the frequency, the more power consumption and more heat dissipation. Power consumption is especially a problem for portable devices.

2. Use Harvard architecture by increasing the number of buses to bring more information (code and data) into the CPU to be processed concurrently. As we will see in this section, the new Arm chips, including the Cortex series, have Harvard architecture.

3. Change the internal architecture of the CPU and use Pipelining and the RISC architecture.

Arm has used all three methods to increase the processing power of the Arm microcontrollers.

Pipelining

In early microprocessors such as the 8085 or 6800, the CPU could either fetch or execute at a given time. In other words, the CPU had to fetch an instruction from memory, decode, and then execute it, and then fetch the next instruction, decode and execute it, and so on as shown in Figure 2-20. All steps of running a program occur serially. The idea of pipelining in its simplest form is to allow the CPU to fetch and execute at the same time. That is an instruction is being fetched while the previous instruction is being executed.

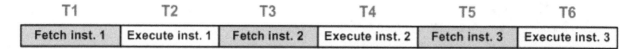

T1	T2	T3	T4	T5	T6
Fetch inst. 1	Execute inst. 1	Fetch inst. 2	Execute inst. 2	Fetch inst. 3	Execute inst. 3

Figure 2-20: Non-pipeline execution

We can use a pipeline to speed up execution of instructions. In pipelining, the process of executing instructions is split into small steps that are executed in parallel. In this way, the executions of many instructions are overlapped. One limitation of pipelining is that the speed of execution is limited to the slowest stage of the pipeline. Compare this to making pizza. You can split the process of making pizza into many stages, such as flattening the dough, putting on the toppings, and baking, but the process is limited to the slowest stage, baking, no matter how fast the rest of the stages are performed.

Arm multistage execution pipeline

As shown in Figure 2-21, in the Arm Cortex-M (except Cortex-M0), each instruction is executed in 3 stages: Fetch, Decode, and Execute.

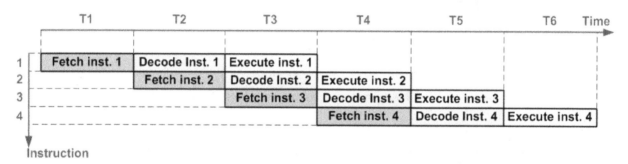

Figure 2-21: Pipeline in Arm

In step 1, the opcode is fetched. In step 2, the opcode is decoded. In step 3, the instruction is executed and result is written into the destination register.

Harvard Architecture

In Chapter 0, we discussed Harvard and Von Neumann architecture. Cortex-M (except Cortex-M0) uses Harvard architecture, which means that there are separate buses for the code and the data memory. See Figure 2-22. The Harvard architecture feeds the CPU with both code and data at the same time via two sets of buses, one for code and one for data. This lets the CPU fetch the next instruction while accessing the memory using the LDR/STR instructions.

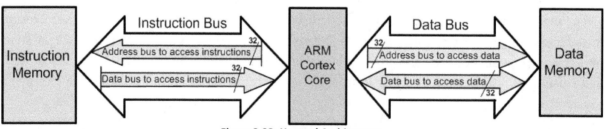

Figure 2-22: Harvard Architecture

In Sections 2-2 and 2-3, we learned about data memory space and how to use the STR and LDR instructions. When the CPU wants to execute the "LDR Rd, [Rx]" instruction, it puts the value of Rx on the address bus of the data bus, and receives data through the data bus. For example, to execute "LDR R2, [R5]", assuming that R5 = 0x20000200, the CPU puts 0x20000200 on the address bus. The location 0x20000200 is in the SRAM (See Figure 2-4). Thus, SRAM puts the contents of location 0x20000200 on the data bus. The CPU gets the contents of location 0x20000200 through the data bus and puts it in R2.

Review Questions
1. True or false. Cortex-M series use a 3-stage pipeline.
2. True or false. Cortex-M uses von Neumann architecture.
3. True or false. Cortex-M series (except Cortex-M0) use Harvard architecture.
4. True or false. Harvard architecture uses the same address and data buses to fetch both code and data.

Section 2.12: RISC Architecture in Arm

In the early 1980s, a controversy broke out in the computer design community, but unlike most controversies, it did not go away. Since the 1960s, in all mainframes and minicomputers, designers put as many instructions as they could think of into the CPU. Some of these instructions performed complex tasks like string operations. Naturally, microprocessor designers followed the lead of minicomputer and mainframe designers. Because these processors used such a large number of instructions, many of which performed highly complex activities, they came to be known as CISC (complex instruction set computer) processors. According to several studies in the 1970s, many of these complex instructions etched into CPUs were never used by programmers and compilers. The huge cost of implementing a large number of instructions (some of them complex) into the microprocessor, plus the fact that a good portion of the transistors on the chip are used by the instruction decoder, made some designers think of simplifying and reducing the number of instructions. As this concept developed, the resulting processors came to be known as RISC (reduced instruction set computer).

Features of RISC

The following are some of the features of RISC as implemented by the Arm microcontroller.

Feature 1

RISC processors have a fixed instruction size. In a CISC microprocessors such as the x86, instructions can be 1, 2, 3, or even 5 bytes. For example, look at the following instructions in the x86:

```
CLR    C                      ; clear Carry flag, a 1-byte instruction
ADD    Accumulator, #mybyte   ; a 2-byte instruction
LJMP   target_address         ; a 5-byte instruction
```

This variable instruction size makes the task of the instruction decoder very difficult because the size of the incoming instruction is never known. In a RISC architecture, the size of all instructions is fixed. Therefore, the CPU can decode the instructions quickly. This is like a bricklayer working with bricks of the same size as opposed to using bricks of variable sizes.

But fixed-size instruction has one drawback as well; the program memory usage is not optimized. In a 32-bit RISC CPU all the instructions are 32-bit and if not all the 32 bits are needed to form the instruction it fills with zeros. In the original Arm all the instructions were 32-bit. To decrease the memory size, Arm introduced the Thumb 16-bit instruction set. Thumb programs use less memory but since the Thumb instruction set is very limited compared to the Arm instruction set, the Thumb programs have lower performance. In the next step, Arm introduced Thumb2. In Thumb2, instructions can be 16-bit and 32-bit and it covers most of the features of the original Arm. So, the performance is almost the same as the original Arm while the program space is optimized.

Feature 2

One of the major characteristics of RISC architecture is a large number of registers. All RISC architectures have at least 8 or 16 registers. Of these 16 registers, only a few are assigned to dedicated functions. One advantage of a large number of registers is that it avoids the need for a large stack to store temporary data. Accessing data on the stack is a memory read/write and is much slower than CPU register access. Although a stack is implemented on a RISC processor, it is not as essential as in CISC because so many registers are available. In Arm the use of a large number of general purpose registers satisfies this RISC feature. The stack for the Arm is covered in Chapter 4.

Feature 3

RISC processors have a smaller instruction set. RISC processors have only basic instructions such as ADD, SUB, MUL, LOAD, STORE, AND, ORR, EOR, CALL, B, and so on. The limited number of instructions is one of the criticisms leveled at the RISC processor because it makes the task of assembly language programmers much more tedious and difficult compared to CISC assembly language programming. It is interesting to note that some defenders of CISC have called it "complete instruction set computer" instead of "complex instruction set computer" because it has a complete set of every kind of instruction. How many of these instructions are used and how often is another matter. In the recent years, almost all the new programs are written in high level languages such as C or Java. The advantage of CISC in this regard is no longer valid. The limited number of instructions in RISC leads to programs that are larger. Although these programs can use more memory, this is not a problem because memory is cheaper. Before the advent of semiconductor memory in the 1960s, however, CISC designers had to pack as much action as possible into a single instruction to get the maximum bang for their buck. In the Arm we have around 50 instructions. We will examine more of the instruction set for the Arm in future chapters.

Feature 4

At this point, one might ask, with all the difficulties associated with RISC programming, what is the gain? The most important characteristic of the RISC processor is that more than 99% of instructions are executed with only one clock cycle because the instructions are much simpler, in contrast to CISC instructions which take various number of clock cycles to execute. Even some of the 1% of the RISC instructions that are executed with two clock cycles can be executed with one clock cycle by juggling instructions around (code scheduling).

Feature 5

Because CISC has such a large number of instructions, each with so many different addressing modes, microinstructions (microcode) are used to implement them. The implementation of microinstructions inside the CPU employs more than 40–60% of transistors in many CISC processors. RISC instructions, however, due to the small set of instructions, are implemented using the hardwire method. Hardwiring of RISC instructions takes no more than 10% of the transistors. With much smaller circuit, the RISC processor consumes much less power. This is a major reason Arm processor is used in majority of the portable devices like cellphone or tablet.

Feature 6

RISC uses load/store architecture. In CISC microprocessors, data can be manipulated while it is still in memory. For example, in instructions such as "ADD Reg, Memory", the microprocessor must bring the contents of the external memory location into the CPU, add it to the contents of the register, then move the result back to the external memory location. The problem is there might be a delay in accessing the data from external memory then the whole process would be stalled, preventing other instructions from proceeding in the pipeline. In RISC, designers did away with these kinds of instructions. In RISC, instructions can only load from external memory into registers or store registers into external memory locations. There is no direct way of doing arithmetic and logic operations between a register and the contents of external memory locations. All these instructions must be performed by first bringing both operands into the registers inside the CPU, then performing the arithmetic or logic operation, and then sending the result back to memory. This idea was first implemented by the Cray 1 supercomputer in 1976 and is commonly referred to as load/store architecture. In the last section, we saw that the arithmetic and logic operations are between the GPRs registers, but none involves a memory location. For example, there is no "ADD R1, RAM-Loc" instruction in Arm. Operating only on the CPU registers guarantees that the memory bus contention will not slow down the instruction execution.

In concluding this discussion of RISC processors, it is interesting to note that RISC technology was explored by the scientists at IBM in the mid-1970s, but it was David Patterson of the University of California at Berkeley who in 1980 brought the merits of RISC concepts to the attention of computer scientists. It must also be noted that in recent years CISC processors such as the Pentium have used some RISC features in their design. This was the only way they could enhance the processing power of the x86 processors and stay competitive. Of course, they had to add circuits in the CPU to translate the x86 instructions into an internal RISC instruction set, because they had to deal with all the CISC instructions of the x86 processors and the legacy software of DOS/Windows.

Review Questions
1. What do RISC and CISC stand for?
2. True or false. The CISC architecture executes the vast majority of its instructions in 2, 3, or more clock cycles, while RISC executes them in one clock.
3. RISC processors normally have a _____ (large, small) number of general-purpose registers.
4. True or false. Instructions such as "ADD R16, ROMmemory" do not exist in RISC microprocessors such as the Arm.

5. True or false. While CISC instructions are of variable sizes, RISC instructions are all the same size.
6. Which of the following operations do not exist for the ADD instruction in RISC?

   (a) register to register (b) immediate to register (c) memory to memory

Problems

Section 2.1: The General Purpose Registers in the Arm

1. Arm is a(n) _____-bit microprocessor.
2. The general purpose registers are _____ bits wide.
3. The value in MOV R2, #value is _____ bits wide.
4. The largest number that an Arm GPR register can have is _____ in hex.
5. What is the result of the following code and where is it kept?

         MOV   R2, #0x15
         MOV   R1, #0x13
         ADD   R2, R1, R2
6. Which of the followings is (are) illegal?

   (a) MOV R1, #0x52   (b) MOV R2, #0x50   (c) MOV R1, #0x00

   (d) MOV R1, 255   (e) MOV R17, #25   (f) MOV R23, #0xF5

   (g) MOV 123, 0x50   (h) MOV R1,#0x1234
7. Which of the following is (are) illegal?

   (a) ADD R2, #20, R1   (b) ADD R1, R1, R2   (c) ADD R5, R16, R3
8. What is the result of the following code and where is it kept?

         MOV R9, #0x25
         ADD R8, R9, #0x1F
9. What is the result of the following code and where is it kept?

         MOV R1, #0x15
         ADD R6, R1, #0xEA
10. True or false. We have 32 general purpose registers in the Arm.
11. True or false. R13 and R14 are special function registers.
12. Show the lowest and highest values (in hex) that the Arm program counter can take.

Section 2.2: The Arm Memory Map

13. True or false. The peripheral registers are mapped to memory space.
14. True or false. The On-chip Flash is the same size in all members of Arm.
15. True or false. The On-chip data SRAM is the same size in all members of Arm.
16. What is the maximum number of bytes that the Arm can access?
17. Find the address of the last location of on-chip Flash for each of the following, assuming the first location is 0:

    (a) Arm with 32 KB   (b) Arm with 8 KB

    (c) Arm with 64 KB   (d) Arm with 16 KB

    (e) Arm with 128 KB   (f) Arm with 256 KB

18. A given Arm has 0x7FFF as the address of the last location of its on-chip ROM. What is the size of on-chip Flash for this Arm?

19. Repeat Question 18 for 0x3FFF.

20. Find the on-chip program memory size in K for the Arm chip with the following address ranges:

    (a) 0x0000–0x1FFF   (b) 0x0000–0x3FFF

    (c) 0x0000–0x7FFF   (d) 0x0000–0xFFFF

    (e) 0x0000–0x1FFFF   (f) 0x00000–0x3FFFF

21. Find the on-chip program memory size in K for the Arm chips with the following address ranges:

    (a) 0x00000–0xFFFFFF   (b) 0x00000–0x7FFFF

    (c) 0x00000–0x7FFFFF   (d) 0x00000–0xFFFFF

    (e) 0x00000–0x1FFFFF   (f) 0x00000–0x3FFFFF

Section 2.3: Load and Store Instructions in Arm

22. Show a simple code to store values 0x30 and 0x97 into locations 0x20000015 and 0x20000016, respectively.

23. Show a simple code to load the value 0x55 into locations 0x20000030–0x20000038.

24. True or false. We cannot load immediate values into the data SRAM directly.

25. Show a simple code to load the value 0x11 into locations 0x20000010–0x20000015.

26. Show a simple code to load the value 0x19 into locations 0x20000034–0x2000003C.

27. Show the contents of the memory locations after the execution of each instruction.

    (a) LDR R2, =0x129F   (b) LDR R4, =0x8C63
        LDR R1, =0x20001450   LDR R1, =0x20002400
        LDR R2, [R1]   LDRH R4, [R1]

    0x20001450 = (.......)   0x20002400 = (.......)
    0x20001451 = (.......)   0x20002401 = (.......)

Section 2.4: Arm CPSR (Current Program Status Register)

28. The status register is a(n) _____ -bit register.

29. Which bits of the status register are used for the C and Z flag bits, respectively?

30. Which bits of the status register are used for the V and N flag bits, respectively?

31. In the ADD instruction, when is C raised?

32. In the ADD instruction, when is Z raised?

33. What is the status of the C and Z flags after the following code?

```
        LDR     R0, =0xFFFFFFFF
        LDR     R1, =0xFFFFFFF1
        ADDS    R1, R0, R1
```

34. Find the C flag value after each of the following codes:

    (a) LDR R0, =0xFFFFFF54   (b) MOV R3, #0   (c) LDR R3, =0xFFFFFFFF
        LDR R5, =0xFFFFFFC4   LDR R6, =0xFFFFFFFF   LDR R8, =0xFFFFFF05
        ADDS R2, R5, R0   ADDS R3, R3, R6   ADDS R2, R3, R8

35. Write a simple program in which the value 0x55 is added 5 times.

Section 2.5: Arm Data Format and Directives

36. State the value (in hex) used for each of the following data:
    MYDAT_1 EQU 55
    MYDAT_2 EQU 98
    MYDAT_3 EQU 'G'
    MYDAT_4 EQU 0x50
    MYDAT_5 EQU 200
    MYDAT_6 EQU 'A'
    MYDAT_7 EQU 0xAA
    MYDAT_8 EQU 255
    MYDAT_9 EQU 2_10010000
    MYDAT_10 EQU 2_01111110
    MYDAT_11 EQU 10
    MYDAT_12 EQU 15
37. State the value (in hex) for each of the following data:
    DAT_1 EQU 22
    DAT_2 EQU 0x56
    DAT_3 EQU 2_10011001
    DAT_4 EQU 32
    DAT_5 EQU 0xF6
    DAT_6 EQU 2_11111011
38. Show a simple code to load the value 0x10102265 into locations 0x20000030–0x2000003F.
39. Show a simple code to (a) load the value 0x23456789 into locations 0x20000060–0x2000006F, and (b) add them together and place the result in R9 as the values are added. Use EQU to assign the names TEMP0–TEMP3 to locations 0x20000060–0x2000006F.

Section 2.6: Assembler data allocation directives

40. Allocate 4 bytes of memory and initialize them with 1, 2, 3, and 4.
41. Using DCB, store your first name in the flash memory.
42. Allocate 60 bytes of SRAM.
43. Allocate 4 bytes of RAM and name it as Temp. ·

Sections 2.7 and 2.8: Introduction to Arm Assembly Programming and Assembling an Arm Program

44. Assembly language is a _____ (low, high)-level language while C is a _____ (low, high)-level language.
45. Of C and assembly language, which is more efficient in terms of code generation (i.e., the amount of program memory space it uses)?
46. Which program produces the .obj file?
47. True or false. The assembly source file may have the extension ".asm".

48. True or false. The source code file can be a non-ASCII file.
49. True or false. Every source file must have EQU directive.
50. Do the EQU and END directives produce opcodes?
51. The file with the _____ extension is downloaded into Arm Flash ROM.
52. Give three file extensions produced by Arm Keil.

Section 2.9: The Program Counter and Program ROM Space in the Arm

53. Every Cortex-M loads PC with _____ when it is powered up.
54. Write a program to add each of your 5-digit ID to a register and place the result into memory location 0x2000100. Use the program listing to show the Flash memory addresses and their contents.

Section 2.10: Some Arm Addressing Modes

55. Give the addressing mode for each of the following:

    (a) MOV R5, R3   (b) MOV R0, #56

    (c) LDR R5, [R3]   (d) ADD R9, R1, R2

    (e) LDR R7, [R2]   (f) LDRB R1, [R4]

Section 2.11: Pipelining and Harvard Architecture in Arm
56. The Arm Cortex-M3 uses a pipeline of _____ stages.
57. Give the names of the pipeline stages in the Cortex.

Section 2.12: RISC Architecture in Arm
58. What do RISC and CISC stand for?
59. In _____ (RISC, CISC) architecture we can have 1-, 2-, 3-, or 4-byte instructions.
60. In _____ (RISC, CISC) architecture instructions are fixed in size.
61. In _____ (RISC, CISC) architecture instructions are mostly executed in one or two cycles.
62. In _____ (RISC, CISC) architecture we can have an instruction to ADD a register to external memory.
63. True or false. Most instructions in CISC are executed in one or two cycles.

Answers to Review Questions

Section 2.1
1. MOV   R2, #0x34
2.

```
MOV    R1, #0x16
MOV    R2, #0xCD
ADD    R1, R1, R2
```

    or

```
MOV    R1, #0x16
ADD    R1, R1, #0xCD
```

3. False
4. 32
1. True
2. general-purpose registers
3. 32
4. Special function registers (SFRs)
5. 32

Section 2.2

1. True
2. The flash ROM is used to store the program code. The memory can also be used for storage of static data such as text strings and look-up tables

Section 2.3

1. True
2.

```
MOV    R1, #0x20
MOV    R2, #0x95
STRB   R2, [R1]
```

3. `STR    R2, [R8]`
4.

```
MOV    R1, #0x20
LDR    R4, [R1]
```

5. 0xFF in hex or 255 in decimal
6. R6
7. It copies the lower 8 bits of R1 into location pointed to by R2.
8. 0xFFFFFFFF in hex or 4,294,967,295 in decimal (2^{32}-1)

Section 2.4

1. CPSR (current program status register)
2. 32 bits
3.

Hex	Binary
FFFFFF9F	1111 1111 1111 1111 1111 1111 1001 1111
+00000061	+ 0000 0000 0000 0000 0000 0000 0110 0001
1 00000000	1 0000 0000 0000 0000 0000 0000 0000 0000

This leads to C = 1 and Z = 1.

4.

	Hex	Binary
	00000022	0000 0000 0000 0000 0000 0000 0010 0010
	+00000022	+ 0000 0000 0000 0000 0000 0000 0010 0010
	0 00000000	0000 0000 0000 0000 0000 0000 0100 0100

This leads to Z = 0.

5.

	Hex	Binary
	0000 0067	0000 0000 0000 0000 0000 0000 0110 0111
	+ 0000 0099	+ 0000 0000 0000 0000 0000 0000 1001 1001
	0000 0100	0000 0000 0000 0000 0000 0001 0000 0000

This leads to C = 0 and Z = 0.

Section 2.5

1. MOV R1, #0x20
2. (a) MOV R2, #0x14   (b) MOV R2, #20   (c) MOV R2, #2_00010100
3. If the value is to be changed later, it can be done once in one place instead of at every occurrence in the file and the code becomes more readable, as well.
4. (a) 0x34   (b) 0x1F
5. 15 in decimal (0x0F in hex)
6. Value of location 0x00000200 = 0x95
7. 0x0C + 0x10 = 0x1C will be in data memory location 0x00000630.

Section 2.6

1. True
2. False
3. True

Section 2.7

1. Assembly directives direct the assembler in doing its job.
2. The instructions, assembler directives
3. False
4. All except (c)
5. True
6. (c)

Section 2.8

1. True
2. True

3. (a)
4. (b), (c) and (d)

Section 2.9
1. 32
2. False
3. 0x00000004

Section 2.10
1. No
2. The general purpose registers (R0 to R15)
3. It is a part of the instruction

Section 2.11
1. True
2. False
3. True
4. False

Section 2.12
1. RISC is Reduced Instruction Set Computer; CISC stands for Complex Instruction Set Computer.
2. True
3. Large
4. True
5. True
6. (c)

Chapter 3: Arithmetic and Logic Instructions and Programs

In this chapter, most of the arithmetic and logic instructions are discussed and program examples are given to illustrate the application of these instructions. Unsigned numbers are used in this discussion of arithmetic and logic instructions. In Section 3.1 we examine the arithmetic instructions for unsigned numbers. The logic instructions and programs are covered in Section 3.2. In Section 3.3 we discuss the Arm instructions for rotate and shift. In Section 3.4 we perform the shift and rotate operations as part of the other data processing instructions. Section 3.5 is dedicated to BCD and ASCII data conversion.

Section 3.1: Arithmetic Instructions

Unsigned numbers are numbers that represent only zero or positive numbers. All the bits are used to represent data and no bits are set aside for the positive or negative sign. This means that the operand can be between 00 and 0xFF (0 to 255 decimal) for 8-bit data and between 0x0000 and 0xFFFF (0 to 65535 decimal) for 16-bit data. For the 32-bit operand it can be between 0 and 0xFFFFFFFF (0 to 2^{32} -1). See Table 3-1. This section covers the ADD, SUB, multiply and divide instructions for unsigned number.

Data Size	Bits	Decimal	Hexadecimal	Load instruction used
Byte	8	0 – 255	0 – 0xFF	STRB
Half-word	16	0 – 65535	0 – 0xFFFF	STRH
Word	32	0 – 2^{32}-1	0 – 0xFFFFFFFF	STR

Table 3-1: Unsigned Data Range Summary in Arm

Affecting flags in Arm instructions

A unique feature of the execution of Arm arithmetic instructions is that it does not affect (updates) the flags in the CPSR register unless we explicitly request it. This is different from most of other microprocessors and microcontrollers. In other processors the arithmetic/logic instructions (and sometimes other instructions) automatically change the N, Z, C, and V flags according to the result of the operation. To update the flags in CPSR register in Arm CPU by the data processing instructions, the S flag in the instruction must be set. This is done by appending the 'S' suffix to the opcode of the instruction. With the S suffix, the Arm assembler will set the S flag in the instruction. For example, we use SUBS instead of SUB if we want the instruction to update the flags in CPSR. The SUBS means subtract and set the flags, while the SUB simply subtracts without having any effect on the flags. See Table 3-2.

Instruction (Flags unchanged)		Instruction (Flags updated)	
ADD	Add	ADDS	Add and set flags
ADC	Add with carry	ADCS	Add with carry and set flags
SUB	SUBS	SUBS	Subtract and set flags
SBC	Subtract with carry	SBCS	Subtract with carry and set flags
RSB	Reverse subtract	RSBS	Reverse subtract and set flags
RSC	Reverse subtract with carry	RSCS	Reverse subtract with carry and set flags
Note: The above instructions affect all the N, Z, C, and V flag bits of CPSR (current program status register) but the N and V flags are for signed data and are discussed in Chapter 5.			

Table 3-2: Arithmetic Instructions and Flag Bits for Unsigned Data

Addition of unsigned numbers

The form of the ADD instruction is

```
ADD    Rd, Rn, Op2          ; Rd = Rn + Op2
```

The instructions ADD and ADC are used to add two operands. The destination operand must be a register. The Op2 (or operand 2) can be a register or an immediate value. Remember that memory-to-register or memory-to-memory arithmetic and logic operations are never allowed in Arm processor since it is a RISC processor. The instruction could change any of the N, Z, C, or V bits of the program status register, as long as we use the ADDS instead of ADD. The effects of the ADDS instruction on the V (overflow) and N (negative) flags are discussed in Chapter 5 since they are used in signed number operations. Look at Examples 3-1 and 3-2 for the effect of ADDS instruction on Z and C flags.

Example 3-1

Show the flag bits of status register for the following cases:

```
a)    LDR    R2, =0xFFFFFFF5    ; R2 = 0xFFFFFFF5 (notice the = sign)
      MOV    R3, #0x0B
      ADDS   R1, R2, R3         ; R1 = R2 + R3 and update the flags


b)    LDR    R2, =0xFFFFFFFF
      ADDS   R1, R2, #0x95      ; R1 = R2 + 95 and update the flags
```

Solution:

a)

```
        0xFFFFFFF5        1111 1111 1111 1111 1111 1111 1111 0101
    +   0x0000000B      + 0000 0000 0000 0000 0000 0000 0000 1011
        0x100000000     1 0000 0000 0000 0000 0000 0000 0000 0000
```

First, notice how the "LDR R2, =0xFFFFFFF5" pseudo-instruction loads the 32-bit value into R2 register. Also notice the use of ADDS instruction instead of ADD since the ADD instruction does not update the flags. Now, after the addition, the R1 register (destination) contains 0 and the flags are as follows:
C = 1, since there is a carry out from D31
Z = 1, the result of the action is zero (for all 32 bits)

b)

```
        0xFFFFFFFF        1111 1111 1111 1111 1111 1111 1111 1111
    +   0x00000095      + 0000 0000 0000 0000 0000 0000 1001 0101
        0x100000094     1 0000 0000 0000 0000 0000 0000 1001 0100
```

After the addition, the R1 register (destination) contains 0x94 and the flags are as follows:
C = 1, since there is a carry out from D31
Z = 0, the result of the action is not zero (for the 32 bits)

Example 3-2

Show the flag bits of status register for the following case:

```
LDR    R2, =0xFFFFFFF1    ; R2 = 0xFFFFFFF1
MOV    R3, #0x0F
ADDS   R3, R3, R2         ; R3 = R3 + R2 and update the flags
ADD    R3, R3, #0x7       ; R3 = R3 + 0x7 and flags unchanged
MOV    R1, R3
```

Solution:

```
   0xFFFFFFF1      1111 1111 1111 1111 1111 1111 1111 0001
+  0x0000000F    + 0000 0000 0000 0000 0000 0000 0000 1111
   0x100000000   1 0000 0000 0000 0000 0000 0000 0000 0000
```

After the ADDS addition, the R3 register (destination) contains 0 and the flags are as follows:

C = 1, since there is a carry out from D31

Z = 1, the result of the action is zero (for the 32 bits)

After the "ADD R3, R3, #0x7" addition, the R3 register (destination) contains 0x7 (0 + 07 = 07) and the flags are unchanged from previous instruction since we used ADD instead of ADDS. Therefore, the Z = 1 and C = 1. If we used "ADDS R3, R3, #0x7" instruction instead of "ADD R3, R3, #0x7", we would have Z = 0 and C = 0. Use the Keil Arm simulator to verify this.

Comment

Microsoft Windows comes with a calculator. Use the Programmer mode to verify the calculations in this and future chapters. The calculator supports data size of up to 64-bit

ADC (add with carry)

This instruction is used for adding multiword (data larger than 32-bit) numbers. The form of the ADC instruction is

```
ADC    Rd, Rn, Op2 ; Rd = Rn + Op2 + Carry
```

In discussing addition, the following two cases will be examined:

- Addition of single word data
- Addition of multiword data

CASE 1: Addition of single word data

The result of adding two 32-bit registers can be more than 32-bit. So, whenever some big 32-bit values are added, after each addition, the carry flag should be considered. See Example 3-3.

Example 3-3: Write a program to calculate the total sum of five words of data. Each data value represents the mass of a planet in integer. The decimal data are as follow: 1000000000, 2000000000, 3000000000, 4000000000, and 4100000000. The results should be in R9:R8.

Solution:

```
      EXPORT  __main
      AREA       EXAMPLE3_3, CODE, READONLY
__main
      LDR   R1, =1000000000
      LDR   R2, =2000000000
      LDR   R3, =3000000000
      LDR   R4, =4000000000
      LDR   R5, =4100000000
      MOV   R8, #0      ; R8 = 0 for saving the lower word
      MOV   R9, #0      ; R9 = 0 for accumulating the carries

      ADDS  R8, R8, R1  ; R8 = R8 + R1
      ADC   R9, R9, #0  ; R9 = R9 + 0 + Carry
                        ; (increment R9 if there is carry)
      ADDS  R8, R8, R2  ; R8 = R8 + R2
      ADC   R9, R9, #0  ; R9 = R9 + 0 + Carry
      ADDS  R8, R8, R3  ; R8 = R8 + R3
      ADC   R9, R9, #0  ; R9 = R9 + 0 + Carry
      ADDS  R8, R8, R4  ; R8 = R8 + R4
      ADC   R9, R9, #0  ; R9 = R9 + 0 + Carry
      ADDS  R8, R8, R5  ; R8 = R8 + R5
      ADC   R9, R9, #0  ; R9 = R9 + 0 + Carry
HERE  B     HERE
      END
```

CASE 2: Addition of multi-word numbers

Assume a program is needed that will add the total U.S. budget for the last 100 years or the mass of all the planets in the solar system. In cases like this, the numbers being added could be up to 8 bytes wide or more. Since Arm registers are only 32 bits wide (4 bytes), it is the job of the programmer to write the code to break down these large numbers into smaller chunks to be processed by the CPU. If a 32-bit register is used and the operand is 8 bytes wide, that would take a total of two iterations. See Example 3-4. However, if a 16-bit register is used, the same operands would require four iterations. This obviously takes more time for the CPU, one reason to have wide registers in the design of the CPU.

Example 3-4

Analyze the following program which adds 0x35F62562FA to 0x21F412963B:

```
      LDR   R0, =0xF62562FA   ; R0 = 0xF62562FA
      LDR   R1, =0xF412963B   ; R1 = 0xF412963B
      MOV   R2, #0x35         ; R2 = 0x35
```

```
MOV    R3, #0x21        ; R3 = 0x21
ADDS   R5, R1, R0       ; R5 = 0xF62562FA + 0xF412963B
                        ; now C = 1
ADC    R6, R2, R3       ; R6 = R2 + R3 + C
                        ;    = 0x35 + 21 + 1 = 0x57
```

Solution:

After the R5 = R0 + R1 the carry flag is one. Since C = 1, when ADC is executed, R6 = R2 + R3 + C = 0x35 + 0x21 + 1 = 0x57.

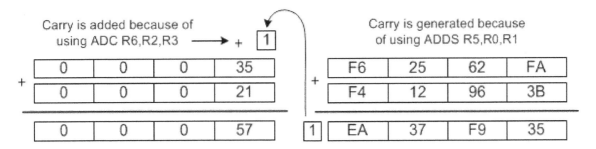

Microsoft Windows calculator support data size of up 64-bit (double word). Use it to verify the above calculations.

Subtraction of unsigned numbers

```
SUB    Rd, Rn, Op2 ; Rd = Rn - Op2
```

In subtraction, the Arm microprocessors (and almost all modern CPUs) use the 2's complement method. All CPUs contain adder circuitry. It would be redundant to design a separate subtractor circuitry if subtraction can be performed with adder. Assuming that the Arm is executing simple subtract instructions, one can summarize the steps of the hardware of the CPU in executing the SUB instruction for unsigned numbers as follows:

1. Take the 2's complement of the subtrahend (Operand 2).
2. Add it to the minuend (Rn operand).
3. Place the result in destination Rd.
4. Update the flags in CPSR if the S flag is set in the instruction.

These four steps are performed for every SUBS instruction by the internal hardware of the Arm CPU. It is after these four steps that the result is obtained and the flags are set. Examples 3-5 through 3-7 illustrates the four steps.

Example 3-5

Show the steps involved for the following cases:

a)
```
MOV    R2, #0x4F        ; R2 = 0x4F
MOV    R3, #0x39        ; R3 = 0x39
SUBS   R4, R2, R3       ; R4 = R2 - R3
```

b)

```
    MOV    R2, #0x4F          ; R2 = 0x4F
    SUBS   R4, R2, #0x05      ; R4 = R2 - 0x05
```

Solution:

a)

```
      0x4F        0000004F
    - 0x39      + FFFFFFC7   2's complement of 0x39
      0x16      1 00000016   (C = 1 step 4)
```

The flags would be set as follows: C = 1, and Z = 0.

b)

```
      0x4F        0000004F
    - 0x05      + FFFFFFFB   2's complement of 0x05
      0x4A      1 0000004A   (C=1 step 4)
```

Example 3-6

Analyze the following instructions:

```
    LDR    R2, =0x88888888    ; R2 = 0x88888888
    LDR    R3, =0x33333333    ; R3 = 0x33333333
    SUBS   R4, R2, R3         ; R4 = R2 - R3
```

Solution:

Following are the steps for "SUB R4, R2, R3":

```
      88888888      88888888
    - 33333333    + CCCCCCCD   (2's complement of 0x33333333)
      55555555    1 55555555   (C = 1 step 4)
```

After the execution of SUBS, if C=1, there was no borrow; if C = 0, borrow occurred at the most significant bit. Since we are only dealing with unsigned numbers in this chapter, the result is incorrect with a borrow.

Example 3-7

Analyze the following instructions:

```
MOV    R1, #0x4C    ; R1 = 0x4C
MOV    R2, #0x6E    ; R2 = 0x6E
SUBS   R0, R1, R2   ; R0 = R1 - R2
```

Solution:

Following are the steps for "SUB R0, R1, R2":

```
  4C      0000004C
- 6E    + FFFFFF92   (2's complement of 0x6E)
- 22    0 FFFFFFDE   (C = 0 step 4) result is incorrect
```

SBC (subtract with borrow)

```
SBC    Rd, Rn, Op2 ; Rd = Rn - Op2 - 1 + C
```

This instruction is used for subtraction of multiword (data larger than 32-bit) numbers. Notice that in some other architectures, the CPU inverts the C flag after subtraction so the content of carry flag is the borrow bit of subtract operation. But in Arm the carry flag is not inverted after subtraction and the carry flag after the subtraction is the invert of the borrow. This difference does not affect the use of SBC instruction because in those architectures the subtract with borrow is implemented as "Rd = Rn – Op2 – C" but in Arm, it is implemented as "Rd = Rn – Op2 – 1 + C". So the polarity of the carry bin in subtraction is compensated by SBC instruction. See Example 3-8.

Example 3-8

Analyze the following program which subtracts 0x21F62562FA from 0x35F412963B:

```
LDR    R0, =0xF62562FA    ; R0 = 0xF62562FA,
                          ; notice the syntax for LDR
LDR    R1, =0xF412963B    ; R1 = 0xF412963B
MOV    R2, #0x21          ; R2 = 0x21
MOV    R3, #0x35          ; R3 = 0x35
SUBS   R5, R1, R0         ; R5 = R1 - R0
                          ;    = 0xF412963B - 0xF62562FA, and C = 0
SBC    R6, R3, R2         ; R6 = R3 - R2 - 1 + C
                          ;    = 0x35 - 0x21 - 1 + 0 = 0x13
```

Solution:

After the R5 = R1 – R0 there is a borrow so the carry flag is cleared. Since C = 0, when SBC is executed, R6 = R3 – R2 – 1 + C = 0x35 – 0x21 – 1 + 0 = 0x35 – 0x21 – 1= 0x13.

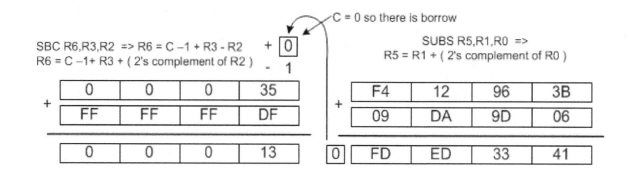

Multiplication and division of unsigned numbers

Because multiplication and division circuits are complex, not all processors have instructions for multiplication and division. All the Arm processors have multiplication instructions but not all have the division. Some family members such as Arm Cortex-A, Cortex-M3, and M4 have both the division and multiplication instructions. In this section we examine the multiplication of unsigned numbers. Signed numbers multiplication is treated in Chapter 5.

Multiplication of unsigned numbers in Arm

The Arm gives you two choices of unsigned multiplication: regular multiply and long multiply. The regular multiply instruction (MUL) is used when the result is less than 32-bit, while the long multiply (MULL) is used when the result is greater than 32-bit. See Table 3-3. In this section we examine both of them.

Instruction	Source 1	Source 2	Destination	Result
MUL	Rn	Op2	Rd (32 bits)	Rd=Rn×Op2
UMULL	Rn	Op2	RdLo, RdHi (64 bits)	RdLo:RdHi=Rn×Op2
Note 1: Using MUL for word × word multiplication preserves only the lower 32-bit result in Rd and the rest are dropped. If the result is greater than 0xFFFFFFFF, then we must use UMULL (unsigned Multiply Long) instruction.				
Note 2: In some CPUs the C flag is used to indicate the result is greater than 32-bit but this is not the case with Arm MUL instruction.				

Table 3-3: Unsigned Multiplication (UMUL Rd, Rn, Op2) Summary

MUL (multiply)
```
MUL    Rd, Rn, Op2 ; Rd = Rn × Op2
```

In multiplication, all the operands must be in register. Immediate value is not allowed as an operand. After the multiplication, the destination register will contain the result. See the following example:

```
MOV    R1, #0x25    ; R1=0x25
MOV    R2, #0x65    ; R2=0x65
MUL    R3, R1, R2   ; R3 = R1 × R2 = 0x65 × 0x25
```

Note that in the case of half-word times half-word or smaller sources since the destination register is 32-bit there is no problem in keeping the result of 65,535 × 65,535, the highest possible unsigned 16-bit data. That is not the case in word times word multiplication because 32-bit × 32-bit can produce a result greater than 32-bit. If the MUL instruction is used, the destination register will only hold the lower word (32-bit) and the portion beyond 32-bit is dropped. So it is not safe to use MUL for multiplication of numbers greater than 65,536. See the following example:

```
LDR    R1, =100000  ; R1=100,000
LDR    R2, =150000  ; R2=150,000
MUL    R3, R2, R1   ; R3 is not 15,000,000,000 because
                    ; it cannot fit in 32 bits.
```

For this reason, we must use UMULL (unsigned multiply long) instruction if the result is going to be greater than 0xFFFFFFFF.

UMULL (unsigned multiply long)

```
UMULL  RdLo, RdHi, Rn, Op2      ; RdHi:RdLoRd = Rn × Op2
```

In unsigned long multiplication, all the operands must be in register and no immediate value is allowed. After the multiplication, the destination registers will contain the result. Notice that the left most register in the instruction, RdLo in our case, will hold the lower word and the higher portion beyond 32-bit is saved in the second register, RdHi. See the following example:

```
LDR    R1, =0x54000000   ; R1 = 0x54000000
LDR    R2, =0x10000002   ; R2 = 0x10000002
UMULL  R3, R4, R2, R1    ; 0x54000000 × 0x10000002 = 0x054000000A8000000
                         ; R3 = 0xA8000000, the lower 32 bits
                         ; R4 = 0x05400000, the higher 32 bits
```

Notice that it is the job of programmer to choose the best type of multiplication depending on the size of operands and the result. See Example 3-9.

Example 3-9

Write a short program to multiply 0xFFFFFFFF by itself.
Solution:

```
MOV R1, #0xFFFFFFFF      ; R1 = 0xFFFFFFFF
UMULL R3, R4, R1, R1
```

Since 0xFFFFFFFF × 0xFFFFFFFF = 0xFFFFFFFE00000001, then R4=0xFFFFFFFE and R3=0x00000001. If we had used MUL instruction, then the 0xFFFFFFFF would have been dropped and only 0x00000001 would have been kept by the destination register.

Notice that in Cortex-M which use Thumb-2 the multiply instructions do not affect the flags.

Division of unsigned numbers in Arm

To divide unsigned numbers UDIV can be used:

```
UDIV   Rd, Rn, Op2  ; Rd = Rn / Op2
```

The following example divides 8 by 3 and stores the result in R5:

```
MOV   R1, #8      ; R1 = 8
MOV   R2, #3      ; R2 = 3
UDIV  R5, R1, R2  ; R5 = 8/3 = 2
```

Other Arithmetic Instructions (Case study)

RSB (reverse subtract)

The format for the RSB instruction is

```
RSB   Rd, Rn, Op2          ; Rd = Op2 - Rn
```

Notice the difference between the RSB and SUB instruction. They are essentially the same except the way the source operands are subtracted is reversed. See Example 3-10.

Example 3-10

Find the result of R0 for the following:

```
MOV   R1, #0x1   ; R1 = 1
RSB   R0, R1, #0  ; R0 = 0 - R1 = 0 - 1
```

Solution:

Following are the steps for "RSB R0, R1, #0":

```
     0      00000000
  - 6E   + FFFFFF92   (2's complement)
  - 6E     FFFFFF92   (C = 0) result is negative
```

Multiply and Accumulate Instructions in Arm

In some applications such as digital signal processing (DSP) we need to multiply two variables and add the result to another variable. The Arm has an instruction to do both in a single instruction. The format of MLA (multiply and accumulate) instruction is as follows:

```
MLA   Rd, Rm, Rs, Rn    ; Rd = Rm × Rs + Rn
```

In multiplication and accumulate, all the operands must be in register. After the multiplication and add, the destination register will contain the result. See the following example:

```
MOV   R1, #100          ; R1 = 100
MOV   R2, #5            ; R2 = 5
```

80

```
MOV    R3, #40            ; R3 = 40
MLA    R4, R1, R2, R3     ; R4 = R1 × R2 + R3 = 100 × 5 + 40 = 540
```

To accumulate the products of the multiplication, just use the same register for Rd and Rn:

```
MLA    R3, R1, R2, R3     ; R3 = R1 × R2 + R3 or R3 += R1 × R2
```

Notice that multiply and accumulate can produce a result greater than 32-bit, if the MLA instruction is used, the destination register will only hold the lower word (32 bits) of the sum and the portion beyond 32-bit is dropped. For this reason, we must use UMLAL (unsigned multiply and accumulate long) instruction if the result is going to be greater than 0xFFFFFFFF. The format of UMLAL instruction is as follows:

```
UMLAL RdLo, RdHi, Rn, Op2      ; RdHi:RdLo = Rn × Op2 + RdHi:RdLo
```

In UMLAL instruction, all the operands must be in register. Notice that the addend and the destination use the same registers, the two left most registers in the instruction. It means that the contents of the registers which have the addend will be changed after execution of UMLAL instruction. See the following example:

```
LDR    R1, =0x34000000    ; R1 = 0x34000000
LDR    R2, =0x2000000     ; R2 = 0x2000000
MOV    R3, #0             ; R3 = 0x00
LDR    R4, =0x00000BBB    ; R4 = 0x00000BBB
UMLAL R4, R3, R2, R1      ; 0x34000000×0x2000000+0xBBB
                          ;   = 0x068000000000000BBB
```

Review Questions

1. Explain the difference between ADDS and ADD instructions.
2. The ADC instruction that has the syntax "ADC Rd, Rn, Op2" means _____.
3. Explain why the Z=0 for the following:

```
MOV          R2, #0x4F
MOV          R4, #0xB1
ADDS         R2, R4, R2
```

4. Explain why the Z=1 for the following:

```
MOV          R2, #0x4F
LDR          R4, =0xFFFFFFB1
ADDS         R2, R4, R2
```

5. Show how the CPU would subtract 0x05 from 0x43.
6. If C = 1, R2 = 0x95, and R3 = 0x4F prior to the execution of "SBC R2, R2, R3", what will be the contents of R2 after the subtraction?
7. In unsigned multiplication of "MUL R2, R3, R4", the product will be placed in register

    _____.

8. In unsigned multiplication of "MUL R1, R2, R4", the R2 can be maximum of _____ if R4 = 0xFFFFFFFF so that there are no bits lost by the operation.

Section 3.2: Logic Instructions

In this section we discuss the logic instructions AND, OR, and Ex-OR in the context of many examples. Just like arithmetic instruction, we must use the S suffix in the instruction if we want to update the flags. If the S suffix is used the Z flag will be set if and only if the result is all zeros, and the N flag will be set to the logical value of bit 31 of the result. The V flag in the CPSR will be unaffected, and the C flag will be updated according to the calculation of the Operand 2. See Table 3-4.

Instruction (Flags Unchanged)	Action	Instruction (Flags Changed)	Hexadecimal
AND	ANDing	ANDS	Anding and set flags
ORR	ORRing	ORS	Oring and set flags
EOR	Exclusive-ORing	EORS	Exclusive ORing and set flags
BIC	Bit Clearing	BICS	Bit clearing and set flags

Table 3-4: Logic Instructions and Flag Bits

AND

```
AND    Rd, Rn, Op2          ; Rd = Rn ANDed Op2
```

Inputs		Output	Symbol
X	**Y**	**X AND Y**	
0	0	0	
0	1	0	
1	0	0	
1	1	1	

This instruction will perform a bitwise logical AND on the operands and place the result in the destination. The destination and the first source operand are registers. The second source operand can be a register or an immediate value of less than 0xFF with even bits of rotate.

If we use ANDS instead of AND it will change the N and Z flags according to the result (and C flag during the calculation of operand 2). As seen in Example 3-11, AND can be used to mask certain bits of the operand.

Example 3-11

Show the results of the following cases

a)
```
MOV    R1, #0x35
AND    R2, R1, #0x0F       ; R2 = R1 ANDed with 0x0F
```

b)
```
MOV    R0, #0x97
MOV    R1, #0xF0
AND    R2, R0, R1          ; R2 = R0 ANDed with R1
```

Solution:

a)

	0x35	0 0 1 1 0 1 0 1
AND	0x0F	0 0 0 0 1 1 1 1
	0x05	0 0 0 0 0 1 0 1

b)

	0x97	1 0 0 1 0 1 1 1
AND	0xF0	1 1 1 1 0 0 0 0
	0x90	1 0 0 1 0 0 0 0

ORR

ORR   Rd, Rn, Op2 ; Rd = Rn ORed Op2

Inputs		Output	Symbol
X	Y	X OR Y	
0	0	0	
0	1	1	
1	0	1	
1	1	1	

The operands are ORed and the result is placed in the destination. ORR can be used to set certain bits of an operand to one. The destination and the first source operand are registers. The second source operand can be either a register or an immediate value of less than 0xFF with even bits of rotate.

If we use ORRS instead of ORR, the flags will be updated, just the same as for the ANDS instruction. See Example 3-12.

Example 3-12

Show the results of the following cases:

a)
```
      MOV    R1, #0x04        ; R1 = 0x04
      ORRS   R2, R1, #0x68    ; R2= R1 ORed 0x68
```

b)
```
      MOV    R0, #0x97
      MOV    R1, #0xF0
      ORR    R2, R0, R1       ; R2= R0 ORed with R1
```

Solution:

a)

	0x04	0000 0100	
OR	0x68	0110 1000	Flag will be: Z = 0
	0x6C	0110 1100	

b)

```
        0x97    1001 0111
OR      0xF0    1111 0000      Flag will be unchanged
        0xF7    1111 0111
```

The ORR instruction can also be used to test for a zero operand. For example, "ORRS R2, R2, #0" will OR the register R2 with zero and make Z = 1 if R2 is zero.

EOR

```
EOR    Rd, Rn, Op2 ; Rd = Rn Ex-ORed with Op2
```

Inputs		Output	Symbol
X	Y	X EOR Y	
0	0	0	
0	1	1	
1	0	1	
1	1	0	

The EOR instruction will perform an Exclusive-OR of the two operands and place the result in the destination register. EOR sets the result bits to 1 if the corresponding source bits are not equal; otherwise, they are clear to 0. The flags are updated if we use EORS instead of EOR. The rules for the operands are the same as in the AND and OR instructions. See Examples 3-13 and 3-14.

Example 3-13

Show the results of the following:

```
MOV    R1, #0x54
EOR    R2, R1, #0x78      ; R2 = R1 ExOred with 0x78
```

Solution:

```
        0x54    0 1 0 1 0 1 0 0
EOR     0x78    0 1 1 1 1 0 0 0
        0x2C    0 0 1 0 1 1 0 0
```

Example 3-14

The EOR instruction can be used to clear the contents of a register by Ex-ORing it with itself. Show how "EOR R1, R1, R1" clears R1, assuming that R1 = 0x45.

Solution:

```
          0x45   0 1 0 0 0 1 0 1
EOR       0x45   0 1 0 0 0 1 0 1
          0x00   0 0 0 0 0 0 0 0
```

Another application of EOR is to toggle bits of an operand. For example, to toggle bit 2 of register R2:

```
EOR   R2, R2, #0x04      ; EOR R2 with 0000 0100
```

This would cause bit 2 of R2 to change to the complement value; all other bits would remain unchanged.

BIC (bit clear)

```
BIC   Rd, Rn, Op2        ; clear certain bits of Rn specified by
                         ; the Op2 and place the result in Rd
```

Inputs		Output
X	Y	X AND (NOT Y)
0	0	0
0	1	0
1	0	1
1	1	0

The BIC (bit clear) instruction is used to clear the selected bits of the Rn register. The selected bits are held by Op2. The bits that are HIGH in Op2 will be cleared and bits with LOW will be left unchanged. For example, assuming that R3 = 0000000000001000 binary, the instruction "BIC R2, R2, R3" will clear bit 3 of R2 and leaves the rest of the bits unchanged. In reality, the BIC instruction performs AND operation on Rn register with the complement of Op2 and places the result in destination register. Look at the following example:

```
MOV   R2, #0xAA
BIC   R3, R2, #0x0F      ; now R3 = 0xAA AND 0xF0 = 0xA0
```

We can use the AND operation with complement to achieve the same result:

```
MOV R2, #0xAA
AND R3, R2, #~0x0F       ; AND R2 with the complement of #0x0F
                        ; and store the result in R3
```

If we want the flags to be updated, then we must use BICS instead of BIC.

MVN (move not)

```
MVN   Rd, Rn             ; move the complement of Rn to Rd
```

The MVN (move not) instruction is used to generate one's complement of an operand. For example, the instruction "MVN R2, #0" will make R2=0xFFFFFFFF. Look at the following example:

```
LDR     R2, =0xAAAAAAAA        ; R2 = 0xAAAAAAAA
MVN     R2, R2                 ; R2 = 0x55555555
```

We can also use Ex-OR instruction to generate one's complement of an operand. Ex-ORing an operand with 0xFFFFFFFF will generate the 1's complement. See the following code:

```
LDR     R2, =0xAAAAAAAA        ; R2 = 0xAAAAAAAA
MVN     R0, #0                 ; R0 = 0xFFFFFFFF
EOR     R2, R2, R0             ; R2 = R2 ExORed with 0xFFFFFFFF
                               ;     = 0x55555555
```

Review Questions

1. Use operands 0x4FCA and 0xC237 to perform:

   (a) AND   (b) OR   (c) XOR

2. ANDing a word operand with 0xFFFFFFFF will result in what value for the word operand? To set all bits of an operand to 0, it should be ANDed with _____.

3. To set all bits of an operand to 1, it could be ORed with _____.

4. XORing an operand with itself results in what value for the operand?

5. Write an instruction that sets bit 4 of R7.

6. Write an instruction that clears bit 3 of R5.

Section 3.3: Shift and Rotate Instructions

In this section we explore the shift and rotate instructions.

LSL (Logical Shift Left) instruction

```
LSL     Rd, Rm, Rn
```

Shift left is a logical shift. It is the reverse of LSR. After every shift, the LSB is filled with 0 and the MSB goes to C flag in CPSR if the 'S' suffix is used in the instruction. One can use an immediate value or a register to hold the number of times it is to be shifted left. See Example 3-15. One can use the LSL to multiply a number by 2. See Example 3-16.

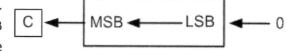

Example 3-15

Show the effects of LSL in the following:

```
LDR     R1, =0x0F000006
LSLS    R2, R1, #8
```

Solution:

```
        00001111 00000000 00000000 00000110
C=0     00011110 00000000 00000000 00001100 (shifted left once)
C=0     00111100 00000000 00000000 00011000
```

86

```
C=0     01111000 00000000 00000000 00110000
C=0     11110000 00000000 00000000 01100000
C=1     11100000 00000000 00000000 11000000
C=1     11000000 00000000 00000001 10000000
C=1     10000000 00000000 00000011 00000000
C=1     00000000 00000000 00000110 00000000 (shifted eight times)
```

After eight shifts left, the R2 register has 0x00000600 and C = 1. The eight MSBs are lost through the carry, one by one, and 0s fill the eight LSBs. Another way to write the above code is:

```
LDR    R1, =0x0F000006
MOV    R0, #0x08
LSLS   R2, R1, R0
```

Notice that the LSL instruction multiplies the content of the register by power of 2 as long as there is no carry out. For example, when a number is shifted left 3 times, it is multiplied by 2^3. See the following example.

Example 3-16

Show the results of LSL in the following:

```
TIMES EQU  0x5
      LDR  R1, #0x7        ; R1=0x7
      MOV  R2, #TIMES      ; R2=0x05
      LSL  R1, R1, R2      ; shift R1 left R2 number of times
                           ; and place the result in R1
```

Solution:
After the five shifts, the R1 will contain 0x000000E0. 0xE0 is 224 in decimal. Notice that $7 \times 2^5 = 7 \times 32 = 224 = 0xE0$. So, it multiplies number by 32 (2 to the power of 5 is 32).

LSR (Logical Shift Right) Instruction

```
LSR    Rd, Rm, Rn
```

The operand is shifted right bit by bit, and for every shift the LSB (least significant bit) will go to the carry flag if the 'S' suffix is used in the instruction and the MSB (most significant bit) is filled with 0. At the end of the execution of the instruction, the carry flag will hold the last bit shifted out if the 'S' suffix is used in the instruction. One can use an immediate value or a register to hold the number of times it is to be shifted. Example 3-17 should help to clarify LSR.

Example 3-17

Show the result of the MOVS instruction with LSR in the following:

```
MOV    R0, #0x9A        ; R0 = 0x9A
LSRS   R1, R0, #3       ; shift R0 to right 3 times
                        ; then store the result in R1
```

Solution:

0x9A = 00000000 00000000 0000000 00000000 10011010

first shift: 00000000 00000000 0000000 00000000 01001101 C = 0

second shift: 00000000 00000000 0000000 00000000 00100110 C = 1

third shift: 00000000 00000000 0000000 00000000 00010011 C = 0

After shifting right three times, R1 = 0x00000013 and C = 0. Another way to write the above code is:

```
MOV    R0, #0x9A
MOV    R2, #0x03
LSRS   R1, R0, R2   ; shift R0 to right R2 times
                    ; and move the result to R1
```

One can use the LSR to divide a number by 2. See Example 3-18.

Example 3-18

Show the results of LSR in the following:

```
LDR    R0, =0x88        ; R0=0x88
MOVS   R1, R0, LSR #3   ; shift R0 right three times (R1 = 0x11)
```

Solution:

After the three shifts, the R1 will contain 0x11. This divides the number by 8 since 2 to the power of 3 is 8.

Table 3-5 lists the logical shift operations in Arm.

Operation	Destination	Source	Number of shifts
LSR (Shift Right)	Rd	Rn	Immediate value
LSR (Shift Right)	Rd	Rn	register Rm
LSL (Shift Left)	Rd	Rn	Immediate value
LSL (Shift Left)	Rd	Rn	register Rm
Note: Number of shift cannot be more than 32.			

Table 3-5: Logic Shift operations for unsigned numbers in Arm

ROR (Rotate Right) instruction

```
ROR    Rd, Rm, Rn   ; Rd=rotate Rm right Rn bit positions
```

As each bit of Rm register is shifted from left to right, they exit from the end (LSB) and entered from left end (MSB). The number of bits to be rotated right is given by Rn and the result is placed in Rd register. To update the flags, use RORS instruction.

Example 1:
```
      LDR   R2,  =0x00000010
      ROR   R0, R2, #8    ; R0=R2 is rotated right 8 times
                          ; now, R0 = 0x10000000, C=0
```

Example 2:
```
      LDR   R0,  =0x00000018
      MOV   R1,  #12
      ROR   R2, R0, R1    ; R2=R0 is rotated right R1 number of times
                          ; now, R2 = 0x01800000, C=0
```

Example 3:
```
      LDR   R0,  =0x0000FF18
      MOV   R1,  #16
      ROR   R2, R0, R1    ; R2=R0 is rotated right R1 number of times
                          ; now, R2 = 0xFF180000, C=0
```

RRX (Rotate Right with extend) instruction

```
      RRXS   Rd,  Rm       ; Rd=rotate Rm right 1 bit through C flag
```

Each bit of Rm register is rotated from left to right one bit through C flag when RRXS instruction is used. If the 'S' suffix is not used, the LSB is lost and the current C flag is shifted into MSB.

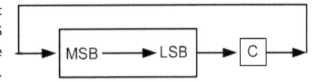

Example:
```
      LDR   R2,  =0x00000002
      RRX   R0, R2         ; R0=R2 is shifted right one bit
                           ; now, R0=0x00000001
```

Table 3-6 lists the rotate instructions of the Arm.

Operation	Destination	Source	Number of Rotates
ROR (Rotate Right)	Rd	Rn	Immediate value
ROR (Rotate Right)	Rd	Rn	register Rm
RRX (Rotate Right Through Carry)	Rd	Rn	1 bit

Table 3-6: Rotate operations for unsigned numbers in Arm

Review Questions
1. Find the contents of R2 after executing the following code:

```
MOV    R1, #0x08
ROR    R2, R1, #2
```

2. Find the contents of R4 after executing the following code:

```
MOV    R3, #0x3
LSL    R4, R3, #2
```

Section 3.4: Rotate and Shift in Data Processing Instructions (Case Study)

In previous sections, we discussed that as the second operand of data process instructions we can use register or immediate values. We can also perform the shift and rotate operations as part of the other data processing instructions (arithmetic and logic instructions) such as MOV, ADD, or SUB. Examples 3-19 through 3-22 should help to clarify.

Example 3-19

Show the result of the MOVS instruction with LSR in the following:

```
MOV    R0, #0x9A          ; R0 = 0x9A
MOVS   R1, R0, LSR #3     ; shift R0 to right 3 times
                          ; then store the result in R1
```

Solution:

0x9A =	00000000 00000000 0000000 00000000 10011010
first shift:	00000000 00000000 0000000 00000000 01001101 C = 0
second shift:	00000000 00000000 0000000 00000000 00100110 C = 1
third shift:	00000000 00000000 0000000 00000000 00010011 C = 0

After shifting right three times, R1 = 0x00000013 and C = 0. Another way to write the above code is:

```
MOV    R0, #0x9A
LSR    R1, R0, #0x03     ; shift R0 to right 3 times
```

Example 3-20

Show the results of the ADDS with LSR in the following:

```
LDR    R1, =0x777            ; R1=0x777
LDR    R2, =0xA6D            ; R2=0xA6D
ADDS   R3, R1, R2, LSR #4    ; shift R2 right 4 times then add it to
                             ; R1 and place the result in R3
                             ; R3 = 0x777 + 0xA6 = 0x81D
```

Solution:

After four shifts, the R2 will contain 0xA6. The four LSBs are lost through the carry, one by one, and 0s fill the four MSBs. 0xA6 is added to 0x777 in R1 and the sum 0x81D is placed in R3. Unlike MOVS operation, which does not affect the C flag itself, the ADDS operation generates C flag depending on the carry out of the MSB by the ADD, which will overwrite the C flag generated from the shift of operand 2. In this example, "R2, LSR #4" generates C = 1 but the add results in C = 0. So at the end of the ADDS instruction, C = 0.

Example 3-21

Show the effects of LSL in the following:

```
LDR   R1,  =0x0F000006
MOVS  R2,  R1,  LSL #5
```

Solution:

	00001111 00000000 00000000 00000110
C=0	00011110 00000000 00000000 00001100 (shifted left once)
C=0	00111100 00000000 00000000 00011000
C=0	01111000 00000000 00000000 00110000
C=0	11110000 00000000 00000000 01100000
C=1	11100000 00000000 00000000 11000000 (shifted five times)

After five shifts left, the R2 register has 0x000000C0 and C = 1. The five MSBs are lost through the carry, one by one, and 0s fill the five LSBs. Another way to write the above code is:

```
LSL   R2,  R1,  #0x05
```

Example 3-22

Show the results of the ADDS with ROR in the following:

```
LDR   R1,  =0x777          ; R1=0x777
LDR   R2,  =0x444          ; R2=0x444
ADDS  R3, R1, R2, ROR #2   ; rotate R2 right 2 times then add it to
                           ; R1 and place the result in R3
                           ; R3 = 0x777 + 0x111 = 0x888
```

Solution:

After two shifts, 0x444 becomes 0x10000011. The six LSBs are rotated to the MSB bits, one by one. 0x10000011 is added to 0x777 in R1 and the sum 0x10000788 is placed in R3.

Table 3-7 lists the available shift and rotate instructions in Cortex-M3.

Operation	Source	Number of Rotates
ASR (Arithmetic Shift Right)	Rn	Immediate value
LSL (Logic Shift Left)	Rn	Immediate value
LSR (Logic Shift Right)	Rn	Immediate value
ROR (Rotate Right)	Rn	Immediate value
RRX (Rotate Right Through Carry)	Rn	1 bit

Table 3-7: Rotate operations for unsigned numbers in Arm

Review Questions

1. Find the contents of R3 after executing the following code:

```
MOV    R0, #0x04
MOV    R3, R0, LSR #2
```

2. Find the contents of R4 after executing the following code:

```
LDR    R1, =0xA0F2
MOV    R2, #0x3
MOV    R4, R1, LSR R2
```

3. Find the contents of R3 after executing the following code:

```
LDR    R1, =0xA0F2
MOV    R2, #0x3
MOV    R3, R1, LSL R2
```

4. Find the contents of R5 after executing the following code:

```
SUBS   R0, R0, R0
MOV    R0, #0xAA
MOV    R5, R0, ROR #4
```

5. Find the contents of R0 after executing the following code:

```
LDR    R2, =0xA0F2
MOV    R1, #0x1
MOV    R0, R2, ROR R1
```

6. Give the result in R1 for the following:

```
MVN    R1, #0x01, #2
```

7. Give the result in R2 for the following:

```
MVN    R2, #0x02, #28
```

Section 3.5: BCD and ASCII Conversion

This section covers binary, BCD, and ASCII conversions with some examples.

BCD number system

BCD stands for Binary Coded Decimal. Most of the computers these days perform arithmetic in binary because binary arithmetic is easier and faster to implement in electronic circuit. But most of the numbers used in real lift are decimal, so it requires to convert the decimal numbers to binary before the computations can be done. Earlier computers did arithmetic in decimal because it does not require the decimal to binary and binary to decimal conversions.

Digit	BCD
0	0000
1	0001
2	0010
3	0011
4	0100
5	0101
6	0110
7	0111
8	1000
9	1001

Table 3-8: BCD Codes

To perform arithmetic in decimal, data need to be encoded in decimal format but using binary system of the computer so binary coded decimal (BCD) is often used. See Table 3-8. In the modern computing, you may still encounter the usage of BCD in some applications. For example, BCD is used in many real-time clock (RTC) of the embedded systems.

There are two formats for BCD numbers: (1) unpacked BCD, and (2) packed BCD.

Unpacked BCD

In unpacked BCD, each decimal digit is represented by a byte (8-bit). The lower 4 bits of the byte represent the BCD number and the rest of the bits are 0. For example, "0000 1001" and "0000 0101" are unpacked BCD for 9 and 5, respectively.

Packed BCD

In the case of packed BCD, two decimal digits are packed in one byte, one in the lower 4 bits and one in the upper 4 bits. For example, "0101 1001" is packed BCD for 59. Obviously, packed BCD is more efficient in memory usage but to perform arithmetic with packed BCD, the circuit has to be able to detect the decimal carry from the lower digit to the upper digit in the same byte. Arm CPU does not do that.

ASCII encoding

The American Standard Code for Information Interchange was established in the early 1960's as a character encoding standard for telegraph in United States. It was adopted by computer developers to be used as the encoding for transmitting text between computer and peripherals, text file storage, and communication between computers. The ASCII code has the advantage over other encode of the earlier time as the code within the three groups of code (numerals, uppercase alphabets, and alphabets) are all in consecutive order. That makes conversion between ASCII and BCD or between uppercase and lowercase easier.

ASCII codes are 7-bit long. The ASCII encoding of numerals starts from "011 0000" (0x30) for "0". Since all the numeral codes are consecutive, "1" is encoded as "011 0001" (0x31) "2" is encoded as "011 0010" (0x32) and so on.

For example, in an ASCII keyboard when a key is pressed, the ASCII encoding of that key is transmitted to the computer. So when key "0" is pressed, "011 0000" (0x30) is sent to the computer. In the same way, when key "5" is pressed, "011 0101" (0x35) is sent. The ASCII codes of numerals are shown in the following table together with the corresponding BCD code:

Key	ASCII	Binary(hex)	BCD (unpacked)
0	30	011 0000	0000 0000
1	31	011 0001	0000 0001
2	32	011 0010	0000 0010
3	33	011 0011	0000 0011
4	34	011 0100	0000 0100
5	45	011 0101	0000 0101
6	36	011 0110	0000 0110
7	37	011 0111	0000 0111
8	38	011 1000	0000 1000
9	39	011 1001	0000 1001

Though we mentioned earlier that processing decimal data in BCD does not require to convert the data to binary. But often the input/output data and the data stored in the files are in ASCII code for ease of human reading. Input/output devices like keyboard and LCD display are usually using ASCII encoding. These ASCII data need to be converted to BCD before performing decimal data processing and be converted back to ASCII afterward. These are the subjects covered next.

ASCII to unpacked BCD conversion

The lower nibble (least significant four bits) of the ASCII codes for numeral contain the binary value of that digit. To convert ASCII data to unpacked BCD, the programmer must get rid of the "011" in the upper 3 bits of the 7-bit ASCII. To do that, each ASCII number is ANDed with "0000 1111" (0x0F).

ASCII to packed BCD conversion

To convert ASCII numbers to packed BCD, they are first converted to unpacked BCD (remove the upper 3 bits) and then combined every two digits to make a packed BCD. For example, if the user typed digit 2 and 7 on an ASCII keyboard, the keyboard transmits ASCII codes 0x32 and 0x37 to the computer. The goal is to produce 0x27 or "0010 0111", which is called packed BCD. This process is illustrated in detail in the program snippet below.

Key	ASCII	Unpacked BCD	Packed BCD
2	32	00000010	
7	37	00000111	00100111 (0x27)

```
MOV    R1, #0x37          ; R1 = 0x37
MOV    R2, #0x32          ; R2 = 0x32
AND    R1, R1, #0x0F      ; mask 3 to get unpacked BCD
AND    R2, R2, #0x0F      ; mask 3 to get unpacked BCD
ORR    R3, R1, R2, LSL #4 ; shift R2 4 bits to the left and combine
                          ; with R1 to get packed BCD in R3 = 0x27
```

Packed BCD to ASCII conversion

For data to be displayed or printed on a device that accepts only ASCII format, they need to be converted to ASCII first. Conversion from packed BCD to ASCII is discussed next. To convert packed BCD to ASCII, it must first be unpacked and then tagged with 011 0000 (0x30) to encode in ASCII. The following code snippet shows the process of converting from packed BCD to ASCII.

Packed BCD	Unpacked BCD	ASCII
0x29	0x02 & 0x09	0x32 & 0x39
0010 1001	0000 0010 & 0000 1001	011 0010 & 011 1001

```
MOV   R0, #0x29
AND   R1, R0, #0x0F     ; mask upper four bits
ORR   R1, R1, #0x30     ; combine with 30 to get ASCII
MOV   R2, R0, LSR #04   ; shift right 4 bits to get unpacked BCD
ORR   R2, R2, #0x30     ; combine with 30 to get ASCII
```

Review Questions

1. For the following decimal numbers, give the packed BCD and unpacked BCD representations in binary

   (a) 15   (b) 99

2. For the following packed BCD numbers, give the decimal and unpacked BCD representations.

   (a) 0x41   (b) 0x09

3. Repeat question 2 for ASCII.

Problems

Section 3.1: Arithmetic Instructions

1. Find C and Z flags for each of the following. Also indicate the result of the addition and where the result is saved.

   (a)

   ```
   MOV   R1, #0x3F
   MOV   R2, #0x45
   ADDS  R3, R1, R2
   ```

   (b)

   ```
   LDR   R0, =0x95999999
   LDR   R1, =0x94FFFF58
   ADDS  R1, R1, R0
   ```

   (c)

   ```
   LDR   R0, =0xFFFFFFFF
   ADDS  R0, R0, #1
   ```

   (d)

   ```
   LDR   R2, =0x00000001
   LDR   R1, =0xFFFFFFFF
   ADDS  R0, R1, R2
   ADCS  R0, R0, #0
   ```

   (e)

```
LDR    R0, =0xFFFFFFFE
ADDS   R0, R0, #2
ADC    R1, R0, #0x0
```

2. State the three steps involved in a SUB and show the steps for the following data.

   (a) 0x23 − 0x12   (b) 0x43 − 0x51   (c) 0x99 − 0x99

Section 3.2: Logic Instructions

3. Assume that the following registers contain these hex contents: R0 = 0xF000, R1 = 0x3456, and R2 = 0xE390. Perform the following operations. Indicate the result and the register where it is stored.

   Note: the operations are independent of each other.

   (a) AND R3, R2, R0   (b) ORR R3, R2, R1

   (c) EOR R0, R0, #0x76   (d) AND R3, R2, R2

   (e) EOR R0, R0, R0   (f) ORR R3, R0, R2

   (g) AND R3, R0, #0xFF   (h) ORR R3, R0, #0x99

   (i) EOR R3, R1, R0   (j) EOR R3, R1, R1

4. Give the value in R2 after the following code is executed:

   ```
   MOV    R0, #0xF0
   MOV    R1, #0x55
   BIC    R2, R1, R0
   ```

5. Give the value in R2 after the following code is executed:

   ```
   LDR    R1, =0x55555555
   MVN    R0, #0
   EOR    R2, R1, R0
   ```

Section 3.3: Shift and Rotate Instructions

6. Assuming C = 0, what is the value of R1 after the following?

   ```
   MOV    R1, #0x25
   RORS   R1, R1, #4
   ```

7. Assuming C = 0, what are the values of R0 and C after the following?

   ```
   LDR    R0, =0x3FA2
   MOV    R2, #8
   RORS   R0, R0, R2
   ```

8. Assuming C = 0 what is the value of R2 and C after the following?

```
MOV    R2, #0x55
RRX    R2, R2
```

9. Assuming C = 0 what is the value of R1 after the following?

```
MOV    R1, #0xFF
MOV    R3, #5
RORS   R1, R1, R3
```

Section 3.4: Rotate and Shift in Data Processing Instructions

10. Find the contents of registers and C flag after executing each of the following codes:

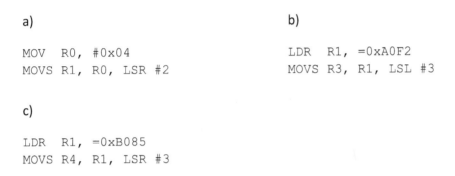

a)

```
MOV  R0, #0x04
MOVS R1, R0, LSR #2
```

b)

```
LDR  R1, =0xA0F2
MOVS R3, R1, LSL #3
```

c)

```
LDR  R1, =0xB085
MOVS R4, R1, LSR #3
```

11. Find the contents of registers and C flag after executing each of the following codes:

a)

```
MOV  R0, #0xAA
MOVS R1, R0, ROR #4
```

b)

```
MOV  R2, #0xAA
MOVS R1, R2, ROR #1
```

c)

```
LDR  R0, =0x1234
MOVS R1, R0, ROR #4
```

d)

```
MOV  R0, #0xAA
MOVS R1, R0, RRX
```

Section 3.5: BCD and ASCII Conversion

12. Write a program to convert 0x76 from packed BCD number to ASCII. Place the ASCII codes into R1 and R2.

13. For "3" and "2" the keyboard gives 0x33 and 0x32, respectively. Write a program to convert 0x33 and 0x32 to packed BCD and store the result in R2.

Answers to Review Questions

Section 3.1: Arithmetic Instructions

1. The ADDS instruction updates the flag bits in CPSR register while ADD does not do that.
2. Rd = Rn + Op2 + C
3. 0x4F + 0xB1 = 0x100, since the result is less than 32-bit the C = 0 and Z = 0.
4. 0x4F + 0xFFFFFFB1 = 0x00000000, since the result is greater than 32-bit, there is a carry out from the MSB and the remaining 32 bits are all 0, the C = 1 and Z = 1.

5.

0x43	0100 0011		00000000000000000000000001000011
−0x05	0000 0101	2's complement =	+ 11111111111111111111111111111011
0x3E			1 00000000000000000000000000111110

C = 1; therefore, the result is positive

6. R2 = R2 − R3 − C + 1 = 0x95 − 0x4F − 1 + 1 = 0x46
7. R2
8. R2 = 1

Section 3.2: Logic Instructions

1. (a) 0x4202   (b) 0xCFFF   (c) 0x8DFD
2. The operand will remain unchanged; all zeros
3. All ones
4. All zeros
5. ORR R7, R7, #0x10   ; R7 = R7 ORed 0001 0000
6. BIC R5, R5, #0x8   ; R5 = R5 ANDed 1111 1111 1111 0111

Section 3.3: Shift and Rotate Instructions

1. 0x02
2. 0x0C

Section 3.4: Rotate and Barrel Shifter Operation

1. R3 = 1
2. R4 = 0x0000141E
3. R3 = 0x00050790
4. R5 = 0xA000000A
5. R0 = 0x00005079
6. 0xBFFFFFFF
7. 0xFFFFFFDF

Section 3.5: BCD and ASCII Conversion

1. (a) 15 = 0001 0101 packed BCD = 0000 0001 0000 0101 unpacked BCD

    (b) 99 = 1001 1001 packed BCD = 0000 1001 0000 1001 unpacked BCD

2. (a) 0x41 = 0000 0100 0000 0001 unpacked BCD = 41 in decimal

    (b) 0x09 = 0000 0000 0000 1001 unpacked BCD = 9 in decimal

3. (a) 0x34, 0x31

    (b) 0x30, 0x39

Chapter 4: Branch, Call, and Looping in Arm

In the sequence of instructions to be executed, it is often necessary to transfer program control to a different location (e.g. when a function is called, execution of a loop is repeated, or an instruction executes conditionally). There are many instructions in Arm to achieve this. This chapter covers the control transfer instructions available in Arm assembly language. In Section 4.1, we discuss instructions used for looping, as well as instructions for conditional and unconditional branches (jumps). In Section 4.2, we examine the instructions associated with calling subroutine. In Section 4.3, instruction timing and time delay subroutines are discussed. The Stack of Arm is discussed in Section 4.4. The Startup file is explored in Section 4.5.

Section 4.1: Looping and Branch Instructions

In this section we first discuss how to perform a looping action in Arm and then the branch (jump) instructions, both conditional and unconditional.

Looping in Arm

Repeating a sequence of instructions or an operation for a certain number of times is called a *loop*. The loop is one of the most widely used programming techniques. In the Arm, there are several ways to repeat an operation many times. One way is to repeat the operation over and over until it is finished, as shown below:

```
MOV   R0, #0       ; R0 = 0
MOV   R1, #9       ; R1 = 9
ADD   R0, R0, R1   ; R0 = R0 + R1, add 9 to R0 (Now R0 is 0x09)
ADD   R0, R0, R1   ; R0 = R0 + R1, add 9 to R0 (Now R0 is 0x12)
ADD   R0, R0, R1   ; R0 = R0 + R1, add 9 to R0 (Now R0 is 0x1B)
ADD   R0, R0, R1   ; R0 = R0 + R1, add 9 to R0 (Now R0 is 0x24)
ADD   R0, R0, R1   ; R0 = R0 + R1, add 9 to R0 (Now R0 is 0x2D)
ADD   R0, R0, R1   ; R0 = R0 + R1, add 9 to R0 (Now R0 is 0x36)
```

In the above program, we add 9 to R0 six times. That makes 6 × 9 = 54 = 0x36. One problem with the above technique is that too much code space would be needed for a large number of repetitions like 50 or 1000. A much better way is to use a loop. Next, we describe the method to do a loop in Arm.

Using instruction BNE for looping

The BNE (branch if not equal) instruction uses the zero flag in the status register (CPSR). The BNE instruction is used as follows:

```
BACK  ........        ; start of the loop
      ........        ; body of the loop
      ........        ; body of the loop
      SUBS  Rn, Rn, #1 ; Rn = Rn - 1, set the flag Z = 1 if Rn = 0
      BNE   BACK       ; branch if Z = 0
```

In the last two instructions, the Rn (e.g. R2 or R3) is decremented; if it is not zero, it branches (jumps) back to the target address referred to by the label. Prior to the start of the loop, the Rn is loaded with the counter value for the number of repetitions (loop count). Notice that the BNE instruction refers to the Z flag of the status register affected by the previous instruction, SUBS. This is shown in Example 4-1.

Example 4-1

Write a program to (a) clear R0, (b) add 9 to R0 a thousand times, then (c) place the sum in R4. Use the zero flag and BNE instruction.

Solution:

```
            ; --- this program adds value 9 to the R0 a 1000 times ---
            EXPORT  __main
            AREA  EXAMPLE4_1,  CODE,  READONLY
__main
            LDR   R2, =1000    ; R2 = 1000 (decimal) for counter
            MOV   R0, #0       ; R0 = 0 (sum)
AGAIN       ADD   R0, R0, #9   ; R0 = R0 + 9 (add 09 to R1, R1 = sum)
            SUBS  R2, R2, #1   ; Decrement counter and set the flags.
            BNE   AGAIN        ; repeat until COUNT = 0 (when Z = 1)
            MOV   R4, R0       ; store the sum in R4
HERE        B     HERE         ; stay here
            END
```

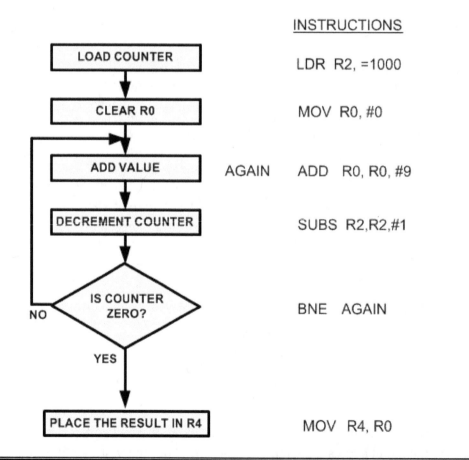

100

In the program in Example 4-1, register R2 is used as a counter. The counter is first set to 1000. In each iteration, the SUBS instruction decrements the R2 and sets the flag bits accordingly. If R2 is not zero (Z = 0), it jumps to the target address associated with the label "AGAIN". This looping action continues until R2 becomes zero. After R2 becomes zero (Z = 1), it falls through the loop and executes the instruction immediately below it, in this case "MOV R4, R0".

It must be emphasized again that we must use SUBS instead of SUB since the SUB instruction will not change (update) the flags in CPSR. As we mentioned in Chapter 3, many of the Arm instructions have the option of affecting the flags. In these instructions the default is not to affect the flags. Therefore, to update the flag we must add 'S' suffix to the instruction. That means SUBS and ADDS instructions are different from SUB and ADD, as far as the flags are concerned. As another example see Example 4-2.

Example 4-2

Write a program to place value 0x55 into 100 consecutive bytes of RAM locations.

Solution:

```
        RAM_ADDR EQU 0x20000000

        EXPORT  __main
        AREA   EXAMPLE4_2, CODE, READONLY
__main
        MOV   R2, #25            ; counter (25 x 4 = 100 byte block size)
        LDR   R1, =RAM_ADDR      ; R1 = RAM Address
        LDR   R0, =0x55555555    ; R0 = 0x55555555

OVER    STR   R0, [R1]           ; send it to RAM
        ADD   R1, R1, #4         ; R1 = R1 + 4 to increment pointer
        SUBS  R2, R2, #1         ; R2 = R2 - 1 for decrement counter
        BNE   OVER               ; keep doing it

HERE    B     HERE
        END
```

Looping a trillion times with loop inside a loop

As shown in Example 4-3, the maximum count is $2^{32}-1$. What happens if we want to repeat an action more times than that? To do that, we use a loop inside a loop, which is called a nested loop. In a nested loop, we use two registers to hold the loop counts. See Example 4-3.

Example 4-3

Explain what is the maximum number of times that the loop in Example 4-1 can be repeated. Then, write a program to load the R0 register with the value 0x55, and complement it 16,000,000,000 (16 billion) times.

Solution:

Because Arm registers are 32-bit long, they can hold a maximum of 0xFFFFFFFF ($2^{32} - 1$ decimal); therefore, the loop can be repeated a maximum of $2^{32} - 1$ times. This example shows how to create a nesting loop to go beyond 4 billion times. Because 16,000,000,000 is larger than 0xFFFFFFFF (the maximum capacity of any R0–R12 registers), we use two registers to hold the counts. The following code shows how to use R2 and R1 as a register for counters in a nesting loop.

```
        EXPORT  __main
        AREA    EXAMPLE4_3, CODE, READONLY
__main
        MOV     R0, #0x55           ; R0 = 0x55
        MOV     R2, #16             ; load 16 into R2 (outer loop count)
L1      LDR     R1, =1000000000     ; R1 = 1,000,000,000 (inner loop count)
L2      EOR     R0, R0, #0xFF       ; complement R0 (R0 = R0 Ex-OR 0xFF)
        SUBS    R1, R1, #1          ; R1 = R1 - 1, decrement R1 (inner loop)
        BNE     L2                  ; repeat it until R1 = 0
        SUBS    R2, R2, #1          ; R2 = R2 - 1, decrement R2 (outer loop)
        BNE     L1                  ; repeat it until R2 = 0
HERE    B       HERE                ; stay here
        END
```

In this program, R1 is used to keep the inner loop count. In the instruction "BNE L2", whenever R1 becomes 0 it falls through and "SUBS R2, R2, #1" is executed. The next instructions force the CPU to load the inner count with 1,000,000,000 if R2 is not zero, and the inner loop starts again. This process will continue until R2 becomes zero and the outer loop is finished. If you use the Keil IDE to verify the operation of the above program use smaller values for counter to go through the iterations. See Figure 4-1.

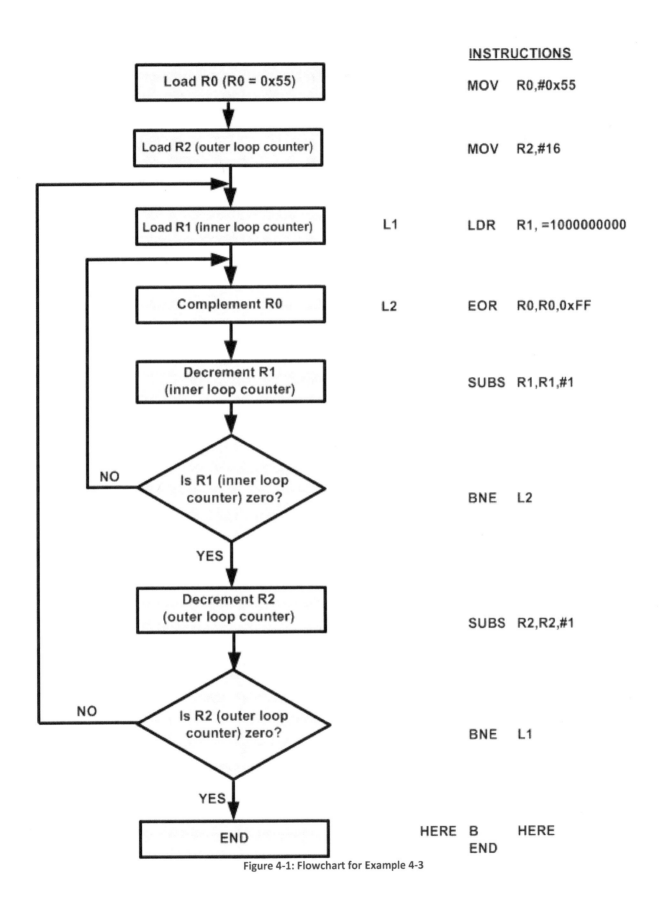

	INSTRUCTIONS	
Load R0 (R0 = 0x55)	MOV	R0,#0x55
Load R2 (outer loop counter)	MOV	R2,#16
Load R1 (inner loop counter) L1	LDR	R1, =1000000000
Complement R0 L2	EOR	R0,R0,0xFF
Decrement R1 (inner loop counter)	SUBS	R1,R1,#1
Is R1 (inner loop counter) zero?	BNE	L2
Decrement R2 (outer loop counter)	SUBS	R2,R2,#1
Is R2 (outer loop counter) zero?	BNE	L1
END	HERE B	HERE
	END	

Figure 4-1: Flowchart for Example 4-3

Other conditional Branches

As we mentioned in Chapter 3, C and Z flags reflect the result of calculation on unsigned numbers. Table 4-1 lists available conditional branches for unsigned numbers that use C and Z flags. More details of each instruction are provided in Appendix A. In Table 4-1 notice that the instructions, such as BEQ (Branch if Z = 1) and BCS (Branch if carry set, C = 1), jump only if a certain condition is met. Next, we examine some conditional branch instructions with examples. The other conditional branch instructions associated with the signed numbers are discussed in Chapter 5 when arithmetic operations for signed numbers are discussed.

Instruction		Action
BCS/BHS	branch if carry set/branch if higher or same	Branch if C = 1
BCC/BLO	branch if carry clear/branch if lower	Branch if C = 0
BEQ	branch if equal	Branch if Z = 1
BNE	branch if not equal	Branch if Z = 0
BLS	branch if lower or same	Branch if Z = 1 or C = 0
BHI	branch if higher	Branch if Z = 0 and C = 1

Table 4-1: Arm Conditional Branch Instructions for Unsigned Data

BCC (branch if carry is clear, branch if C = 0)

In this instruction, the carry flag bit in program status registers (CPSR) is used to make the decision whether to branch or not. In executing "BCC label", the processor looks at the carry flag to see if it is cleared (C = 0). If it is, the CPU starts to fetch and execute instructions from the address of the label. If C = 1, it will not jump but will execute the next instruction below BCC. See Example 4-4.

Example 4-4

Examine the following code and give the result in registers R0, R1, and R2.

```
        MOV    R1, #0             ; clear high word (R1 = 0)
        MOV    R0, #0             ; clear low word (R0 = 0)
        LDR    R2, =0x99999999    ; R2 = 0x99999999
        ADDS   R0, R0, R2         ; R0 = R0 + R2 and set the flags
        BCC    L1                 ; if C = 0, jump to L1 and add next number
        ADDS   R1, R1, #1         ; ELSE, increment (R1 = R1 + 1)
L1      ADDS   R0, R0, R2         ; R0 = R0 + R2 and set the flags
        BCC    L2                 ; if C = 0, add next number
        ADDS   R1, R1, #1         ; if C = 1, increment
L2      ADDS   R0, R2             ; R0 = R0 + R2 and set the flags
        BCC    L3                 ; if C = 0, add next number
        ADDS   R1, R1, #1         ; C = 1, increment
L3      ADDS   R0, R2             ; R0 = R0 + R2 and set the flags
        BCC    L4                 ; if C = 0, add next number
        ADDS   R1, R1, #1         ; if C = 1, and set the flags
L4
```

Solution:

This program adds 0x99999999 together four times.

	R1 (high word)	R0 (low word)
At first	0	0
Just before L1	0	0x99999999
Just before L2	1	0x33333332
Just before L3	1	0xCCCCCCCB
Just before L4	2	0x66666664

Here is the loop version of the above program that runs 10 times.

```
        EXPORT  __main
        AREA    EXAMPLE4_4, CODE, READONLY
__main
        MOV     R1, #0           ; clear high word (R1 = 0)
        MOV     R0, #0           ; clear low word (R0 = 0)
        LDR     R2, =0x99999999  ; R2 = 0x99999999
        MOV     R3, #10          ; counter
L1      ADDS    R0, R2           ; R0 = R0 + R2 and set the flags
        BCC     NEXT             ; if C = 0, add next number
        ADD     R1, R1, #1       ; if C = 1, increment the upper word
NEXT    SUBS    R3, R3, #1       ; R3 = R3 - 1 and set the flags
                                 ; (Decrement counter)
        BNE     L1               ; next round if Z = 0
HERE    B       HERE             ; stay here
        END
```

Note that there is also a "BCS label" instruction. In the BCS instruction, if C = 1 it jumps to the target address. We will give more examples of these instructions in the context of applications.

Comparison of unsigned numbers
```
        CMP     Rn, Op2      ; compare Rn with Op2 and set the flags
```

The CMP instruction compares two operands and set or clear the flags according to the result of the comparison. The operands themselves remain unchanged. There is no destination register and the second source operands can be a register or an immediate value (an 8-bit value with even number or rotate). It must be emphasized that "CMP Rn, Op2" instruction is really a subtract operation (SUBS) without a destination. Op2 is subtracted from Rn (Rn – Op2), the result is discarded and flags are set accordingly. Although all the C, S, Z, and V flags reflect the result of the comparison, only C and Z are used for unsigned numbers, as outlined in Table 4-2.

Instruction	C	Z
Rn > Op2	1	0
Rn = Op2	1	1
Rn < Op2	0	0

Table 4-2: Flag Settings for Compare (CMP Rn, Op2) of Unsigned Data

Look at the following case:

```
        LDR   R1, =0x35F   ; R1 = 0x35F
        LDR   R2, =0xCCC   ; R2 = 0xCCC
        CMP   R1, R2       ; compare 0x35F with 0xCCC
        BCC   OVER         ; branch if C = 0
        MOV   R1, #0       ; if C = 1, then clear R1
OVER    ADD   R2, R2, #1   ; R2 = R2 + 1 = 0xCCC + 1 = 0xCCD
```

Figure 4-2 shows the diagram and the C language version of the code.

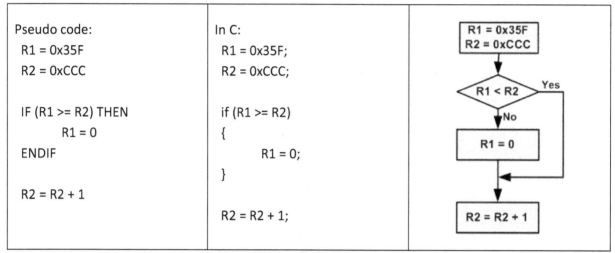

Figure 4-2: Flowchart of if Instruction

In the above program, R1 is less than the R2 (0x35F < 0xCCC); therefore, C = 0 and BCC (branch if carry clear) will go to target OVER. In contrast, look at the following:

```
        LDR   R1, =0xFFF
        LDR   R2, =0x888
        CMP   R1, R2            ; compare 0xFFF with 0x888
        BCC   NEXT
        ADD   R1, R1, #0x40
NEXT    ADD   R1, R1, #0x25
```

In the above, R1 is greater than R2 (0xFFF > 0x888), which sets C = 1, the branch, "BCC NEXT," is not taken and the execution falls through so that "ADD R1, R1, 0x40" is executed.

Again, it must be emphasized that in CMP instructions, the operands are unaffected regardless of the result of the comparison. Only the flags are affected. It also may be noted that, unlike other arithmetic and logic instructions, there is no need to put the 'S' suffix in the CMP instruction to update the flags. In other words, the CMP instruction always updates the flags.

Program 4-1 uses the CMP instruction to search for the highest byte in a series of 5 data bytes. To search for the highest value, the instruction "CMP R1, R3" works as follows where R1 is the contents of the memory location brought into R1 register by the [R2] pointer.

a) If R1 < R3, then C = 0 and R3 becomes the basis of the new comparison.

b) If R1 ≥ R3, then C = 1 and R1 is the larger of the two values and remains the basis of comparison.

Program 4-1

Assume that there is a class of five people with the following grades:

69, 87, 96, 45, and 75. Find the highest grade.

```
; searching for highest value in a list
COUNT       RN      R0              ; COUNT is the new name of R0
MAX         RN      R1              ; MAX is the new name of R1
                                    ; (MAX has the highest value)
POINTER     RN      R2              ; POINTER is the new name of R2
NEXT        RN      R3              ; NEXT is the new name of R3

            AREA    PROG_4_1D, DATA, READONLY
MYDATA      DCD     69, 87, 96, 45, 75

            EXPORT  __main
            AREA    PROG_4_1, CODE, READONLY
__main
            MOV     COUNT, #5               ; COUNT = 5
            MOV     MAX, #0                 ; MAX = 0
            LDR     POINTER, =MYDATA        ; POINTER has the address of first data
AGAIN       LDR     NEXT, [POINTER]         ; load NEXT with contents at address
                                            ; in POINTER
            CMP     MAX, NEXT               ; compare MAX and NEXT
            BHS     CTNU                    ; if MAX > NEXT branch to CTNU
            MOV     MAX, NEXT               ; MAX = NEXT
CTNU        ADD     POINTER, POINTER, #4    ; increment POINTER for next word
            SUBS    COUNT, COUNT, #1        ; decrement counter
            BNE     AGAIN                   ; branch AGAIN if counter is not zero

HERE        B       HERE
            END
```

Program 4-1 searches through five data items to find the highest value. The program has a variable called "MAX" that holds the highest grade found so far. One by one, the grades are brought into the register and compared to MAX. If any of them is higher, that value is placed in MAX. This continues until all data items are checked. A REPEAT-UNTIL structure was chosen in the program design. Figure 4-3 shows the flowchart for Program 4-1. This design could be used to code the program in many different languages.

Program 4-1 also demonstrates using aliasing for registers. This practice improves the readability of the small programs.

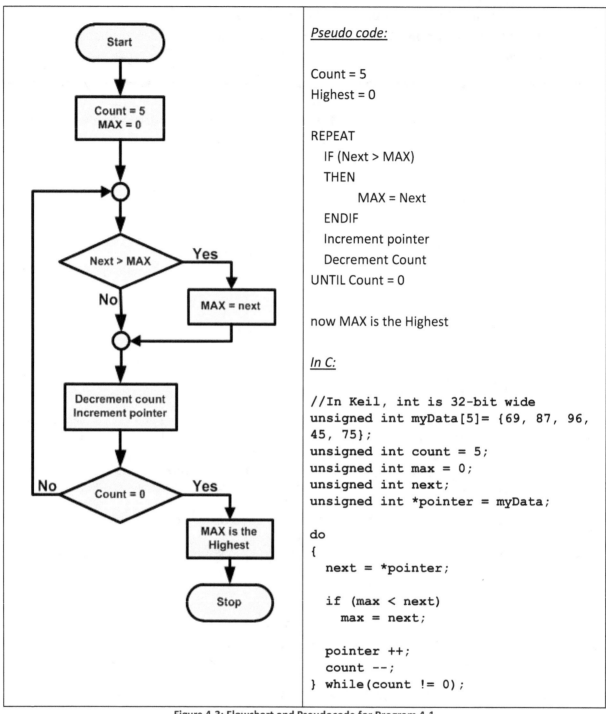

Pseudo code:

```
Count = 5
Highest = 0

REPEAT
    IF (Next > MAX)
    THEN
            MAX = Next
    ENDIF
    Increment pointer
    Decrement Count
UNTIL Count = 0

now MAX is the Highest
```

In C:

```c
//In Keil, int is 32-bit wide
unsigned int myData[5]= {69, 87, 96,
45, 75};
unsigned int count = 5;
unsigned int max = 0;
unsigned int next;
unsigned int *pointer = myData;

do
{
  next = *pointer;

  if (max < next)
    max = next;

  pointer ++;
  count --;
} while(count != 0);
```

Figure 4-3: Flowchart and Pseudocode for Program 4-1

Using CMP instruction followed by conditional branches we can make comparison on numbers, as shown in Table 4-3. Although BCS (branch carry set) and BCC (branch carry clear) check the carry flag and can be used after a compare instruction, it is recommended that BHS (branch higher or same) and BLO (branch lower) be used because "branch higher" and "branch lower" are easier to understand than "branch carry set" and "branch carry clear, " since it is more immediately apparent that one number is larger than another than whether a carry would be generated if the two numbers were subtracted.

Instruction		Action
BCS/BHS	branch if carry set/branch if higher or same	Branch if Rn ≥ Op2
BCC/BLO	branch if carry clear/branch lower	Branch if Rn < Op2
BEQ	branch if equal	Branch if Rn = Op2
BNE	branch if not equal	Branch if Rn ≠ Op2
BLS	branch if less or same	Branch if Rn ≤ Op2
BHI	branch if higher	Branch if Rn > Op2

Table 4-3: Arm Conditional Branch Instructions for Unsigned Data

Division of unsigned numbers in Arm

Some of the older Arm family members do not have instructions for division since it took too many gates to implement it. In ARMs with no divide instructions we can use SUB instruction to perform the division. Program 4-2 shows an example of an unsigned division using simple subtract operation. In the program the numerator is placed in a register and the denominator is subtracted from it repeatedly. The quotient is the number of times we subtracted and the remainder is in the register upon completion. This program is to demonstrate the used of conditional branch in a loop. The program is not efficient in calculating the quotient. There are much more efficient algorithms to perform division but they are beyond the scope here. See Figure 4-4 for the flowchart of the simple division program.

Program 4-2: Division by Repeated Subtractions

```
        EXPORT  __main
        AREA    PROG_4_2, CODE, READONLY     ; Division by subtractions
__main
        LDR   R0, =2012    ; R0 = 2012 (numerator)
                           ; it will contain remainder
        MOV   R1, #10      ; R1 = 10 (denominator)
        MOV   R2, #0       ; R2 = 0 (quotient)
L1      CMP   R0, R1       ; Compare R0 with R1 to see if less than 10
        BLO   FINISH       ; if R0 < R1 jump to finish
        SUB   R0, R0, R1   ; R0 = R0 - R1 (division by subtraction)
        ADD   R2, R2, #1   ; R2 = R2 + 1 (quotient is incremented)
        B     L1           ; go to L1 (B is discussed in the next section)
FINISH B    FINISH
```

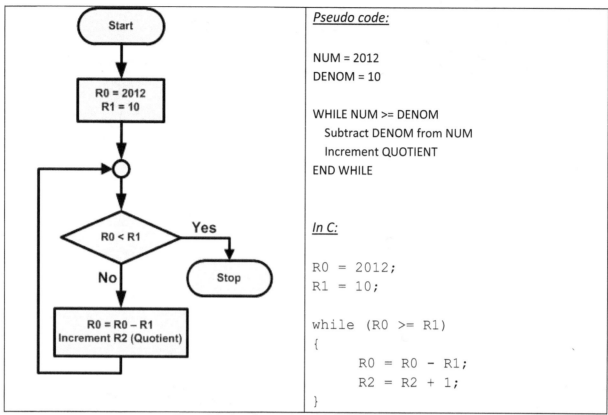

Figure 4-4: Flowchart and Pseudo-code for Program 4-2

TST (Test)

```
        TST    Rn, Op2              ; Rn AND with Op2 and flag bits are updated
```

The TST instruction is used to test the contents of register to see if one or multiple bits are HIGH. Similar to CMP instruction, TST is an ANDS instruction without a destination. After the operands are ANDed together the flags are updated. If the result is zero, then Z flag is raised and one can use BEQ (branch equal) to make decision. In the following example below, the program execution stays in the loop between OVER and BEQ OVER until bit 2 (0x04) of the content at "myport" becomes high.

```
        MOV    R0, #0x04            ; R0=00000100 in binary
        LDR    R1, =myport          ; port address
OVER    LDRB   R2, [R1]             ; load R2 from myport
        TST    R2, R0               ; is bit 2 HIGH?
        BEQ    OVER                 ; keep checking
```

In TST, like other data processing instructions, the Op2 can be an immediate value (an 8-bit value with even number of rotate). Look at the following example, which does the same as the program snippet above.

```
        LDR    R1, =myport          ; port address
OVER    LDRB   R2, [R1]             ; load R2 from myport
        TST    R2, #0x04            ; is bit 2 HIGH?
        BEQ    OVER                 ; keep checking
```

See Example 4-5.

Example 4-5

Assume address location 0x40010808 is assigned to an input port address and connected to 8 DIP switches. Write a short program to check the input port and whenever both pins 4 or 6 are LOW, R4 register is incremented.

Solution:

```
MYPORT EQU 0x40010808
       MOV   R0, #2_01010000    ; R0=0x50 (01010000 in binary)
       LDR   R1, =MYPORT        ; R1 = port address
OVER   LDRB  R2, [R1]           ; get a byte from PORT and place it in R2
       TST   R2, R0             ; are bits 4 and 6 LOW?
       BNE   OVER               ; keep checking
       ADD   R4, R4, #1
```

TEQ (test equal)

```
       TEQ   Rn, Op2            ; Rn EX-ORed with Op2 and flag bits are set
```

The TEQ instruction is used to test to see if the contents of two registers or one register and the immediate value are equal. Like CMP and TST, TEQ is an EORS instruction without a destination. After the source operands are Ex-ORed together the flag bits are set according to the result. If result is 0, then Z flag is raised and one can use BEQ (branch zero) to make decision. Recall that if we Exclusive-OR a value with itself, the result is zero. Look at the following example for checking to see whether the temperature on a given port is equal to 100 or not:

```
TEMP  EQU   100
      MOV   R0, #TEMP           ; R0 = Temp
      LDR   R1, =myport         ; port address
OVER  LDRB  R2, [R1]            ; load R2 from myport
      TEQ   R2, R0              ; is it 100?
      BNE   OVER                ; keep checking
```

Unconditional branch (jump) instruction

The unconditional branch is a jump in which control is transferred unconditionally to the target location. In the Arm there are two unconditional branches: B (branch) and BX (branch and exchange). This is discussed next.

B (Branch)

B (branch) is an unconditional jump that can go to any memory location within the $\pm32M$ byte address range.

B has different usages like implementing if/else, while, and for instructions. In the following code you see an example of implementing the if/else instruction:

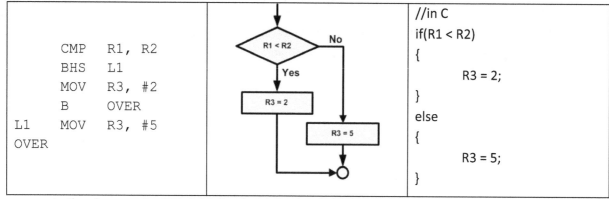

```
          CMP    R1, R2
          BHS    L1
          MOV    R3, #2
          B      OVER
L1        MOV    R3, #5
OVER
```

	//in C
	if(R1 < R2)
	{
	R3 = 2;
	}
	else
	{
	R3 = 5;
	}

In the above code, R3 is initialized with 2 when R1 is lower than R2. Otherwise, it is initialized with 5.

As an example of implementing the while instruction see the following program. It calculates the sum of numbers between 1 and 5:

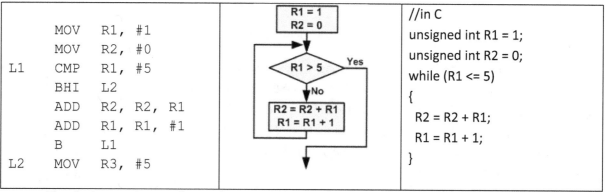

```
          MOV    R1, #1
          MOV    R2, #0
L1        CMP    R1, #5
          BHI    L2
          ADD    R2, R2, R1
          ADD    R1, R1, #1
          B      L1
L2        MOV    R3, #5
```

```
//in C
unsigned int R1 = 1;
unsigned int R2 = 0;
while (R1 <= 5)
{
  R2 = R2 + R1;
  R1 = R1 + 1;
}
```

The *for* instruction can be implemented the same way as the *while* instruction. For example, the above assembly program can be considered as a *for* loop.

In cases where there is no operating system or monitor program, we use the "branch to itself" in order to keep the program from running away. In a stand-alone program, if we allow it to continue beyond the end of program, there is no telling what it is going to happen. A simple way of keeping the program from running away is shown below:

```
HERE   B       HERE   ; stay here
```

Calculating the branch address

The branch instruction is made of two parts: the opcode and the relative address. See Figure 4-5. The target address is relative to the value in the program counter. If the relative address is positive, the jump is forward. If the relative address is negative, then the jump is backward. Because the Thumb-2 instructions are either 2-byte or 4-byte long, the lowest bit of the addresses for instructions are always 0.

There is no need to keep the lowest bit in the relative address and the offset in the instruction does not hold the lowest bit. When the instruction is decoded, the offset is shifted left for one bit to form the offset.

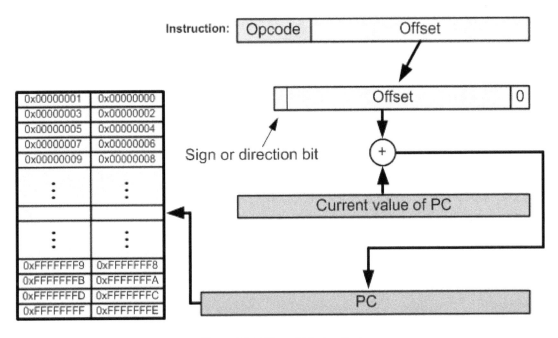

Figure 4-5: B (Branch) Instruction

Notice that in Cortex-M series (except Cortex-M0) pipeline has 3 stages: fetch, decode, and execute. So, when the branch instruction is executed, the next instruction is already fetched into the pipeline and the program counter is pointing to 4 bytes below. So, we add the relative address to the address of 4 bytes below the current instruction. See Example 4-6.

Example 4-6

In Cortex-M, the program counter points to 4 bytes below the current executing instruction. Using the following list file verify the jump forward address calculation.

LINE	ADDRESS	Machine	Mnemonic		Operand
1	00000000			EXPORT	__main
2	00000000			AREA	EXAMPLE_4_6, CODE, READONLY
3	00000000	F04F 0115	__main	MOV	R1, #0x15 ; R1 = 0x15
4	00000004	E005		B	THERE
5	00000006	F04F 0125		MOV	R1, #0x25 ; R1 = 0x25
6	0000000A	F04F 0235		MOV	R2, #0x35 ; R2 = 0x35
7	0000000E	F04F 0345		MOV	R3, #0x45 ; R3 = 0x45
8	**00000012**	F04F 0455	THERE	MOV	R4, #0x55 ; R4 = 0x55
9	00000016	E7FE	H	B	H
10	00000018	END			

Solution:

First notice that the B instruction in line 4 jumps forward. To calculate the target address, the relative address (offset) is shifted left and added to the PC. The value of PC is 4 bytes below the current

113

instruction and the current instruction has address 00000004. So the current value of PC is 0000004 + 4 = 0000008.

In line 4 the instruction "B THERE" has the machine code of E005. If we compare it with the B instruction format, we see that the operand is 000005. Recall that to calculate the target address, the relative address (offset) is shifted left and added to the current value of the PC (Program Counter). Shifting the offset (000005) left results in 00000A and then adding it to the PC (00000008) we have 000008 + 0000000A = 00000012 which is exactly the address of THERE label.

It must also be noted that for the backward branch the relative value is negative (2's complement). That is shown in Example 4-7.

Example 4-7

Verify the calculation of backward jumps for the listing of Example 4-1, shown below.

LINE	ADDRESS	Machine	Mnemonic		Operand
1	00000000			EXPORT	__main
2	00000000			AREA	EXAMPLE_4_7, CODE, READONLY
3	00000000	F44F 727A	__main	LDR	R2, =1000 ; R2 = 1000
4	00000004	F04F 0000		MOV	R0, #0 ; R0 = 0, sum
5	00000008	F100 0009	AGAIN	ADD	R0, R0, #9 ; R0 = R0 + 9
6	0000000C	1E52		SUBS	R2, R2, #1 ; R2 = R2 - 1
7	0000000E	D1FB		BNE	AGAIN ; repeat
8	00000010	4604		MOV	R4, R0 ; store the sum in R4
9	00000012	E7FE	H	B	H
10	00000014			END	

Solution:

In the program list, "BNE AGAIN" in line 7 has machine code D1FB. To separate the operand and opcode, we compare the instruction with the branch instruction format. The operand (relative offset address) is FB. The FB gives us –5, which means the displacement is (–5 × 2 = –10 = **–0x0A**).

The branch is located in address 0x000E. The current value of PC is 0x000E + 4 = **0x0012**.

When the relative address of –0x0A is added to 00000012, we have –0x000A + 0x0012 = 0x08

Notice that 00000008 is the address of the label AGAIN.

FC is a negative number and that means it will branch backward. For further discussion of the addition of negative numbers, see Chapter 5.

Branching beyond the limits

Although branch instruction does not cover the whole 4 GB memory space of Arm, it is more than adequate for most of the applications. In rare cases that there is need to branch to whole 4 GB, we use BX (branch and exchange) instruction. The "BX Rn" instruction uses register Rn to hold target address. Since Rn can be any of the R0–R14 registers and they are 32-bit registers, the "BX Rn" instruction can land anywhere in the 4G bytes address space of the Arm. In the instruction "BX R2" the content of R2 is loaded into the program counter (R15) and CPU starts to fetch instructions from the target address pointed to by the program counter. See Figure 4-6.

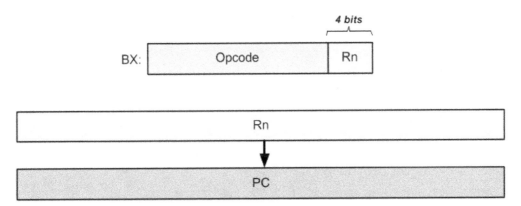

Figure 4-6: BX (Branch and exchange) Instruction Target Address

Since the instructions are either 16-bit or 32-bit long, the lowest bit of the Rn are 0s. The BX instruction is also used to switch between Arm and THUMB modes using bit 0 of the register operand. If bit 0 is set, the mode changes to Thumb mode; otherwise, the mode will be changed to Arm mode.

Review Questions
1. The mnemonic BNE stands for _____.
2. True or false. "BNE BACK" makes its decision based on the last instruction affecting the Z flag.
3. "BNE HERE" is a ___ -byte instruction.
4. In "BEQ NEXT", which flag bit is checked to see if it is high?
5. B(ranch) is a(n) ___ -byte instruction.
6. Compare B and BX instructions.

Section 4.2: Calling Subroutine with BL

Another control transfer instruction is the BL (branch with link) instruction, which is used to call a subroutine. Subroutines are often used to perform tasks that need to be performed frequently. This makes a program more structured in addition to saving memory space.

BL (Branch and Link) instruction and calling subroutine

The BL instruction is made of two parts: the opcode and the offset. The offset is used to address the target subroutine, as shown in Figure 4-7.

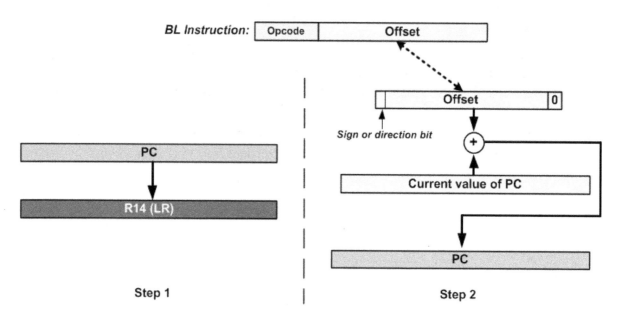

Figure 4-7: BL (Branch and Link) Instruction

The link register and returning from subroutine

To make sure that the Arm knows where to return to after execution of the called subroutine, the BL instruction automatically saves the address of the instruction immediately below the BL (the return address) in the link register (LR), the R14. After finishing the subroutine, the program execution should return to where the caller is left off. This is done by putting the return address into the program counter. To return, we may use "BX LR" instruction, which copies the content of LR to PC, to transfer control back to the caller.

To further understand the role of the R14 register in BL instruction and the return, examine the Examples 4-8. The following points should be noted for the Example 4-8:

1. Notice the DELAY subroutine. Upon executing the first "BL DELAY", the address of the instruction right below it, "MOV R0, #0xAA", is saved onto the R14 register, and the CPU starts to execute instructions at DELAY subroutine.

2. In the DELAY subroutine, first the counter R3 is set to 5 (R3 = 5); therefore, the inner loop is repeated 5 times. When R3 becomes 0, control falls to the "BX LR" instruction, which restores the address into the program counter and returns to main program to resume executing the instructions after the BL.

Example 4-8

Write a program to toggle all the bits of address 0x40000000 by sending to it the values 0x55 and 0xAA continuously. Put a time delay between each issuing of data to address 0x40000000 location.

Solution:

```
        EXPORT      __main
        AREA    EXAMPLE4_8, CODE, READONLY
RAM_ADDR    EQU   0x40000000  ; change the address for your Arm
__main
        LDR   R1, =RAM_ADDR     ; R1 = RAM address
AGAIN MOV   R0, #0x55    ; R0 = 0x55
        STRB  R0, [R1]     ; send it to RAM
        BL    DELAY        ; call delay (R14 = PC of next instruction)
        MOV   R0, #0xAA    ; R0 = 0xAA
        STRB  R0, [R1]     ; send it to RAM
        BL    DELAY        ; call delay
        B     AGAIN        ; keep doing it

        ; -------------------DELAY SUBROUTINE
DELAY LDR   R3, =5       ; R3 =5, modify this value for different delay
L1      SUBS  R3, R3, #1  ; R3 = R3 - 1
        BNE   L1
        BX    LR           ; return to caller
        ; -------------------end of DELAY subroutine
        END              ; notice the place for END directive
```

Use Keil IDE simulator for Arm to simulate the above program and examine the registers and memory location 0x40000000. You might have to change the address 0x40000000 to some other value depending on the RAM address of the Arm chip you use.

In above program, in place of "BX LR" for return, we could have used "BX R14", "MOV R15, R14", or "MOV PC, LR" instructions. All of them will copy the content of LR to PC; but it is recommended to use the "BX LR" instruction.

The amount of time delay in Example 4-8 depends on the frequency of the Arm chip. The time calculation will be explained in the next section of this chapter.

PROC and ENDP directives

The PROC (procedure) and ENDP (end procedure) assembler directives are used to mark the beginning and the end of subroutines in Keil. If the directives are not used, Keil does not go into the subroutine if it is called from another file, while debugging. For example, the DELAY subroutine should be defined as follows in the Keil IDE:

```
DELAY PROC
   ...
   BX LR
   ENDP
```

Main Program and Calling Subroutines

In real world projects we divide the programs into small subroutines (also called functions) and the subroutines are called from the main program. Figure 4-8 shows the format.

```
        ; MAIN program calling subroutines
        AREA   ProgramName, CODE, READONLY


__main      PROC
     BL     SUBR_1              ; Call Subroutine 1
     BL     SUBR_2              ; Call Subroutine 1
     BL     SUBR_3              ; Call Subroutine 1
HERE   B     HERE          ; stay here
     ENDP  ; ----end of MAIN


     ; ------------------SUBROUTINE 1
SUBR_1      PROC

     ....

     ....
     BX    LR    ; return to main
     ENDP  ; --- end of subroutine 1


     ; ------------------SUBROUTINE 2
SUBR_2      PROC

     ....

     ....
     BX    LR    ; return to main
     ENDP  ; ------   end of subroutine 2


     ; ------------------SUBROUTINE 3
SUBR_3      PROC

     ....

     ....
     BX    LR    ; return to main
     ENDP  ; ------   end of subroutine 3
     END          ; notice the END of file
```

Figure 4-8: Arm Assembly Main Program That Calls Subroutines

Program 4-3 shows an example of the main program calling subroutine.

Program 4-3

```
     ; This program fills a block of memory with a fixed value and
     ; then transfers (copies) the block to new area of memory
RAM1_ADDR   EQU   0x40000000   ; Change the address for your Arm
RAM2_ADDR   EQU   0x40000100   ; Change the address for your Arm
     EXPORT __main
     AREA  PROGRAM4_3, CODE, READONLY
__main      PROC
     BL    FILL                ; call block fill subroutine
     BL    COPY                ; call block transfer subroutine
```

```
HERE    B       HERE                    ; Brach here
        ENDP
        ; ----------------BLOCK FILL SUBROUTINE
FILL    PROC
        LDR     R1, =RAM1_ADDR          ; R1 = RAM Address pointer
        MOV     R0, #10                 ; counter
        LDR     R2, =0x55555555
L1      STR     R2, [R1]                ; send it to RAM
        ADD     R1, R1, #4              ; R1 = R1 + 4 to increment pointer
        SUBS    R0, R0, #1              ; R0 = R0 - 1 to decrement counter
        BNE     L1                      ; keep doing it until R0 is 0
        BX      LR                      ; return to caller
        ENDP
        ; ----------------BLOCK COPY SUBROUTINE
COPY    PROC
        LDR     R1, =RAM1_ADDR          ; R1 = RAM Address pointer (source)
        LDR     R2, =RAM2_ADDR          ; R2 = RAM Address pointer (destination)
        MOV     R0, #10                 ; counter
L2      LDR     R3, [R1]                ; get from RAM1
        STR     R3, [R2]                ; send it to RAM2
        ADD     R1, R1, #4              ; R1 = R1 + 4 to increment pointer for RAM1
        ADD     R2, R2, #4              ; R2 = R2 + 4 to increment pointer for RAM2
        SUBS    R0, R0, #1              ; R0 = R0 - 1 for decrementing counter
        BNE     L2                      ; keep doing it
        BX      LR                      ; return to caller
        ENDP    ; ----------
        END
```

Register usage in a subroutine

The registers can be used to pass data between the caller and the subroutine. When calling a subroutine, the parameters may be stored in the registers. When exiting the subroutine, the return value may also be left in the register. To improve the compatibility of the reusable software modules, Arm published Arm Architecture Procedure Call Standard (AAPCS), which defines the register usages among other things. According to AAPCS, the first four registers (R0-R3) are used to pass data between caller and subroutine. Caller should not expect the data in these four registers to be preserved. The rest of the registers except PC (program counter, R15) and SP (stack pointer, R13) should be preserved across a subroutine call.

Review Questions

1. The mnemonic BL stands for _____.
2. True or false. "BL DELAY" saves the address of the instruction below BL in LR register.
3. "BL DELAY" is a ___ -byte instruction.
4. LR is an ___ -bit register.
5. LR is the same as _____ register.
6. Explain the difference between B and BL instructions.

Section 4.3: Time Delay

In this section we discuss how to generate various time delays and calculate time delays for the Arm. We will also discuss the impact of pipelining on execution time.

Delay calculation for the Arm

In creating a time delay using assembly language instructions, one must be mindful of two factors that can affect the accuracy of the delay:

1. **The core clock frequency:** The frequency of the core clock connected to the CPU is one factor in the time delay calculation. The duration of the clock period for the instruction cycle is a function of this core clock frequency.

2. **The Arm design:** Since the 1970s, both the field of IC technology and the architectural design of microprocessors have seen great advancements. Due to the limitations of IC technology and limited CPU design experience for many years, the instruction cycle duration was longer. Advances in both IC technology and CPU design in the 1980s and 1990s have made the single instruction cycle a common feature of many microprocessors. Indeed, one way to increase performance without losing code compatibility with the older generation of a given family is to reduce the number of instruction cycles it takes to execute an instruction. One might wonder how microprocessors such as Arm are able to execute an instruction in one cycle. There are three ways to do that: (a) Use Harvard architecture to get the maximum amount of code and data into the CPU, (b) use RISC architecture features, and finally (c) use pipelining to overlap fetching and execution of instructions.

Instruction cycle time for the Arm

It takes certain amount of time for the CPU to execute an instruction. The unit of time is referred to as *machine cycles*. Thanks to the RISC architecture, Arm executes most instructions in one machine cycle. The length of the machine cycle depends on the frequency of the oscillator connected to the core clock of the CPU. The oscillator circuitry with external crystal or on-chip clock reference, provides the clock source for the Arm CPU. To calculate the machine cycle for the CPU, we take the inverse of the oscillator frequency, as shown in Example 4-9.

Example 4-9

The following shows the oscillator frequency for four different Arm-based systems. Find the period of the instruction cycle in each case.
(a) 8 MHz   (b) 72 MHz   (c) 100 MHz   (d) 50 MHz

Solution:

(a) instruction cycle is 1/8 MHz = 0.125 ms (microsecond) = 125 ns (nanosecond)
(b) instruction cycle = 1/72 MHz = 0.01389 ms = 13.89 ns
(c) instruction cycle = 1/100 MHz = 0.01 ms = 10 ns

(d) instruction cycle = 1/50 MHz = 0.02 ms = 20 ns

Branch penalty

The overlapping of fetch and execution of the instruction is widely used in today's microprocessors such as Arm. For the concept of pipelining to work, we need a buffer or queue in which instructions are pre-fetched and ready to be executed. In some circumstances, the CPU must flush out the queue. For example, when a branch is taken and the CPU starts to fetch code from a new memory location, the code in the queue that was previously fetched becomes useless. In this case, the execution unit must wait until the new instruction is fetched. This is called a branch penalty. The penalty is an extra instruction cycle time to fetch the instruction from the new location instead of executing the instruction already in the queue. This means that while the vast majority of Arm instructions take only one machine cycle, some instructions take three machine cycles. These are Branch, BL (call), and all the conditional branch instructions such as BNE, BLO, and so on. The conditional branch instruction can take only one machine cycle if the condition is not met and the branch is not taken. For example, the BNE will jump if Z = 0 and that takes three machine cycles. If Z = 1, then it falls through and it takes only one machine cycle. See Examples 4-10 and 4-11.

Example 4-10

For an Arm system with the core clock running at 100 MHz, find how long it takes to execute each of the following instructions:

(a) MOV	(b) SUB	(c) B
(d) ADD	(e) NOP	(f) BHI
(g) BLO	(h) BNE	(i) EQU

Solution:

The machine cycle for a system of 100 MHz clock is 10 ns, as shown in Example 4-9. Therefore, we have:

Instruction	Instruction cycles	Time to execute
(a) MOV	1	1 × 10 ns = 10 ns
(b) SUB	1	1 × 10 ns = 10 ns
(c) B	3	3 × 10 ns = 30 ns
(d) ADD	1	1 × 10 ns = 10 ns
(e) NOP	1	1 × 10 ns = 10 ns

For the following, due to branch penalty, 3 clock cycles if taken and 1 if it falls through:

(f) BHI	3/1	3 × 10 ns = 30 ns
(g) BLO	3/1	3 × 10 ns = 30 ns
(h) BNE	3/1	3 × 10 ns = 30 ns
(i) EQU	0	(directives do not produce machine instructions)

Delay calculation for Arm

A delay subroutine consists of two parts: (1) setting a counter, and (2) a loop. Most of the time delay is performed by the body of the loop, as shown in Example 4-11.

Example 4-11

Find the size of the delay of the code snippet below if the system clock frequency is 100 MHz:

```
DELAY MOV    R0, #255
AGAIN PROC
      NOP
      NOP
      SUBS  R0, R0, #1
      BNE   AGAIN
      BX    LR          ; return
      ENDP
```

Solution:

We have the following machine cycles for each instruction of the DELAY subroutine:

	Instruction		Machine Cycle
DELAY	PROC		
	MOV	R0, #255 ;	1
AGAIN	NOP	;	1
	NOP	;	1
	SUBS	R0, R0, #1 ;	1
	BNE	AGAIN ;	3/1
	BX	LR ;	3
	ENDP		

Therefore, we have a time delay of [1 + ((1+1+1+3) × 255) + 3] × 10 ns = 15, 340 ns.
Notice that BNE takes three instruction cycles if it jumps back, and takes only one cycle when falling through the loop. That means the above number should be 15,320 ns. Because the last time, when R0 is zero, the BNE takes only one cycle because it falls through the loop

---

Often we calculate the time delay based on the instructions inside the loop and ignore the clock cycles associated with the instructions outside the loop.

In Example 4-11, the largest value the R0 register can take is 2^{32} = 4G. One way to increase the delay is to use many NOP instructions within the loop. NOP, which stands for "no operation," simply wastes time, but takes 2 bytes of program memory and that is too heavy a price to pay for just one instruction cycle. A better way is to use a nested loop.

Loop inside a loop delay

Another way to get a large delay is to use a loop inside a loop, which is also called a *nested loop*. See Example 4-12.

Example 4-12

In a given Arm trainer an I/O port is connected to 8 LEDs. The following program toggles the LEDs by sending to it 0x55 and 0xAA values continuously. Calculate the time delay for toggling of LEDs. Assume the system clock frequency of 100 MHz.

Solution:

```
        AREA  Example4_12, CODE, READONLY
        EXPORT  __main
PORT_ADDR   EQU   0x4001080C  ; change the address for your Arm and PORT
__main      PROC
        LDR   R1, =PORT_ADDR    ; R1 = port address
AGAIN MOV   R0, #0x55   ; R0 = 0x55
        STRB  R0, [R1]     ; send it to LEDs
        BL    DELAY        ; call delay
        MOV   R0, #0xAA   ; R0 = 0xAA
        STRB  R0, [R1]     ; send it to LEDs
        BL    DELAY        ; call delay
        B     AGAIN        ; keep doing it forever
        ENDP


        ; -------------------DELAY SUBROUTINE
DELAY PROC
        MOV   R3, #100   ; R3 = 100, modify this value for different size delay
L1      LDR   R4, =250000 ; R4 = 250, 000 (inner loop count)
L2      SUBS  R4, R4, #1  ; 1 clock
        BNE   L2          ; 3 clock
        SUBS  R3, R3, #1  ; R3 = R3 - 1
        BNE   L1
        BX    LR    ; return to caller
        ENDP
        END
```

Ignoring the delay associated with the outer loop, we have the following time delay:
$[(1 + 3) \times 250, 000 \times 100] \times 10$ ns = 1 second since 1/100 MHz = 10 ns.

Examine the working frequency for your Arm trainer, change the above address 0x4001080C to your Arm trainer port address and verify the time delay using oscilloscope.

From these discussions we conclude that the use of instructions in generating time delay is not the most reliable method. To complicate the matter, newer performance enhancements of the CPU hardware or the compiler software may affect the loop timing.

To get more accurate time delay Timers are used. All Arm microcontrollers come with on-chip Timers. We can use Keil uVision's simulator to verify delay time and number of cycles used. Meanwhile, to get an accurate time delay for a given Arm microcontroller, we must use an oscilloscope to verify the exact time delay.

Review Questions

1. True or false. In the Arm, the machine cycle lasts 1 clock period of the core clock frequency.
2. The minimum number of machine cycles needed to execute an Arm instruction is _____.
3. Find the machine cycle for a core clock frequency of 66 MHz.
4. Assuming a core clock frequency of 100 MHz, find the time delay associated with the loop section of the following DELAY subroutine:

```
DELAY       PROC
            LDR    R2, =50000000
HERE        NOP
            NOP
            NOP
            NOP
            NOP
            SUBS   R2, R2, #1
            BNE    HERE
            MOV    PC, LR
            ENDP
```

5. Find the machine cycle for an Arm if the core clock frequency is 50 MHz.
6. True or false. In the Arm, the instruction fetching and execution are done at the same time.
7. True or false. B and BL will always take 2 machine cycles.
8. True or false. The BNE instruction will always take 3 machine cycles.

Section 4.4: Stack in Arm Cortex

Stack is like a stack of pancakes that you usually put a new one on the top or take the one on the top off. Similarly, stack is a part of RAM memory. You store data on top of the stack and you get the top most data. Storing data on to the stack is called push and getting data from the stack is called pop.

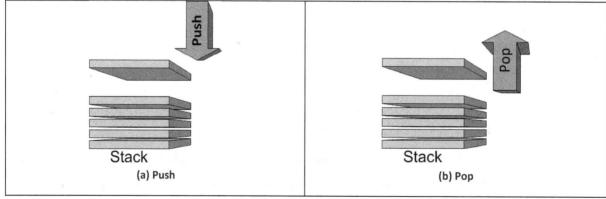

Figure 4-9: Push and Pop

124

Since stack is used extensively in handling subroutine call and interrupt, most of the processors have hardware support to facilitate the creation of stacks in assembly language programming.

Each stack has a stack pointer (SP) that points to the top-of-stack where data is pushed onto or popped off. In Arm Cortex, register R13 is used as stack pointer. The PUSH instruction stores the contents of registers onto the stack and POP pops off the data from top of stack to registers.

Pushing onto the stack

To push registers onto stack the PUSH instruction is used:

```
PUSH {register list}    ;push the contents of the registers on to the stack
```

The register list can contain any of the CPU registers (R0-R15). For example, to store the value of R10 we can write the following instruction:

```
PUSH {R10}    ;store R10 onto the stack
```

The register list can be more than one register, as well. See the following examples:

```
PUSH {R4,R9,R11}   ;store R4, R9, and R11
PUSH {R5-R9}       ;store R5, R6, R7, R8, and R9 onto the stack
```

When we push data onto the stack, the SP is decremented by 4 to point to the word above the top of stack and then the content of a register is copied into that space. Assuming that SP is pointing to location 0x194, and R4 contains 20, the following figure shows pushing R4 onto the stack.

Popping from the stack

Popping the contents of the stack back into a given register is the opposite process of pushing. When the POP instruction is executed, the data in the top location of the stack is copied the registers and the SP is incremented by 4. The POP instruction is used to pop off data from top of stack:

```
POP {register list}     ;pop from the top of stack to the register list
```

For example, the following instruction pops from the top of stack and copies to R7:

```
POP {R7}
```

See Example 4-13.

Example 4-13

The following program places some data into registers and pushes them onto the stack. Assuming that SP is initialized with 0x20000600, examine the stack, stack pointer, and the registers after the execution of each instruction.

```
        EXPORT  __main
        AREA    STACK_SAMPLE1, CODE, READONLY
__main      PROC
        LDR   R0, =0x123         ; R0 = 0x123
```

```
        LDR    R1, =0x455          ; R1 = 0x455
        LDR    R2, =0x6677         ; R2 = 0x6677
        PUSH   {R0}
        PUSH   {R1}
        PUSH   {R2}
        MOV    R0,#0
        MOV    R1,#0
        MOV    R2,#0
        POP    {R2}
        POP    {R1}
        POP {R0}
HERE    B      HERE                 ; stay here
        ENDP
```

After the execution of	Contents of some the registers (in Hex)				Stack
	R0	R1	R2	SP (R13)	

LDR R0, =0x123
 	
LDR R1, =0x455
 	
LDR R2, =0x6677
	123	455	6677	20000600	MSB ...... LSB
					200005F4
					200005F8
					200005FC
					20000600 ◄ SP

PUSH {R0}	123	455	6677	200005FC	200005F4 200005F8 200005FC 00 00 01 23 ◄ SP 20000600
PUSH {R1}	123	455	6677	200005F8	200005F4 200005F8 00 00 04 55 ◄ SP 200005FC 00 00 01 23 20000600
PUSH {R2}	123	455	6677	200005F4	200005F4 00 00 66 77 ◄ SP 200005F8 00 00 04 55 200005FC 00 00 01 23 20000600

Instruction	R0	R1	R2	SP	Memory

MOV R0,#0
MOV R1,#0
MOV R2,#0
	0	0	0	200005F4	200005F4: 00 00 66 77 ◄SP
					200005F8: 00 00 04 55
					200005FC: 00 00 01 23
					20000600:

POP {R2}	0	0	6677	200005F8	200005F4: 200005F8: 00 00 04 55 ◄SP 200005FC: 00 00 01 23 20000600:
POP {R1}	0	455	6677	200005FC	200005F4: 200005F8: 200005FC: 00 00 01 23 ◄SP 20000600:
POP {R0}	123	455	6677	20000600	200005F4: 200005F8: 200005FC: 20000600: ◄SP

Initializing the stack pointer in Arm Cortex

When the Cortex is powered up, the R13 (SP) register is loaded with the contents of memory location 0. Therefore, the address of stack must be stored in locations 0x00000000 to 0x00000003 of memory so that SP points to somewhere in the internal SRAM. In Arm, when we push onto the stack, the SP is decremented and then data is stored. So, the stack pointer should be initialized with the address of the location next to the last location of stack memory. For example, if we want to use locations 0x20000000 to 0x200000FF for stack, we should store 0x20000100 in location 0x00000000. In the case, when the Arm is powered up, the SP is loaded with 0x20000100 and when the first PUSH is executed, the SP is decremented by 4 and the data is stored in the last word of stack (0x200000FC to 0x200000FF).

Some Stack Usages

Nested calls

In Arm, the stack is used for subroutine calls and interrupt handling. We must remember that upon calling a subroutine from the main program using the BL instruction, R14, the linker register, keeps track of where the CPU should return to after completing the subroutine. Now, if we have another call inside the subroutine using the BL instruction, then it is our job to store the original R14 on the stack.

Failure to do that will end up crashing the program. In the Program 4-4, FUNC2 is called in FUNC1. The execution of BL changes the link register (LR). So, before calling FUNC2, the LR register is stored onto the stack and it is restored after returning.

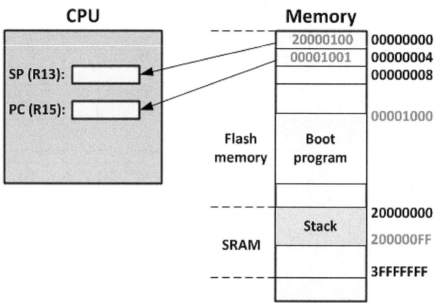

Figure 4-10: Power-up Initialization in Cortex

Program 4-4

```
      EXPORT  __main
      AREA    MY_CODE, CODE, READONLY
__main
      BL      FUNC1
HERE  B       HERE


      ; subroutine FUNC1
FUNC1
      PUSH    {LR}   ;store the LR on the stack
      BL      FUNC2  ;the func. call changes the LR
      POP     {LR}   ;restore the LR value from the stack
      BX      LR


      ; subroutine FUNC2
FUNC2
      ;do something
      BX LR ; return
      END
```

Preserving registers values

Each subroutine may use some registers to hold data temporarily. The subroutine has no knowledge whether the caller left any data in the registers that need to be preserved. So each subroutine should preserve any register it is going to use and restore them before return. In Program 4-5, R7 is used in the delay subroutine. So, its value is preserved using the stack.

Program 4-5

```
        EXPORT  __main
        AREA    MY_CODE, CODE, READONLY
__main
        BL      DELAY
HERE    B       HERE
DELAY
        PUSH    {R7}   ;store R7 onto the stack
        LDR     R7,=120000
D_1     SUBS    R7,R7,#1
        BNE     D_1
        POP     {R7}   ;restore R7
        END
```

Review Questions

1. The _____ register is the default stack pointer.
2. Write an instruction that pushes R5, R6, R7, and R8 into the stack.
3. Write an instruction that pops R5, R6, R7, and R8 from the stack.
4. On power-up, the SP is loaded with the contents of location _____ .

Section 4-5: Exploring the Startup File

In your real projects, you will need to change the Startup file. So, in this section we will explore the contents of the startup file. Figure 4-11 is a generic startup file which shows the important parts of startup files. The file has 4 important parts: stack, heap, vector table, and reset handler.

Figure 4-11: A Generalized startup.s file

```
1                     ;---- Stack ------------------------------------------
2       Stack_Size       EQU     0x00000400 ;stack size in bytes
3                        AREA    STACK, NOINIT, READWRITE, ALIGN=3
4       Stack_Mem        SPACE   Stack_Size ;allocating memory for stack
5       __initial_sp
6
7                     ;---- Heap -------------------------------------------
8       Heap_Size        EQU     0x00000200 ;Heap size in bytes
9
10                       AREA    HEAP, NOINIT, READWRITE, ALIGN=3
11      __heap_base
12      Heap_Mem         SPACE   Heap_Size
13      __heap_limit
14
15
16                    ;---- Vector Table Mapped to Address 0 at Reset ----
```

```
17                    AREA    RESET, DATA, READONLY
18                         EXPORT  __Vectors
19                         EXPORT  __Vectors_End
20                         EXPORT  __Vectors_Size
21
22      __Vectors          DCD     __initial_sp         ; Top of Stack
23                         DCD     Reset_Handler        ; Reset Handler
24                         DCD     NMI_Handler          ; NMI Handler
25                         DCD     HardFault_Handler    ; Hard Fault Handler
26                         DCD     MemManage_Handler    ; MPU Fault Handler
27                         DCD     BusFault_Handler     ; Bus Fault Handler
28                         DCD     UsageFault_Handler   ; Usage Fault Handle
29                         DCD     0                    ; Reserved
30                         DCD     0                    ; Reserved
31                         DCD     0                    ; Reserved
32                         DCD     0                    ; Reserved
33                         DCD     SVC_Handler          ; SVCall Handler
34                         DCD     DebugMon_Handler     ; Debug Monitor Handler
35                         DCD     0                    ; Reserved
36                         DCD     PendSV_Handler       ; PendSV Handler
37                         DCD     SysTick_Handler      ; SysTick Handler
38
39
40                    ;---- Reset handler -------------------------------
41                         AREA    |.text|, CODE, READONLY
42      Reset_Handler      PROC
43                         EXPORT  Reset_Handler                [WEAK]
44                         IMPORT  __main
45                         IMPORT  SystemInit
46                         LDR     R0, =SystemInit
47                         BLX     R0
48                         LDR     R0, =__main
49                         BX      R0
50                         ENDP
```

Stack

Lines 1 to 5 are related to stack memory allocation. The AREA is defined as READWRITE, since the stack memory must be allocated from the RAM memory. In line 4, the space is allocated for the stack. Since Stack_Size is equal to 0x400, 0x400 bytes (1024 bytes) are allocated for the stack. If you like to change the stack size, you can change the value of Stack_Size in line 1. As we saw in the stack section, the stack pointer should be initialized with the address of the next byte to the last location of the stack space. The next byte to the stack space is labeled as __initial_sp and it is used in the vector table to initialize the stack pointer.

Heap

The heap memory is used in C language for dynamic variables. Lines 7 to 13, allocate a part of RAM for heap. If you like to change the heap size, you can change the value of Heap_Size.

130

Vector Table

Lines 16 to 38 are for vector table. The AREA is defined as READONLY in line 17. So, the vector table will be placed in the flash memory. Since it is labeled as __vector in line 18, it will be placed in first locations of memory starting from location 0x0000. As we saw in this chapter and Chapter 2, when the Arm is powered up, the contents of memory locations 0000 to 0x0003 are loaded to the stack pointer, and the PC is loaded with contents of locations 0x0004 to 0x0007. In line 18, the value of __initial_sp is stored in location 0 (the first location of vector table). DCD allocates 4 bytes of memory. So, __initial_sp is stored in locations 0x0000 to 0x0003. For example, if the stack space ends in location 0x200005FF, __initial_sp has the address of 0x20000600; and 0x20000600 will be stored in locations 0 to 3. Similarly, the address of Reset_Handler is stored in locations 0x0004 to 0x0007. See Figure 4-12.

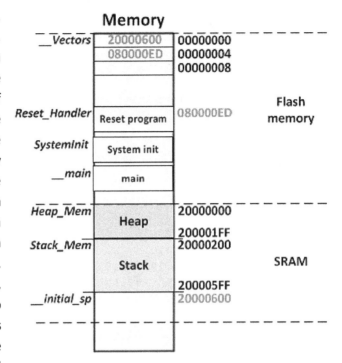

Figure 4-12: Memory Allocation for the Program

The Vector table is discussed in more detail in the interrupt chapter.

Reset Handler

Lines 40 to 50 are for Reset Handler. The address of Reset_Handler is stored in locations 0x0004 to 0x0007. So, when the CPU is powered up, the program counter is loaded with the address of Reset_Handler. Reset Handler is a piece of code which is executed first.

In line 46, R0 is loaded with the address of the SystemInit subroutine and then SystemInit is called in line 47. SystemInit sets the CPU clock frequency and initializes the system. SystemInit is in the system_xxx.c file.

In lines 48 and 49, R0 is loaded with the address of __main and then branches to the __main subroutine. That is why we label our first line of code as __main. In C programs, the programs begin from the main function, as well.

Problems

Section 4.1: Looping and Branch Instructions

1. In the Arm, looping action using a single register is limited to _____ iterations.
2. If a conditional branch is not taken, what is the next instruction to be executed?

3. In calculating the target address for a branch, a displacement is added to the contents of register _____.
4. The mnemonic BNE stands for _____.
5. What is the advantage of using BX over B?
6. True or false. The target of a BNE can be anywhere in the 4G word address space.
7. True or false. All Arm branch instructions can branch to anywhere in the 4G byte address space.
8. Dissect the B instruction and indicate how it can branch.
9. True or false. The program counter has the address of the instruction which the CPU is decoding.
10. Show code for a nested loop to perform an action 10, 000, 000, 000 times.
11. Show code for a nested loop to perform an action 200, 000, 000, 000 times.
12. Find the number of times the following loop is performed:

```
        MOV   R0, #0x55
        MOV   R2, #40
L1      LDR   R1, =10000000
L2      EOR   R0, R0, #0xFF
        SUB   R1, R1, #1
        BNE   L2
        SUB   R2, R2, #1
        BNE   L1
```

13. Indicate the status of Z and C after CMP is executed in each of the following cases.

(a)
```
MOV   R0, #50
MOV   R1, #40
CMP   R0, R1
```

(b)
```
MOV   R1, #0xFF
MOV   R2, #0x6F
CMP   R1, R2
```

(c)
```
MOV   R2, #34
MOV   R3, #88
CMP   R2, R3
```

(d)
```
SUB   R1, R1, R1
MOV   R2, #0
CMP   R1, R2
```

(e)
```
EOR   R2, R2, R2
MOV   R3, #0xFF
CMP   R2, R3
```

(f)
```
EOR   R0, R0, R0
EOR   R1, R1, R1
CMP   R0, R1
```

(g)
```
MOV   R4, #0x78
MOV   R2, #0x40
CMP   R4, R2
```

(h)
```
MOV   R0, #0xAA
AND   R0, R0, #0x55
CMP   R0, #0
```

14. Rewrite Program 4-1 to find the lowest grade in that class.
15. The target address of a BNE is backward if the relative address portion of opcode is _____ (negative, positive).
16. The target address of a BNE is forward if the relative address portion of opcode is _____ (negative, positive).

Section 4.2: Calling Subroutine with BL

17. BL is used to _____.
18. In Arm, which register is the linker register?
19. True or false. The BL target address can be anywhere in the 4G byte address space.

20. Describe how we can return from a subroutine in Arm.
21. In Arm, which address is saved when BL instruction is executed.

Section 4.3: Arm Time Delay and Instruction Pipeline

22. Find the core clock frequency if the machine cycle = 1.25 ns.
23. Find the machine cycle if the core clock frequency is 200 MHz.
24. Find the machine cycle if the core clock frequency is 100 MHz.
25. Find the machine cycle if the core clock frequency is 160 MHz.
26. Find the time delay for the delay subroutine shown below if the system has an Arm with a core clock frequency of 80 MHz:

```
            MOV    R8, #200
BACK        LDR    R1, =400000000
HERE        NOP
            SUBS   R1, R1, #1
            BNE    HERE
            SUBS   R8, R8, #1
            BNE    BACK
```

27. Find the time delay for the delay subroutine shown below if the system has an Arm with a core clock frequency of 50 MHz:

```
            MOV    R2, #100
BACK        LDR    R0, =50000000
HERE        NOP
            NOP
            SUBS   R0, R0, #1
            BNE    HERE
            SUBS   R2, R2, #1
            BNE    BACK
```

28. Find the time delay for the delay subroutine shown below if the system has an Arm with a core clock frequency of 40 MHz:

```
            MOV    R1, #200
BACK        LDR    R0, #20000000
HERE        NOP
            NOP
            NOP
            SUBS   R0, R0, #1
            BNE    HERE
            SUBS   R1, R1, #1
            BNE    BACK
```

29. Find the time delay for the delay subroutine shown below if the system has an Arm with a core clock frequency of 100 MHz:

```
            MOV    R8, #500
```

```
BACK        LDR    R1, =20000
HERE        NOP
            NOP
            NOP
            SUBS   R1, R1, #1
            BNE    HERE
            SUBS   R8, R8, #1
            BNE    BACK
```

Section 4.4: Stack and Stack Usage in Arm

30. True or false. In Arm the R13 is designated as stack pointer.
31. In Arm, stack pointer is a_____ bit register.

Answers to Review Questions

Section 4.1: Looping and Branch Instructions

1. Branch if not Equal
2. True
3. 4
4. Z flag of CPSR (status register)
5. 4
6. The B uses immediate value for offset and can only branch to an address location within ± 32 MB address space, while the BX uses register operand to hold the branch target address and can go anywhere in the 4 GB address space of Arm.

Section 4.2: Calling Subroutine with BL

1. Branch and Link
2. True
3. 4
4. 32
5. R14
6. In both of them the target address is relative to the value of the program counter and the relative address can cover memory space of ± 32MB from current location of program counter. The BL instruction saves the address of the next instruction in the LR register before jumping, while the B instruction just jumps without saving anything.

Section 4.3: Arm Time Delay and Instruction Pipeline

1. True
2. 1
3. MC = 1/66 MHz = 0.015 ms = 15 ns
4. [50, 000, 000 × (1 + 1 + 1 + 1 + 1 + 1 + 3)] × 10 ns = 4.5 seconds
5. Machine Cycle = 1 / 50 MHz = 0.02 ms = 20 ns
6. True
7. False
8. False. It takes 3 cycles, only if it branches to the target address.

Section 4.4: Stack and Stack Usage in Arm

1. R13
2. PUSH {R5-R8}
3. POP {R5-R8}
4. 0x00000000 to 0x00000003

Chapter 5: Signed Integer Numbers Arithmetic

This chapter deals with signed integer number instructions and operations. In Section 5.1, we focus on the concept of signed numbers in software engineering. Signed number arithmetic operations and instructions are explained along with examples in Section 5.2. Signed number comparison is discussed in Section 5-3 and Sign extension is covered in Section 5-4.

Section 5.1: Signed Numbers Concept

All data items used so far have been unsigned integer numbers, meaning that the entire 8-bit, 16-bit or 32-bit operand was used for the magnitude and the numbers represented are all positive or zero. Many applications require the use of negative numbers or signed data. In this section the concept of signed integer numbers is discussed.

Concept of signed numbers in computers

In everyday life, numbers are used that could be positive or negative or zero. For example, a temperature of 5 degrees below zero can be represented as -5, and 20 degrees above zero as +20. Computers must be able to accommodate such numbers. To do that, computer scientists have devised the following arrangement for the representation of signed positive and negative numbers: The most significant bit (MSB) is set aside for the sign (+ or -) and the rest of the bits are used for the magnitude. The sign is represented by 0 for positive (+) numbers and 1 for negative (-) numbers. Signed byte and word representations are discussed below.

Sign-magnitude format

In sign-magnitude format the sign and magnitude of the number are represented independently. For a byte, D7 (MSB) is the sign and D0 to D6 are set aside for the magnitude of the number. If D7 = 0, the number is positive, and if D7 = 1, it is negative.

The range of magnitude that can be represented by the above format is 2^7 (0 to 127). And the range of the number that can be represented is -127 to +127.

Dec.	Binary
0	0000 0000
+1	0000 0001
...	....
+5	0000 0101
...	....
+127	0111 1111

Dec.	Binary
-0	1000 0000
-1	1000 0001
...	....
-5	1000 0101
...	....
-127	1111 1111

The sign-magnitude format is easier for human to understand but more complex for computer to process.

Negative numbers using 2's complement

To simplify ALU circuitry, we often use 2's complement for the negative number representation. Adding a negative number in 2's complement has the same result as a subtraction. Using 2's complement representation, the adder in the ALU will be able to perform both add and subtract. With 2's complement, the most significant bit is still 0 for positive numbers and 1 for negative numbers like sign magnitude format.

In writing negative numbers in program source file, we usually use sign-magnitude format (e.g.: -75 for negative 75) and the assembler/compiler will convert the negative number to 2's complement. We will demonstrate the following process used to convert a positive number to a negative number represented in 2's complement to help you understand the 2's complement representation. Follow these steps:

1. Write the positive number in binary.
2. Invert bit.
3. Add 1 to it.

Unlike sign-magnitude format that has a positive zero and a negative zero, with 2's complement representation, there is only one zero. And there is one more negative number than positive.

Dec.	Binary
0	0000 0000
+1	0000 0001
...	....
+5	0000 0101
...	....
+127	0111 1111

Dec.	Binary
0	0000 0000
-1	1111 1111
...	....
-5	1111 1011
...	....
-127	1000 0001
-128	1000 0000

Examples 5-1, 5-2, and 5-3 demonstrate these three steps.

Example 5-1

Show how the computer would represent -5 in 8-bit 2's complement.

Solution:

1. 0000 0101   5 in 8-bit binary
2. 1111 1010   invert each bit
3. 1111 1011   add 1 (0xFB)

This is the signed number representation in 2's complement for -5.

Example 5-2

Show -34 hex as it is represented in 2's complement.

Solution:

1. 0011 0100   (0x34)
2. 1100 1011
3. 1100 1100   (which is 0xCC)

Example 5-3

Show the 2's complement representation for -128_{10}.

Solution:

1. 1000 0000   (128_{10})
2. 0111 1111
3. 1000 0000   Notice that this is not negative zero (−0).

From the examples above it is clear that the range of byte-sized negative numbers is -1 to -128. The following lists byte-sized signed number ranges:

Decimal	Binary	Hex
-128	1000 0000	80
-127	1000 0001	81
-126	1000 0010	82
...	....	..
-2	1111 1110	FE
-1	1111 1111	FF
0	0000 0000	00
+1	0000 0001	01
+2	0000 0010	02
...	....	..
+127	0111 1111	7F

Halfword-sized signed numbers

In Arm CPU a half-word is 16 bits in length. Using 2's complement representation, the MSB (D15) is used for the sign leaving a total of 15 bits (D14–D0) for the magnitude. This gives a range of −32,768 (−2^{15}) to +32,767 (2^{15}−1).

D15	D14	...	D0
sign	magnitude		

The following table shows the range of signed half-word numbers. To convert a half-word positive number to a negative half-word number in 2's complement representation, the same steps discussed above for byte size number are used.

Decimal	Binary	Hex
-32,768	1000 0000 0000 0000	8000
-32,767	1000 0000 0000 0001	8001
-32,766	1000 0000 0000 0010	8002
...	....	..
-2	1111 1111 1111 1110	FFFE
-1	1111 1111 1111 1111	FFFF
0	0000 0000 0000 0000	0000
+1	0000 0000 0000 0001	0001
+2	0000 0000 0000 0010	0002
...	....	...
+32,766	0111 1111 1111 1110	7FFE
+32,767	0111 1111 1111 1111	7FFF

Using Microsoft Windows calculator for signed numbers

All Microsoft Windows operating systems come with a handy calculator. Use it in programmer's mode to verify the signed number operations in this section.

Word-sized signed numbers

In Arm CPU a word is 32 bits in length. Using 2's complement representation, the MSB (D31) is used for the sign leaving a total of 31 bits (D30–D0) for the magnitude. This gives a range of -(2^{31}) to +(2^{31}-1).

D31	D30	...	D0
sign	magnitude		

To convert a word-size positive number to a negative word-size number in 2's complement representation, the same steps discussed above for byte size number are used. See Example 5-4.

Example 5-4

Show how the computer would represent -5 in 2's complement for (a) 8-bit, (b) 16-bit, and (c) 32-bit data sizes.

Solution:

(a) 8-bit

     1. 0000 0101   5 in 8-bit binary

     2. 1111 1010   invert each bit

     3. 1111 1011   add 1   (0xFB)

(b) 16-bit

     1. 0000 0000 0000 0101   5 in 16-bit binary

     2. 1111 1111 1111 1010   invert each bit

     3. 1111 1111 1111 1011   add 1 (0xFFFB)

(c) 32-bit

     1. 0000 0000 0000 0000 0000 0000 0000 0101 5 in 32-bit binary

     2. 1111 1111 1111 1111 1111 1111 1111 1010 invert each bit

     3. 1111 1111 1111 1111 1111 1111 1111 1011 add 1   (0xFFFFFFFB)

Use the Windows calculator to verify these examples.

If a number is larger than 32-bit, it must be treated as a 64-bit double-word number and be processed word by word the same way as unsigned numbers. The following shows the range of signed word-size numbers.

Decimal	Binary	Hex
-2,147,483,648	10000000000000000000000000000000	80000000
-2,147,483,647	10000000000000000000000000000001	80000001
-2,147,483,646	10000000000000000000000000000010	80000002
...	...	...
-2	11111111111111111111111111111110	FFFFFFFE
-1	11111111111111111111111111111111	FFFFFFFF
0	00000000000000000000000000000000	00000000
+1	00000000000000000000000000000001	00000001
+2	00000000000000000000000000000010	00000002
...	...	...
+2,147,483,646	01111111111111111111111111111110	7FFFFFFE
+2,147,483,647	01111111111111111111111111111111	7FFFFFFF

Table 5-1 shows a summary of signed data ranges.

Data Size	Bits	2^n	Decimal	Hexadecimal
Byte	8	-2^7 to $+2^7-1$	-128 to +127	0x80–0x7F
Half-word	16	-2^{15} to $+2^{15}-1$	-32,768 to +32,767	0x8000–0x7FFF
Word	32	-2^{31} to $+2^{31}-1$	-2,147,483,648 to +2,147,483,647	0x80000000–0x7FFFFFFF

Table 5-1: Signed Data Range Summary

Review Questions
1. In an 8-bit number, bit _____ is used for the sign bit, whereas in a 16-bit number, bit _____ is used for the sign bit. Repeat for 32-bit signed data.
2. Compute the byte-sized 2's complement of 0x16.
3. The range of byte-sized signed operands is -_____ to +_____. The range of half word-sized signed numbers is -_____ to +_____.
4. The range of word-sized signed numbers is -_____ to +_____.
5. Compute the 2's complement of 0x00500000.

Section 5.2: Signed Number Instructions and Operations

In this section we examine issues associated with signed number arithmetic operations. We will also discuss the Arm instructions for signed numbers and how to use them.

N flag

In Arm the N flag bit in CSPR is the sign bit. For positive results, N becomes 0 and for negative results it becomes 1. See Example 5-5.

Example 5-5

Write the following program in Keil and monitor the N flag:

```
      EXPORT  __main
      AREA MY_PROG, CODE, READONLY
__main
      MOV   R1,#6
      SUBS  R0,R1,#8
      ADDS  R3,R1,#3
H     B     H
```

Solution:

Following are the steps for "SUB R4, R2, R3":

After the execution of	Result	N
SUBS R0,R1,#8	6 – 8 = -2	1 (negative)
ADDS R3,R1,#3	-2 + 3 = +1	0 (positive)

141

Overflow problem in signed number operations

When using signed numbers, a serious problem arises that must be dealt with. This is the overflow problem. The CPU indicates the existence of the problem by raising the V (oVerflow) flag, but it is up to the programmer to take care of it. Now what is an overflow? If the result of an operation on signed numbers is too large for the register and resulted in an error, an overflow occurs and the programmer is notified. Look at Example 5-6.

Example 5-6

Look at the following case for 8-bit data size:

$$
\begin{array}{rlr}
+96 & 0110\ 0000 & +96 \\
+70 & +0100\ 0110 & ++70 \\
\hline
+166 & 1010\ 0110 & -90
\end{array}
$$

We are adding two positive numbers together and the result is -90 in 2's complement notation, which is wrong.

In the example above, +96 is added to +70 and the result according to 2's complement notation is -90. Why? The reason is that the result was more than 8 bits could handle. The largest positive number an 8-bit registers can hold is +127. The sum of +96 and +70 is +166, which is more than +127. The designers of the CPU created the overflow flag specifically for the purpose of informing the programmer that the result of the signed number operation is erroneous.

Overflow flag in Arm

In a 32-bit operation, V is set to 1 in either of two cases:

1. There is a carry from D30 to D31 but no carry out of D31 (C = 0).

2. There is a carry from D31 out (C = 1) but no carry from D30 to D31.

The overflow flag is set to 1 when there is a carry into the most significant bit (D31) or out of the most significant bit, but not both. See Examples 5-7 and 5-8.

Example 5-7

Observe the result of executing the following program:

```
        EXPORT   __main
        AREA MY_PROG, CODE, READONLY
__main
        LDR R1,=0x6E2F356F
        LDR R2,=0x13D49530
        ADDS R3,R1,R2
H       B       H
        END
```

Solution:

```
 +6E2F356F    0110 1110 0010 1111 0011 0101 0110 1111
++13D49530   +0001 0011 1101 0100 1001 0101 0011 0000
 +8203CA9F    1000 0010 0000 0011 1100 1010 1001 1111   = −0x7DFC3561
```

The result is incorrect and the V flag will be set to show the over flow. (V = 1, C = 0, N = 1)

Example 5-8

Observe the result of executing the following instructions:

```
LDR R1,=0x6E2F356F
LDR R2,=0x13D49530
ADDS R3,R1,R2
```

Solution:

```
 +542F356F    0101 0100 0010 1111 0011 0101 0110 1111
++12E09530    0001 0010 1110 0000 1001 0101 0011 0000
 +670FCA9F    0110 0111 0000 1111 1100 1010 1001 1111   = +670FCA9F
```

The result is correct; V = 0, C = 0, N = 0

Avoiding Overflow

To avoid the overflow problems associated with signed number operations, the variables that we use in our programs should be big enough to be able to store the results.

Signed number multiplication

Signed number multiplication is similar in its operation to the unsigned multiplication described in Chapter 3. The only difference between them is that the operands including the result in signed number operations are treated as 2's complement representation of positive or negative numbers. In Arm we have SMULL (signed multiply long) that multiplies two 32-bit signed numbers and resulted in a 64-bit signed number. Arm also have 16-bit × 16-bit and 32-bit × 16-bit signed multiplication instructions but they are not available in all versions of the processors. Table 5-2 shows the 32-bit × 32-bit signed multiplication; it is similar to Table 3-3 in Chapter 3. See Examples 5-9 and 5-10.

Multiplication	Operand 1	Operand 2	Result
word×word	Rm	Rs	RdHi= upper 32-bit,RdLo=lower 32-bit
Note: Using SMULL (signed multiply long) for word × words multiplication provides the 64-bit result in RdLo and RdHi register. This is used for 32-bit × 32-bit numbers in which result can go beyond 0xFFFFFFFF.			

Table 5-2: Signed Multiplication (SMULL RdLo, RdHi, Rm, Rs) Summary

Example 5-9

Observe the results of the following multiplication of signed numbers:

```
LDR    R1, =-3500   ; R1 = -3500 (0xFFFFF254)
LDR    R0, =-100    ; R0 = -100 (0xFFFFFF9C)
SMULL R2, R3, R0, R1
```

Solution:

-3500 × -100 = 350,000 = 0x55730 in hex. After executing the above program R2 and R3 will contain 0x55730 and 00000000, respectively.

Example 5-10

The following program is similar to Example 5-9. But, instead of SMULL, the UMULL instruction is used. Observe the results of the following multiplication:

```
LDR    R1, =-3500   ; R1 = -3500 (0xFFFFF254)
MOV    R0, #-100    ; R0 = -100 (0xFFFFFF9C)
UMULL  R2, R3, R0, R1
```

Solution:

0xFFFFF254 × 0xFFFFFF9C = 0xFFFFF1F000055730. Thus, R2 and R3 will contain 0x00055730 and 0xFFFFF1F0, respectively. As you can see, the results of the programs are completely different. In the previous program the SMULL instruction considers the operands signed numbers and the product of two negative numbers becomes positive. As a result, the sign bit becomes zero, but in this example the operands are considered as unsigned numbers.

Arithmetic shift

There are two types of shifts: logical and arithmetic. Logical shift, which is used for unsigned numbers, was discussed in Chapter 3. The arithmetic shift is used for signed numbers. It is basically the same as the logical shift, except that the old sign bit is copied to the new sign bit so that the sign of the number does not change.

ASR (arithmetic shift right)
```
ASR    Rn, Op2, count
```

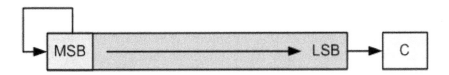

The number of bits to shift can be a register or an immediate value. As the bits of the source are shifted to the right into C, the empty bits are filled with the original sign bit. One can use the ASR instruction to divide a signed number by 2, as shown below:

```
MOV   R0, #-10    ; R0 = -10 = 0xFFFFFFF6
ASR   R3, R0, #1  ; R0 is arithmetic shifted right once
                  ; R3 = 0xFFFFFFFB = -5
```

Review Questions
1. Explain the difference between an overflow and a carry.
2. The instruction for signed long multiplication is _____.

Section 5.3: Signed Number Comparison

In Chapter 4 we saw that the CMP instruction affects the Z and C flags; using the flags we compared unsigned numbers. This instruction affects the N and V flags as well. We can use flags Z, V, and N to compare signed numbers. The Z flag shows if the numbers are equal or not. When the numbers are equal the Z flag is set to one. N and V flags show if the left operand is bigger than the right operand or not. When N and V have the same value, the first operand has a greater value.

In summary, after executing the instruction *CMP Rn, Op2* the flags are changed as follows:

Op2 > Rn	V = N
Op2 = Rn	Z = 1
Op2 < Rn	N ≠ V

Instruction		Action
BEQ	Branch equal	Branch if Z = 1
BNE	Branch not equal	Branch if Z = 0
BMI	Branch minus (branch negative)	Branch if N = 1
BPL	Branch plus (branch positive)	Branch if N = 0
BVS	Branch if V set (branch overflow)	Branch if V = 1
BVC	Branch if V clear (branch if no overflow)	Branch if V = 0
BGE	Branch greater than or equal	Branch if N = V
BLT	Branch less than	Branch if N ≠ V
BGT	Branch greater than	Branch if Z = 0 and N = V
BLE	Branch less than or equal	Branch if Z = 1 or N ≠ V

Table 5-3: Arm Conditional Branch (Jump) Instructions for Signed Data

Table 5-3 lists the branch instructions which check the Z, V, and N flags. The instructions can be used together with the CMP instruction to compare signed numbers.

Program 5-1 finds the lowest number among a list of numbers. The lowest number known so far is kept in R2. The numbers are brought into R1 and compared to R2. If a smaller one is found, it replaces the one in R2. The program starts by putting the first number in R2 since it is the lowest number known so far.

Program 5-1

```
        ; Finding the lowest of signed numbers
        AREA    PROG5_1, CODE, READONLY
__main  LDR R0, =SIGN_DAT
        MOV R3, #9
        LDRSB   R2, [R0]    ; bring first number into R2 and sign extend it
LOOP    ADD     R0, R0, #1  ; point to next
        SUBS    R3, R3, #1  ; decrement counter
        BEQ     DONE        ; if R3 is zero, done
        LDRSB   R1, [R0]    ; bring next number into R1 and sign extend it
        CMP     R1, R2      ; compare R1 and R2
        MOVLT   R2, R1      ; if R1 is smaller, keep it in R2
        B       LOOP
DONE    LDR     R0, =LOWEST ; R0 = address of LOWEST
        STR     R2, [R0]    ; store R2 in location SUM
HERE    B       HERE

SIGN_DAT DCB    +13, -10, +19, +14, -18, -9, +12, -19, +16
        ALIGN
        AREA    VARIABLES, DATA, READWRITE
LOWEST      DCD     0
        END
```

CMN instruction

```
    CMN     Rn, Op2
```

In Arm we have two compare instructions: CMP and CMN. While the CMP instruction sets the flags by subtracting operand2 from operand1, the CMN sets the flags by adding operand2 from operand1. As the result CMN compares the destination operand with the negative of the source operand:

destination > (-1 × source)	V = N
destination = (-1 × source)	Z = 1
destination < (-1 × source)	N ≠ V

When the source operand is an immediate value, the instructions can be used interchangeably. Example 5-11 is an example of using the CMN instruction.

Example 5-11

Assuming R5 has a positive value, write a program that finds its negative match in an array of data (OUR_DATA).

Solution:

```
            EXPORT  __main
            AREA    EXAMPLE5_11, CODE, READONLY
__main      MOV     R5, #13
            LDR     R0, =OUR_DATA
            MOV     R3, #9
BEGIN
            LDRSB R1, [R0]      ; R1 = contents of loc. pointed to by R0
                                ; (sign extended)
            CMN     R1, R5      ; compare R1 and negative of R5
            BEQ     FOUND       ; branch if R1 is equal to negative of R5

            ADDS    R0, R0, #1  ; increment pointer
            SUBS    R3, R3, #1  ; decrement counter
            BNE     BEGIN       ; if R3 is not zero branch BEGIN

NOT_FOUND   B       NOT_FOUND
FOUND       B       FOUND

OUR_DATA    DCB     +13, -10, -13, +14, -18, -9, +12, -19, +16
            END
```

In the above program R5 is initialized with 13. Therefore, it finishes searching when it gets to −13.

Review Questions
1. For each of the following instructions, indicate the flag condition necessary for each branch to occur: (a) BLE (b) BGT

Section 5-4: Sign Extension

The Arm arithmetic instructions work on the 32-bit general purpose registers. But we might have 8-bit or 16-bit signed variables in the memory. If we load them using LDRB or LDRH, the most significant bits, including the sign bit, will be filled with zeros and the result of calculations might be incorrect. See Example 5-12 for instance.

Example 5-12

Run the following program in Keil and watch the value of R3.

```
      EXPORT  __main
      AREA    NotExtendingExample, CODE, READONLY
__main
      LDR   R0,=AA
      LDRB  R1,[R0]      ;read AA

      LDR   R0,=BB
      LDRB  R2,[R0]      ;read BB

      SDIV  R3,R1,R2     ;R3 = R1 / R2
```

```
HERE    B   HERE

AA      DCB     -25
BB      DCB     -2
```

Solution:

The program initializes AA and BB with -25 and -2. So, AA and BB are loaded with 0xE7 and 0xFE, respectively. Then, R1 and R2 are loaded with AA and BB. So, they will contain 0xE7 and 0xFE. Then, they are divided using the SDIV instruction. Considering 0x000000E7 and 0x000000FE as 32-bit numbers, they are in fact 231 and 254. So, the result becomes 231/254 = 0 and R3 will be loaded with 0.

To solve the problem, we need to sign extend the 8-bit and 16-bit signed variables before doing calculations. The LDRSB (load register signed byte) instruction and the LDRSH (load register signed half-word) do just that. They work as follows:

LDRSB loads into the destination register a byte from memory and sign extends (copy D7, the sign bit) to the remaining 24 bits. This is illustrated in Figure 5-1.

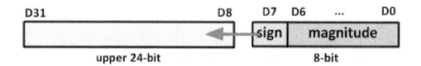

Figure 5-1: Sign Extending a Byte

Look at the following example:

```
; assume memory location 0x80000 has +96 = 0110 0000 and R1=0x80000
LDRSB R0, [R1]      ; now R0 =   00000000000000000000000001100000
; assume memory location 0x80000 contains -2 = 1111 1110 and R2=0x80000
LDRSB R4, [R2]   ; now R4 = 11111111111111111111111111111110
```

As can be seen in the above examples, LDRSB does not alter the lower 8 bits. The sign bit of the 8-bit data is copied to the rest of the 32-bit register.

LDRSH loads the destination register with a 16-bit signed number and sign-extends to the rest of the 16 bits of the 32-bit register. This is used for signed half-word operand and is illustrated in Figure 5-2.

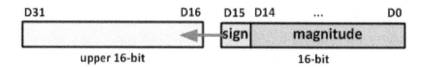

Figure 5-2: Sign Extending a Half-word

Look at the following example:

```
; assume 0x80000 contains +260 = 0000 0001 0000 0100 and R1=0x80000
LDRSH R0, [R1]   ; R0=0000 0000 0000 0000 0000 0001 0000 0100
```

Another example:

```
; assume location 0x20000 has -327660=0x8002 and R2=0x20000
LDRSH R1, [R2]          ; R1=FFFF8002
```

As we see in the above examples, LDRSH does not alter the lower 16 bits. The sign bit of the 16-bit data is copied to the rest of the 32-bit register. In Example 5-13, we correct the program of Example 5-13 using sign extending.

Example 5-13

Rewrite the program of Example 5-12 and correct the problem using sign extending.

Solution:

```
      EXPORT __main
      AREA  ExtendingExample, CODE, READONLY
__main
      LDR   R0,=AA
      LDRSB R1,[R0]      ;read AA

      LDR   R0,=BB
      LDRSB R2,[R0]      ;read BB

      SDIV R3,R1,R2      ; R3 = R1 / R2
HERE  B HERE

AA    DCB -25
BB    DCB   -2
```

In the above program, LDRSB sign extends the values of AA and BB. So, R1 and R2 are loaded with 0xFFFFFFE7 and 0xFFFFFFFE, respectively. Now, the result is -25/-2 = 12 and R3 will be loaded with 12.

Sign extending can be used to avoid overflow errors, as well. In Example 5-14, the calculation of Example 5-6 is done using 32-bit variables and the overflow problem is avoided.

Example 5-14

Write a program for Example 5-5 to handle the overflow problem.

Solution:

```
      EXPORT __main
      AREA  EXAMPLE5_14, CODE, READONLY
__main
      LDR   R1, =DATA1
      LDR   R2, =DATA2
      LDR   R3, =RESULT
```

```
        LDRSB R4, [R1]      ; R4 = +96
        LDRSB R5, [R2]      ; R5 = +70
        ADD   R4, R4, R5    ; R4 = R4 + R5 = 96 + 70 = +166
        STR   R4, [R3]      ; Store +166 in location RESULT
HL      B     HL

DATA1         DCB   +96
DATA2         DCB   +70
        ALIGN
        AREA  VARIABLES, DATA, READWRITE    ; The following is stored in RAM
RESULT        DCW   0
        END
```

The following is an analysis of the values in Example 5-14. Each is sign-extended and then added as follows:

Sign	Binary numbers	Decimal
0	000 0000 0000 0000 0000 0000 0110 0000	+96 after sign ext.
0	000 0000 0000 0000 0000 0000 0100 0110	+70 after sign ext.
0	000 0000 0000 0000 0000 0000 1010 0110	+166

As a rule, if the possibility of overflow exists, all byte-sized signed numbers should be sign-extended into a word, and similarly, all halfword-sized signed operands should be sign-extended to a word before they are processed. This is shown in Program 5-2. Program 5-2 finds total sum of a group of signed number data.

Program 5-2

```
    ; This program calculates the sum of signed numbers

        AREA  PROG5_2, CODE, READONLY

        LDR   R0, =SIGN_DAT
        MOV   R3, #9
        MOV   R2, #0
LOOP    LDRSB       R1, [R0]
        ; Load into R1 and sign extend it.
        ADD   R2, R2, R1   ; R2 = R2 + R1
        ADD   R0, R0, #1   ; point to next
        SUBS  R3, R3, #1   ; decrement counter
        BNE   LOOP
        LDR   R0, =SUM
        STR   R2, [R0]     ; Store R2 in location SUM
HERE    B     HERE

SIGN_DAT DCB      +13, -10, +19, +14, -18, -9, +12, -19, +16
```

```
        AREA    VARIABLES, DATA, READWRITE
SUM     DCD     0
        END
```

Review Questions

1. Explain the purpose of the LDRSB and LDRSH instructions.
2. Demonstrate the effect of LDRSB on R0 = 0xF6.
3. Demonstrate the effect of LDRSH on R1 = 0x124C.

Problems

Section 5.1: Signed Numbers Concept

1. Show how the 32-bit computers would represent the following numbers in 2's complement notation and verify each with a calculator.

   (a) -23   (b) +12   (c) -0x28
   (d) +0x6F   (e) -128   (f) +127
   (g) +365   (h) -32,767

2. Show how the 32-bit computers would represent the following numbers in 2's complement and verify each with a calculator.

   (a) -230   (b) +1200   (c) - 0x28F
   (d) +0x6FF

Section 5.2: Signed Number Instructions and Operations

3. In a program, A and B are defined as 8-bit signed integer variables. They are loaded with -65 and -98 respectively. Then B is added to A (A = A + B;). Check if the result is valid or overflow occurs.
4. In a program, A and B are defined as 8-bit signed integer variables. They are loaded with 15 and -95 respectively. Then B is subtracted from A (A = A – B;). Check if the result is valid or overflow occurs.

Section 5.3: Signed Number Comparison

5. Modify Program 5-2 to find the highest number. Verify your program.

Section 5.4: Sign Extension

6. Find the overflow flag for each case and verify the result using an Arm IDE. Do byte-sized calculation on them.

   (a) (+15) + (-12)   (b) (-123) + (-127)   (c) (+0x25) + (+34)
   (d) (-127) + (+127)   (e) (+100) + (-100)

7. Sign-extend the following values into 32 bits using Arm instructions in the Keil IDE.

(a) -122   (b) -0x999   (c) +0x17
(d) +127   (e) -129

Answers to Review Questions

Section 5.1

1. D7, D15, and D31 for 32-bit signed data.
2. 0x16 = 0001 0110; its 2's complement is: 1110 1001 + 1 = 1110 1010
3. −128 to +127; −32,768 to +32,767 (decimal)
4. -2,147,483,648 to +2,147,483,647
5. 0x500000 = 0000 0000 0101 0000 0000 0000 0000 0000;

   Its 2's complement is: 1111 1111 1010 1111 1111 1111 1111 1111 + 1 =

   1111 1111 1011 0000 0000 0000 0000 0000 = 0xFFB00000

Section 5.2

1. C flag is raised when there is a carry out from the operation, but V flag is raised when there is a carry into the sign bit and no carry out of the sign bit or when there is no carry into the sign bit and there is a carry out of the sign bit. C flag is used to indicate overflow in unsigned arithmetic operations while V flag is involved in signed operations.
2. SMULL

Section 5.3

1.

   (a) BLE will jump if V is different from N, or if Z = 1.

   (b) BGT will jump if V equals N, and if Z = 0.

Section 5.4

1. The LDRSB instruction sign extends the sign bit of a byte into a word; the LDRSH instruction sign extends the sign bit of a half-word into a word.
2. In 0xF6 the sign bit is 1; thus, it is sign-extended into 0xFFFFFFF6
3. 0x124C sign-extended into R1 would be 0x0000124C.

152

Chapter 6: Arm Addressing Modes

This chapter discusses the issue of memory access and the stack. Section 6.1 is dedicated to Arm memory map and memory access. We will also explain the concepts of align, non-align, little endian, and big endian data access. Advanced indexed addressing mode is explained in Section 6.2. In Section 6.3, we discuss the bit-addressable (bit-banding) SRAM and peripherals. In Section 6.4, we describe the PC relative addressing mode and its use in implementing ADR and LDR.

Section 6.1: Arm Memory Access

The Arm CPU uses 32-bit addresses to access memory and peripherals. This gives us a maximum of 4 GB (gigabytes) of memory space. This 4GB of directly accessible memory space has addresses 0x00000000 to 0xFFFFFFFF, meaning each byte is assigned a unique address (Arm is a byte-addressable CPU). See Figure 6-1.

D31 — D24	D23 — D16	D15 — D8	D7 — D0	
0x00000003	0x00000002	0x00000001	0x00000000	0x00000000
0x00000007	0x00000006	0x00000005	0x00000004	0x00000004
0x0000000B	0x0000000A	0x00000009	0x00000008	0x00000008
0x0000000F	0x0000000E	0x0000000D	0x0000000C	0x0000000C
⋮	⋮	⋮	⋮	
0xFFFFFFF3	0xFFFFFFF2	0xFFFFFFF1	0xFFFFFFF0	0xFFFFFFF0
0xFFFFFFF7	0xFFFFFFF6	0xFFFFFFF5	0xFFFFFFF4	0xFFFFFFF4
0xFFFFFFFB	0xFFFFFFFA	0xFFFFFFF9	0xFFFFFFF8	0xFFFFFFF8
0xFFFFFFFF	0xFFFFFFFE	0xFFFFFFFD	0xFFFFFFFC	0xFFFFFFFC

Figure 6-1: Memory Byte Addressing in Arm

The Arm buses and memory access

D31–D0 Data bus

See Figure 6-2. The 32-bit data bus of the Arm provides the 32-bit data path to the on-chip and off-chip memory and peripherals. They are grouped into 8-bit data bytes, D0–D7, D8–D15, D16–D23, and D24–D31.

A31–A0

These signals provide the 32-bit address path to the on-chip and off-chip memory and peripherals. Since the Arm supports data access of byte (8 bits), half word (16 bits), and word (32 bits), the buses must be able to access any of the 4 banks of memory connected to the 32-bit data bus. The A0 and A1 are used to select one of the 4 bytes of the D31-D0 data bus. See Figure 6-3.

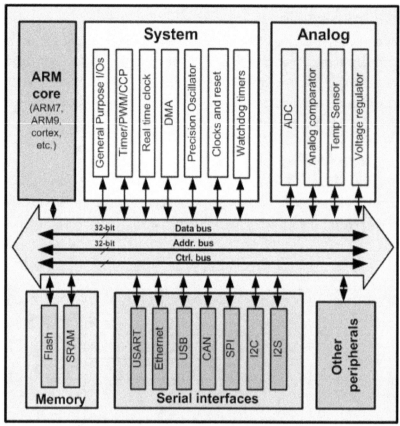

Figure 6-2: Memory Connection Block Diagram in Arm

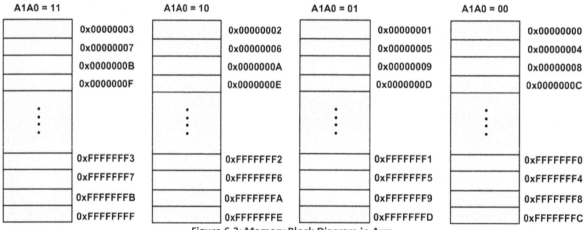

Figure 6-3: Memory Block Diagram in Arm

AHB and APB buses

The Arm CPU is connected to the on-chip memory via an AHB (advanced high-performance bus). The AHB is used not only for connection to on-chip ROM and RAM, it is also used for connection to some of the high speed I/Os (input/output) such as GPIO (general purpose I/O). Arm chip also has the APB (advanced peripherals bus) bus dedicated for communication with the on-chip peripherals such as timers, ADC, UART, SPI, I2C, and other peripheral ports.

While we need the 32-bit data bus between CPU and the memory (RAM and ROM), many slower peripherals have no need for fast data bus pathway. For this reason, Arm uses the AHB-to-APB bridge to access the slower on-chip devices such as peripherals. Also since peripherals do not need a high speed bus, a bridge between AHB and APB allows going from the higher speed bus of AHB to lower speed bus of peripherals. The AHB bus allows a single-cycle access. See Figure 6-4 for AHB-to-APB bridge.

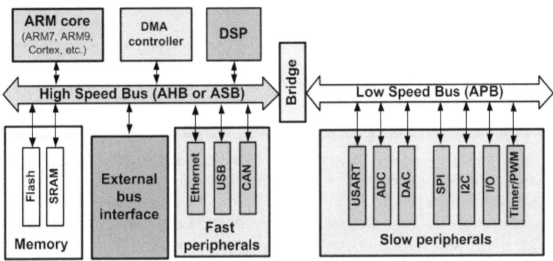

Figure 6-4: AHB and APB in Arm

Bus cycle time

To access a device such as memory or I/O, the CPU provides a fixed amount of time called a bus cycle time. During this bus cycle time, the read or write operation of memory or I/O must be completed. The bus cycle time used for accessing memory is often referred to as MC (memory cycle) time. The time from when the CPU provides the addresses at its address pins to when the data is expected at its data pins is called memory read cycle time. While for on-chip memory the cycle time can be 1 clock, in the off-chip memory the cycle time is often 2 clocks or more. If memory is slow and its access time does not match the MC time of the CPU, extra time can be requested from the CPU to extend the read cycle time. This extra time is called a wait state (WS). In the 1980s, the clock speed for memory cycle time was the same as the CPU's clock speed. For example, in the 20 MHz processors, the buses were working at the same speed of 20 MHz. This resulted in 2 × 50 ns = 100 ns for the memory cycle time (1/20 MHz = 50 ns). See Example 6-1.

Example 6-1

Calculate the memory cycle time of a 50-MHz bus system with
(a) 0 WS,
(b) 1 WS, and
(c) 2 WS.
Assume that the bus cycle time for off-chip memory access is 2 clocks.

Solution:

1/50 MHz = 20 ns is the bus clock period. Since the bus cycle time of zero wait states is 2 clocks, we have:

(a) Memory cycle time with 0 WS	$2 \times 20 = 40$ ns
(b) Memory cycle time with 1 WS	$40 + 20 = 60$ ns
(c) Memory cycle time with 2 WS	$40 + 2 \times 20 = 80$ ns

It is preferred that all bus activities be completed with 0 WS. However, if the read and write operations cannot be completed with 0 WS, we request an extension of the bus cycle time. This extension is in the form of an integer number of WS. That is, we can have 1, 2, 3, and so on WS, but not 1.25 WS.

When the CPU's speed was under 100 MHz, the bus speed was comparable to the CPU speed. In the 1990s the CPU speed exploded to 1 GHz (gigahertz) while the bus speed maxed out at around 200 MHz. The gap between the CPU speed and the bus speed is one of the biggest challenges in the design of high-performance systems. To avoid the use of too many wait states in interfacing memory to CPU, cache memory and other high-speed DRAMs are used.

Bus bandwidth

The rate of data transfer is generally called bus bandwidth. In other words, bus bandwidth is a measure of how fast buses transfer information between the CPU and memory or peripherals. The wider the data bus, the higher the bus bandwidth. However, the advantage of the wider external data bus comes at the cost of increasing the die size for system on-chip (SOC) or the printed circuit board size for off-chip memory. Now you might ask why we should care how fast buses transfer information between the CPU and outside, as long as the CPU is working as fast as it can. The problem is that the CPU cannot process information that it does not have. This is like driving a Porsche or Ferrari in first gear; it is a terrible under usage of CPU power. Bus bandwidth is measured in MB (megabytes) per second and is calculated as follows:

bus bandwidth = (1/bus cycle time) × bus width in bytes

In the above formula, bus cycle time can be for both memory and I/O since the Arm uses the memory mapped I/O. Example 6-2 clarifies the concept of bus bandwidth. As can be seen from Example 6-2, there are two ways to increase the bus bandwidth: Either use a wider data bus or shorten the bus cycle time (or do both). That is exactly what many processors have done. Again, it must be noted that although the processor's speed can go to 1 GHz or higher, the bus speed for off-chip memory is limited to around 200 MHz. The reason for this is that the signals become too noisy for the circuit board if they are above 200 MHz.

Example 6-2

Calculate memory bus bandwidth for the following CPU if the bus speed is 100 MHz.

(a) Arm Thumb with 0 WS and 1 WS (16-bit data bus)

(b) Arm with 0 WS and 1 WS (32-bit data bus)

Assume that the bus cycle time for off-chip memory access is 2 clocks.

Solution:

The memory cycle time for both is 2 clocks, with zero wait states. With the 100 MHz bus speed we have a bus clock of 1/100 MHz = 10 ns.

(a)   Bus bandwidth = (1/(2 × 10 ns)) × 2 bytes = 100M bytes/second (MB/s)
        With 1 wait state, the memory cycle becomes 3 clock cycles
        3 × 10 = 30 ns and the memory bus bandwidth is = (1/30 ns) × 2 bytes = 66.6 MB/s

(b)   Bus bandwidth = (1/(2 × 10 ns)) × 4 bytes = 200 MB/s
        With 1 wait state, the memory cycle becomes 3 clock cycles
        3 × 10 = 30 ns and the memory bus bandwidth is = (1/30 ns) × 4 bytes = 126.6 MB/s

        From the above it can be seen that the two factors influencing bus bandwidth are:

        1. The read/write cycle time of the CPU
        2. The width of the data bus

Code memory region

The 4 GB of Arm memory space is organized as 1G × 32 bits since the Arm instructions are 32-bit. The internal data bus of the Arm is 32-bit, allowing the transfer of one instruction into the CPU every clock cycle. This is one of the benefits of the RISC fixed instruction size. The fetching of an instruction in every clock cycle can work only if the code is word aligned, meaning each instruction is placed at an address location ending with 0, 4, 8, or C. Example 6-3 shows the placement of code in Arm memory. Notice that the code addresses go up by 2 or 4 since the Thumb-2 Arm instructions are 2 bytes or 4 bytes. While compilers ensure that codes are word aligned, it is job of the programmer to make sure the data in SRAM is word aligned too. We will examine this important topic soon.

Example 6-3

Compile and debug the following code in Keil and see the placement of instructions in memory locations.

```
        EXPORT  __main
        AREA   ARMex, CODE, READONLY
__main PROC
```

```
        MOV    R2, #0x00    ; R2=0x00
        MOV    R3, #0x35    ; R3=0x35
        ADD    R4, R3, R2
HERE    B      HERE
        ENDP
        END                 ; Mark end of code
```

Solution

As you can see in the figure, the first MOV instruction starts from location 0x08000134, the second MOV instruction starts from location 0x08000138 and the ADD instruction starts from location 0x0800013C.

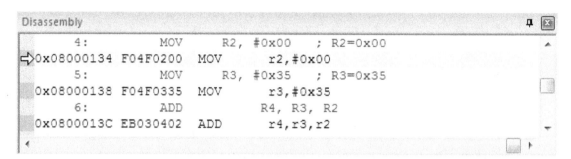

The following image displays the first locations of memory. The code of the first MOV instruction is in location 0x08000134 of memory which is word aligned. The same rule applies for the other instructions. Note that the code of MOV R2, #0x00 is F0 4F 02 00 but 4F F0 00 02 is stored in the memory. We will discuss the reason in this chapter when we focus on the concept of big endian and little endian.

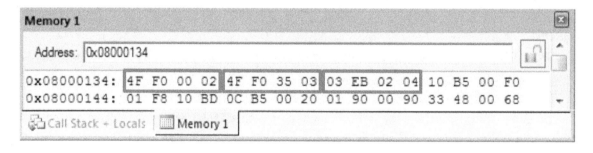

SRAM memory region

A section of the memory space is used by SRAM. The SRAM can be on-chip or off-chip (external). For small embedded systems, this on-chip SRAM is used by the CPU for scratch pad to store parameters and is also used by the CPU for the purpose of the stack. We will examine the stack usage by the Arm in the next section. For larger systems, the operating system and application programs may be run in Flash ROM or copied into the SRAM and run everything in the SRAM just like your laptop computer.

In using the SRAM memory for storing parameters, we must be careful when loading or storing data in the SRAM lest we use unaligned data access. Next, we discuss this important issue.

Data misalignment in SRAM

The case of misaligned data has a major effect on the Arm bus performance. If the data is aligned, for every memory read cycle, the Arm brings in 4 bytes of information (data or code) using the D31–D0 data bus. Such data alignment is referred to as word alignment. To make data word aligned, the least significant digits of the hex addresses must be 0, 4, 8, or C (in hex).

While the compilers make sure that program codes (instructions) are always aligned (Example 6-3), it is the placement of data in SRAM by the programmer that can be nonaligned and therefore subject to memory access penalty. In other words, the single cycle access of memory is also used by Arm to bring into registers 4 bytes of data every clock cycle assuming that the data is aligned. To make sure that data are also aligned we use the ALIGN directive. The use of ALIGN directive for RAM data makes sure that each word is located at an address location ending with address of 0, 4, 8, or C. If our data is word size (using DCDU directive) then the use of ALIGN directive at the start of the data section guaranties all the data placements will be word aligned. When a word size data is defined using the DCD directive, the assembler aligns it to be word aligned.

Accessing non-aligned data

As we have stated many times before, Arm defines 32-bit data as a word. The address of a word can start at any address location. For example, in the instruction "LDR R1, [R0]" if R0 = 0x20000004, the address of the word being fetched into R1 starts at an aligned address. In the case of "LDR R1, [R0]" if R0 = 0x20000001 the address starts at a non-aligned address. In systems with a 32-bit data bus, accessing a word from a non-aligned addressed location can be slower. This issue is important and applies to all 32-bit processors.

In the 8-bit system, accessing a word (4 bytes) is treated like accessing four consecutive bytes regardless of the address location. Since accessing a byte takes one memory cycle, accessing 4 bytes will take 4 memory cycles. In the 32-bit system, accessing a word with an aligned address takes one memory cycle. That is because each byte is carried on its own data path of D0–D7, D8–D15, D16–D23, and D24–D31 in the same memory cycle. However, accessing a word with a non-aligned address requires two memory cycles. For example, see how accessing the word in the instruction "LDR R1, [R0]" works as shown in Figure 6-5. As a case of aligned data, assume that R0 = 0x80000000. In this instruction, the contents of 4 bytes of memory (locations 0x80000000 through 0x80000003) are being fetched in one cycle. In only one cycle, the Arm CPU accesses locations 0x80000000 through 0x80000003 and puts them in R1.

Now assuming that R0 = 0x80000001 in this instruction, the contents of 8 bytes of memory (locations 0x80000000 through 0x80000007) are being fetched in two consecutive cycles but only 4 bytes of it are used. In the first cycle, the Arm CPU accesses locations 0x80000000 through 0x80000003 and puts them in R1 only the desired three bytes of locations 0x800000001 through 0x80000003. In the second cycle, the contents of memory locations 0x8000004 through 0x80000007 are accessed and only the desired byte of 0x80000004 is put into R1. See Example 6-4.

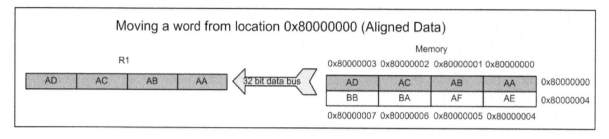

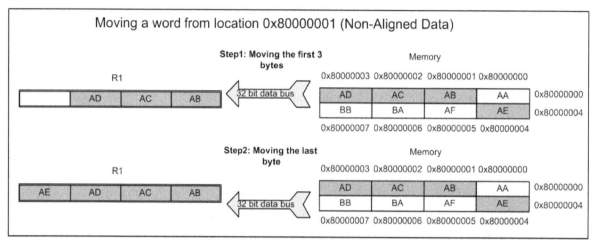

Figure 6-5: Memory Access for Aligned and Non-aligned Data

Example 6-4

Show the data transfer of the following cases and indicate the number of memory cycle times it takes for data transfer. Assume that R2 = 0x4598F31E.

```
LDR   R1, =0x40000000    ; R1=0x40000000
LDR   R2, =0x4598F31E    ; R2=0x4598F31E
STR   R2, [R1]           ; Store R2 to location 0x40000000
ADD   R1, R1, #1         ; R1 = R1 + 1 = 0x40000001
STR   R2, [R1]           ; Store R2 to location 0x40000001
ADD   R1, R1, #1         ; R1 = R1 + 1 = 0x40000002
STR   R2, [R1]           ; Store R2 to location 0x40000002
ADD   R1, R1, #1         ; R1 = R1 + 1 = 0x40000003
STR   R2, [R1]           ; Store R2 to location 0x40000003
```

Solution:

For the first STR R2, [R1] instruction, the entire 32 bits of R2 is stored into locations with addresses of 0x40000000, 0x40000001, 0x40000002, and 0x40000003. The 4-byte content of register R2 is stored into memory locations with starting address of 0x40000000 via the 32-bit data bus of D31–D0. This address is word aligned since address of the least significant digit is 0. Therefore, it takes only one memory cycle to transfer the 32-bit data.

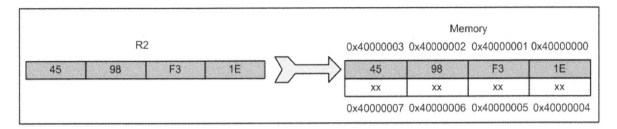

For the second STR R2, [R1] instruction, in the first memory cycle, the lower 24 bits of R2 is stored into locations 0x40000001, 0x40000002, and 0x40000003. In the second memory cycle, the upper 8 bits of R2 is stored into the 0x40000004 location.

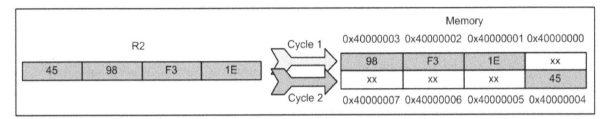

For the third STR R2, [R1] instruction, in the first memory cycle, the lower 16 bits of R2 is stored into locations 0x40000002 and 0x40000003. In the second memory cycle, the upper 16 bits of R2 is stored into locations 0x40000004 and 0x40000005.

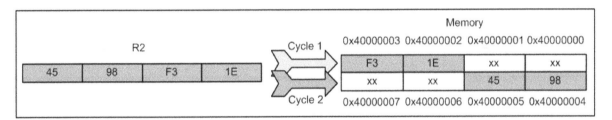

For the fourth STR R2, [R1] instruction, in the first memory cycle, the lower 8 bits of R2 is stored into locations 0x40000003. In the second memory cycle, the upper 24 bits of R2 is stored into the locations 0x40000004, 0x40000005, and 0x40000006.

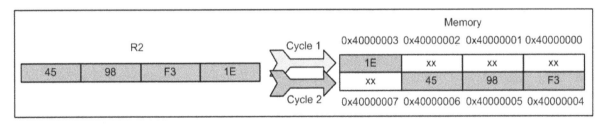

The lesson to be learned from this is to try not to put any words on a non-aligned address location in a 32-bit system. Indeed, this is so important that directive ALIGN is specifically designed for this purpose. Next, we discuss the issue of aligned data.

Using LDR instruction with DCD and ALIGN directives

The DCD and DCDU directives are used for 32-bit (word) data. The DCD directive ensures 32-bit data types are aligned, in contrast to DCDU which does not. DCD is used as follows:

```
VALUE1        DCD     0x99775533
```

This ensures that VALUE1, a word-sized operand, is located in a word aligned address location. Therefore, an instruction accessing it will take only a single memory cycle. Since performance of the CPU depends on how fast it can fetch the data we must ensure that any memory access reading 32-bit data is done in a single clock cycle. This means we must make sure all 32-bit data are word aligned. This is so important that Arm has an interrupt (exception) dedicated to misaligned data, meaning any time it accesses misaligned data, it lets us know that there is a problem. The one-time use of ALIGN directive at the beginning of data area using DCDU makes the data aligned for that group of data.

Different versions of Arm handle unaligned access differently. Some may allow unaligned access without generating interrupt. In this case, the programmer must be careful to allocate data on the word aligned boundary so that the system will perform at its optimal bus bandwidth.

Using LDRH with DCW and ALIGN directives

The problem of misaligned data is also an issue when the data size is in half-words (16-bit). In many cases using DCWU, we must use the ALIGN directive multiple times in the data area of a given program to ensure they are aligned. This is in contrast to the DCW directive which ensures data type to be half-word aligned. This is especially the case when we use the LDRH instruction. See Example 6-5. Aligned data is also an issue for the Thumb version of the Arm.

Example 6-5

Show the data transfer of the following LDRH instructions and indicate the number of memory cycle times it takes for data transfer.

```
LDR    R1, =0x80000000    ; R1=0x80000000
LDR    R3, =0xF31E4598    ; R3=0xF31E4598
LDR    R4, =0x1A2B3D4F    ; R4=0x1A2B3D4F
STR    R3, [R1]           ; (STR R3, [R1]) stores R3 to location 0x80000000
STR    R4, [R1, #4]       ; (STR R4, [R1+4]) stores R4 to location 0x80000004
LDRH   R2, [R1]           ; loads two bytes from location 0x80000000 to R2
LDRH   R2, [R1, #1]       ; loads two bytes from location 0x80000001 to R2
LDRH   R2, [R1, #2]       ; loads two bytes from location 0x80000002 to R2
LDRH   R2, [R1, #3]       ; loads two bytes from location 0x80000003 to R2
```

Solution:

In the LDRH R2, [R1] instruction, locations with addresses of 0x80000000, 0x80000001, 0x80000002, and 0x80000003 are accessed but only 0x80000000 and 0x80000001 are used to get the 16 bits to R2. This address is halfword aligned since the least significant digit is 0. Therefore, it takes only one memory cycle to transfer the data. Now, R2=0x00004598

162

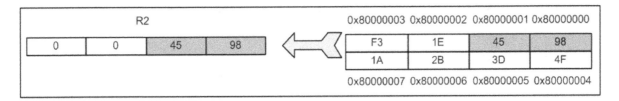

For the LDRH R2, [R1, #1], instruction, locations with addresses of 0x80000000, 0x80000001, 0x80000002, and 0x80000003 are accessed, but only 0x80000001 and 0x80000002 are used to get the 16 bits to R2. Therefore, it takes only one memory cycle to transfer the data. Now, R2=0x00001E45.

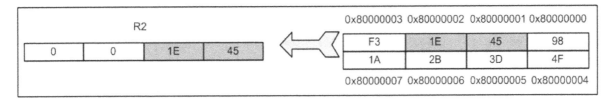

For the LDRH R2, [R1, #2], instruction, locations with addresses of 0x80000000, 0x80000001, 0x80000002, and 0x80000003 are accessed, but only 0x80000002 and 0x80000003 are used to get the 16 bits to R2. Therefore, it takes only one memory cycle to transfer the data. Now, R2=0x0000F31E.

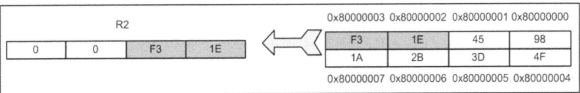

For the LDRH R2, [R1, #3] instruction, in the first memory cycle, locations with addresses of 0x80000000, 0x80000001, 0x80000002, and 0x80000003 are accessed, but only 0x80000003 is used to get the lower 8 bits to R2. In the second memory cycle, the address locations 0x80000004, 0x80000005, 0x80000006, and 0x80000007 are accessed where only the 0x80000004 location is used to get the upper 8 bits to R2. Now, R2=0x00004FF3.

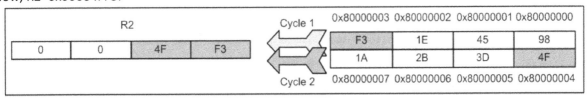

Using LDRB with DCB and ALIGN directives

The problem of misaligned data does not exist when the data size is bytes. A single byte of data will never straddle across a word boundary. In cases such as using the string of ASCII characters with the DCB directive, accessing a byte takes the same amount of time (one memory cycle) as an aligned word (4 bytes), regardless of the address location of the data. See Example 6-6.

Example 6-6

Show the data transfer of the following LDRB instructions and indicate the number of memory cycle times it takes for data transfer.

```
LDR    R1, =0x80000000    ; R1=0x80000000
LDR    R3, =0xF31E4598    ; R3=0xF31E4598
LDR    R4, =0x1A2B3D4F    ; R4=0x1A2B3D4F
STR    R3, [R1]       ; Store R3 to location 0x80000000
STR    R4, [R1, #4] ; (STR R4, [R1+4]) Store R4 to location 0x80000004
LDRB   R2, [R1]       ; load one byte from location 0x80000000 to R2
LDRB   R2, [R1, #1] ; (LDRB R2, [R1+1]) load one byte from location 0x80000001
LDRB   R2, [R1, #2] ; (LDRB R2, [R1+2]) load one byte from location 0x80000002
LDRB   R2, [R1, #3] ; (LDRB R2, [R1+3]) load one byte from location 0x80000003
```

Solution:

In the LDRB R2, [R1] instruction, locations with addresses of 0x80000000, 0x80000001, 0x80000002, and 0x80000003 are accessed but only 0x80000000 is used to get the 8 bits to R2. Therefore, it takes only one memory cycle to transfer the data. Now, R2=0x00000098.

In the LDRB R2, [R1, #1] instruction, locations with addresses of 0x80000000, 0x80000001, 0x80000002, and 0x80000003 are accessed but only 0x80000001 is used to get the 8 bits to R2. Therefore, it takes only one memory cycle to transfer the data. Now, R2=0x00000045.

In the LDRB R2, [R1, #2] instruction, locations with addresses of 0x80000000, 0x80000001, 0x80000002, and 0x80000003 are accessed but only 0x80000002 is used to get the 8 bits to R2. Therefore, it takes only one memory cycle to transfer the data. Now, R2=0x0000001E.

In the LDRB R2, [R1, #3] instruction, locations with addresses of 0x80000000, 0x80000001, 0x80000002, and 0x80000003 are accessed but only 0x80000003 is used to get the 8 bits to R2. Therefore, it takes only one memory cycle to transfer the data. Now, R2=0x000000F3.

Little Endian vs. Big Endian war

In storing data in memory, there are two major byte orderings used. The little endian places the least significant byte (little end of the data) in the low address and the big endian places the most significant byte in the low address. The origin of the terms *big endian* and *little endian* was from a Gulliver's Travels story about how an egg should be opened: from the big end or the little end. Arm supports both little and big endian. In most of the Arm devices little endian is the default. Some Arm chip manufacturers provide an option for changing the endian by software. See Example 6-7 to understand little endian and big endian data storage.

Example 6-7

Show how data is placed after execution of the following code using
a) little endian and

b) big endian.

```
LDR    R2,  =0x7698E39F    ;  R2=0x7698E39F
LDR    R1,  =0x80000000
STR    R2,  [R1]
```

Solution:

a) For little endian we have:
  Location 80000000 = (9F)
  Location 80000001 = (E3)
  Location 80000002 = (98)
  Location 80000003 = (76)

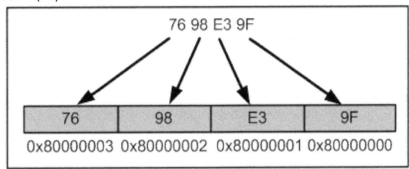

b) For big endian we have:
  Location 80000000 = (76)
  Location 80000001 = (98)
  Location 80000002 = (E3)
  Location 80000003 = (9F)

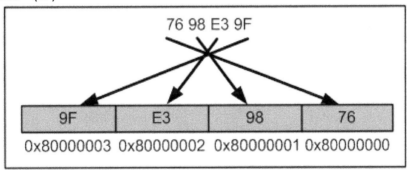

In Example 6-7, notice how the least significant byte (the little end of the data) 0x9F goes to the low address 0x80000000, and the most significant byte of the data 0x76 goes to the high address 0x80000003. This means that the little end of the data goes in first, hence the name little endian. In the Arm with big endian option enabled, data is stored the opposite way: The big end (most significant byte) goes into the low address first, and for this reason it is called big endian. Many of recent RISC processors allow selection of mode in software, big endian or little endian.

Review Questions

1. Who makes sure that instructions are aligned on word boundary?
2. In most of the Arm devices, the _____ endian is the default.
3. A 66 MHz system has a memory cycle time of _____ ns if it is used with a zero wait state.
4. To interface a 100 MHz processor to a 50 ns access time ROM, how many wait states are needed?
5. True or false. Arm uses big endian format when is powered up.

Section 6.2: Advanced Indexed Addressing Modes

In previous chapters we discussed the use of STR and LDR instructions in the form of "LDR Rd, [Rx]" and "STR Rx, [Rd]", where the registers within the brackets hold the pointer (the address where the data resides). These registers within the brackets are referred as the index register or base register. Arm provides three advanced indexed addressing mode that allow the modification of the value in the index register. We will discuss them in this section.

Base plus offset addressing modes

The Arm provides three advanced indexed addressing modes called base plus offset addressing modes. In addition to the base register specified within the bracket, an offset can be added to the value of the base register. These modes are: pre-index, pre-index with writeback, and post-index modes. Table 6-1 summarizes these modes. Each of these addressing modes can be used with offset of fixed value. The pre-index addressing mode can be used with offset of fixed value, register, or a shifted register. See Table 6-2. In this section we will discuss each mode in detail.

Addressing Mode	Syntax	Effective Address of Memory	Rm Value After Execution
Pre-index	LDR Rd, [Rm, #k]	Rm + #k	Rm
Pre-index with WB*	LDR Rd, [Rm, #k]!	Rm + #k	Rm + #k
Post-index	LDR Rd, [Rm], #k	Rm	Rm + #k
*WB means Writeback			
** Rd and Rm are any of registers and #k is a signed immediate value			

Table 6-1: Indexed Addressing in Arm

Offset	Syntax	Pointing Location
Fixed value	LDR Rd, [Rm, #k]	Rm + #k
Register	LDR Rd, [Rm, Rn]	Rm + Rn
Shifted register	LDR Rd, [Rm, Rn, <shift>]	Rm + (Rn shifted <shift>)
* Rn and Rm are any registers and #k is a signed immediate value		
** <shift> is any of the shift operations studied in Chapter3 like LSL #2		

Table 6-2: Offset of Fixed Value vs. Offset of Shifted Register

Pre-indexed addressing mode with fixed offset

In this addressing mode, a register and a positive or negative immediate value are used as a pointer to the data's memory location. The value of register does not change after instruction is executed.

See Figure 6-6. This addressing mode can be used with STR, STRB, STRH, LDR, LDRB, and LDRH. See Example 6-8.

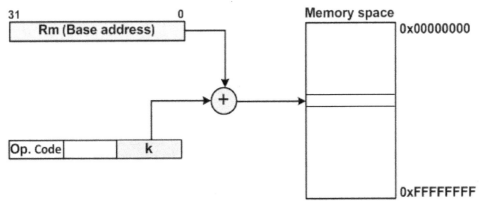

Figure 6-6: Pre-indexed Addressing Mode with Fixed Offset

Example 6-8

Write a program to store contents of R5 to the SRAM location 0x20000000 to 0x20000000F using pre-indexed addressing mode with fixed offset.

Solution:

```
LDR    R5,  =0x55667788
LDR    R1,  =0x20000000    ; load the address of first location
STR    R5,  [R1]           ; store R5 to location 0x10000000
STR    R5,  [R1, #4] ; store R5 to location 0x20000000 + 4  (0x20000004)
STR    R5,  [R1, #8] ; store R5 to location 0x20000000 + 8  (0x20000008)
STR    R5,  [R1, #0x0C]
                     ; store R5 to location 0x20000000 + 0x0C (0x2000000C)
```

Notice that after running this code the content of R1 is still 0x20000000

It is a common practice to use a register to point to the first location of the memory space and access the different locations using proper offsets. For example, see the following program:

```
          ADR    R0, OUR_DATA      ; point to OUR_DATA
          LDRB   R2, [R0, #1]      ; load R2 with offset of BETA
          ...
OUR_DATA
ALFA      DCB    0x30
BETA      DCB    0x21
```

Pre-indexed addressing mode with writeback and fixed offset

This addressing mode is like pre-indexed addressing mode with fixed offset except that the calculated pointer is written back to the pointing register. We put '!' after the instruction to tell the assembler to enable writeback in the instruction. See Figure 6-7 and Example 6-9.

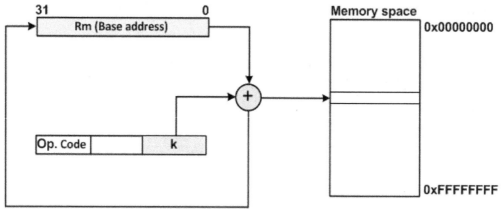

Figure 6-7: Pre-indexed addressing mode with writeback and fixed offset

---

Example 6-9

Rewrite Example 6-8 using pre-indexed addressing mode with writeback and fixed offset.

Solution:

```
LDR   R1, =0x20000000    ; load the address of first location
STR   R5, [R1]           ; store R5 to location 0x20000000
STR   R5, [R1, #4]!
                ; store R5 to location 0x20000000 + 4 (0x20000004)
                ; writeback makes R1 = 0x20000004
STR   R5, [R1, #4]!
                ; store R5 to location 0x20000004 + 4 (0x20000008)
                ; writeback makes R1 = 0x20000008
STR   R5, [R1, #4]!
                ; store R5 to location 0x20000008 + 4 (0x2000000C)
                ; writeback makes R1 = 0x2000000C
```

Notice that after running this code the content of R1 is 0x2000000C

Post-indexed addressing mode with fixed offset

This addressing mode is like pre-indexed addressing mode with fixed offset and writeback except that the instruction is executed on the location that Rn is pointing to regardless of offset value. See Figure 6-8. The new value of the pointer is calculated after the load/store operation and written back to the index register. Examine the following instructions:

```
STR   R1, [R2], #4        ; store R1 into memory pointed to by
                          ; R2 and then write back R2 + 4 to R2
LDRB  R5, [R3], #1        ; load a byte from memory pointed to
                          ; by R3 and then write back R3 + 1 to R3
```

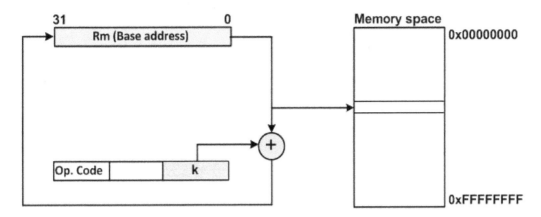

Figure 6-8: Post-indexed addressing mode

Notice that writeback is by default enabled in post-indexed addressing and there is no need to put '!' after instructions because in post-indexing without writeback the offset is neither used in the load/store operation nor written back to the index register. See Example 6-10.

Example 6-10

Rewrite Example 6-9 using post-indexed addressing mode with fixed offset.

Solution:

```
LDR    R1, =0x20000000    ; load the address of first location
STR    R5, [R1], #4       ; store R5 to location 0x20000000 and writeback
                          ; 0x20000000 + 4 (0x20000004) to R1
STR    R5, [R1], #4       ; store R5 to location 0x20000004 and writeback
                          ; 0x20000004 + 4 (0x20000008) to R1
STR    R5, [R1], #4       ; store R5 to location 0x20000008 and writeback
                          ; 0x20000008 + 4 (0x2000000C) to R1
STR    R5, [R1], #4       ; store R5 to location 0x2000000C and writeback
                          ; 0x2000000C + 4 (0x20000010) to R1
```

Notice that after running this code the content of R1 is 0x20000010.

Pre-indexed address mode with offset of a shifted register
See Figure 6-9. This advanced addressing mode is an important feature in the Arm. We start describing this mode from simple cases with no shift and then we will move on to more complex formats.

Simple format of pre-indexed address mode with offset register
The following is the simple syntax for LDR and STR.

```
LDR    Rd, [Rm, Rn]       ; Rd is loaded from location Rm + Rn of memory
STR    Rs, [Rm, Rn]       ; Rs is stored to location Rm + Rn of memory
```

This addressing mode is often used in implementing array access. Rm holds the base address of the array (the address of the first element of the array) and Rn holds the array index. Example 6-11 shows how we use this addressing mode in accessing different locations of an array with byte size elements in memory.

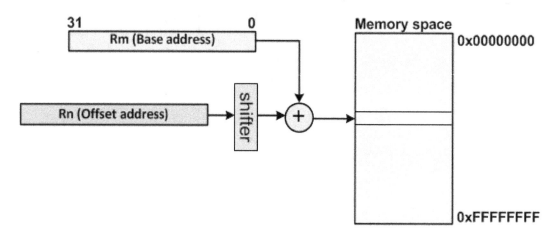

Figure 6-9: Pre-indexed address mode with offset of a shifted register

---

Example 6-11

Examine the value of R5 and R6 after the execution of the following program.

```
INDEX         RN     R2
ARRAY1        RN     R1
       EXPORT __main
       AREA   EXAMPLE_6_11, CODE, READONLY
__main
       LDR   ARRAY1, =MYDATA    ; use array address as base address
       LDRB  R4, [ARRAY1]
             ; load R4 with first element of ARRAY1 (R4= 0x45)

       MOV   INDEX, #1   ; INDEX = 1 to point to location 1 of array
       LDRB  R5, [ARRAY1, INDEX]
                        ; Load R5 with second element of ARRAY1 (R5 = 0x24)
       MOV   INDEX, #2   ; INDEX = 2 to point to location 2 of array
       LDRB  R6, [ARRAY1, INDEX]
                        ; Load R5 with third element of ARRAY1 (R6 = 0x18)
HERE   B     HERE
MYDATA        DCB   0x45, 0x24, 0x18, 0x63
       END
```

Solution:

After running the LDRB R4, [ARRAY1] instruction, first element with offset 0 of MYDATA is loaded into R4. Now R4=0x45.

Next, after running the LDRB R5, [ARRAY1, INDEX] instruction, second element with offset 1 of MYDATA is loaded into R5. Now R5 = 0x24.

Next, after running the LDRB R6, [ARRAY1, INDEX] instruction, third element with offset 2 of MYDATA is loaded into R6. So the content of R6 = 0x18.

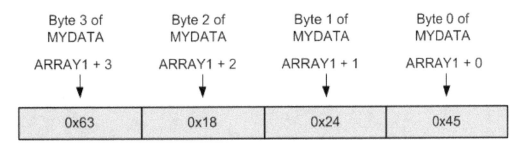

Byte 3 of MYDATA	Byte 2 of MYDATA	Byte 1 of MYDATA	Byte 0 of MYDATA
ARRAY1 + 3	ARRAY1 + 2	ARRAY1 + 1	ARRAY1 + 0
0x63	0x18	0x24	0x45

Notice that in Example 6-11, the array MYDATA contains byte size element so DCB and LDRB were used. It will not work if the data size of the array elements is different from a byte. In the next example, the array elements are word size (4 bytes each). We define the array using DCD, then we will not be able to use LDRB R5, [ARRAY1, INDEX] to load the INDEX location of ARRAY1. See Example 6-12 for clarification.

Example 6-12

In Example 6-11, change MYDATA DCB 0x45, 0x24, 0x18, 0x63 to MYDATA DCD 0x45, 0x2489ACF5 and examine the value of R5 and R6 after the execution of the following program.

```
INDEX       RN    R2
ARRAY1      RN    R1
      EXPORT  __main
      AREA   EXAMPLE_6_12, CODE, READONLY
__main
      LDR    ARRAY1, =MYDATA   ; use array address as base address
      LDRB   R4, [ARRAY1]      ; load R4 with first element of ARRAY1
                               ; (R4= 0x45)
      MOV    INDEX, #1         ; INDEX = 1 to point to location 1 of array
      LDRB   R5, [ARRAY1, INDEX]
                               ; Load INDEX location of ARRAY1 to R5
      MOV    INDEX, #2         ; INDEX = 2 to point to location 2 of array
      LDRB   R6, [ARRAY1, INDEX]
                               ; load INDEX location of ARRAY1 to R6
HERE  B      HERE
MYDATA      DCD    0x45, 0x2489ACF5
      END
```

Solution:
After running the LDRB R4, [ARRAY1] instruction, location 0 of MYDATA is loaded to R4. Now R4=0x45.
Next, after running the LDRB R5, [ARRAY1, INDEX] instruction, location 1 of MYDATA is loaded to R5. Now R5 = 0x00.
Next, after running the LDRB R6, [ARRAY1, INDEX] instruction, location 2 of MYDATA is loaded to R6. So the content of R6 = 0x00.

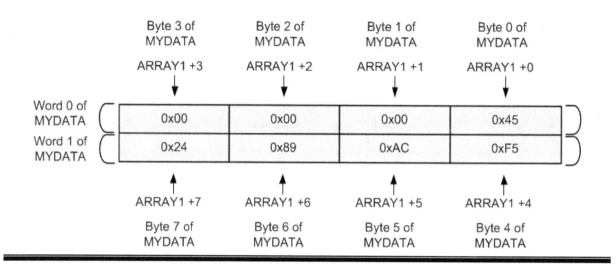

To access locations of a word size array we have to multiply the array index by four to yield the offset. Similarly, to access locations of a half-word size array we have to multiply the array index by two to get the offset. For example, we can correct program of Example 6-12 by replacing instruction

```
MOV    INDEX, #2    ; INDEX = 2 to point to location 2 of array
```

with following instructions:

```
MOV    INDEX, #2    ; INDEX = 2
MOV    INDEX, INDEX, LSL #2    ; INDEX is shifted left two bits (×4)
                               ; to point to word 2 of the array
```

Notice that by shifting left a value by two bits, we multiply it by four. Next, we will see how we can use indexed addressing with shifted registers to combine multiplication with the LDR and STR instructions.

General format of pre-indexed address mode with offset register

The general format of indexed addressing with shifted register for LDR and STR is as follows:

```
LDR Rd, [Rm, Rn, <shift>]  ; (Shifted Rn) + Rm is used as the address
STR Rd, [Rm, Rn, <shift>]  ; (Shifted Rn) + Rm is used as the address
```

In the above instructions <shift> can be any of shift instructions studied in Chapter 3 such as LSL, LSR, ASR and ROR. But for array indexing, LSL is most often used because it is the equivalent of signed multiply by power of two. Examine the following instructions:

```
LDR    R1, [R2, R3, LSL #2]    ; R2 + (R3 × 4) is used as the address
                ; content at location R2 + (R3 × 4) is loaded into R1
STR    R1, [R2, R3, LSL #1]    ; R2 + (R3 × 2) is used as the address
                ; R1 is stored at location R2+ (R3 × 2)
STRB   R1, [R2, R3, LSL #2]    ; R2 + (R3 × 4) is used as the address
     ; least significant byte of R1 is stored at location R2 + (R3 × 4)
LDR    R1, [R2, R3, LSR #2]    ; R2 + (R3 / 4) is used as the address
                ; content at location R2 + (R3 / 4) is loaded into R1
```

From the above code we can see that indexed addressing with shifted register is used to multiply the offset by a power of two and that is why it is also called indexed addressing with scaled register. Examine Example 6-13 to see how we can use scaled register indexing to access an array of words.

Example 6-13

Examine the value of R5 and R6 after the execution of the following program.

```
INDEX          RN    R2
ARRAY1         RN    R1
       EXPORT __main
       AREA   EXAMPLE_6_13, CODE, READONLY
__main
       LDR    ARRAY1, = MYDATA
       MOV    INDEX, #0                ; INDEX = 0
       LDR    R4, [ARRAY1, INDEX, LSL #2]    ;

       MOV    INDEX, #1                ; INDEX = 1
       LDR    R5, [ARRAY1, INDEX, LSL #2]    ;

       MOV    INDEX, #2                ; INDEX = 2
       LDR    R6, [ARRAY1, INDEX, LSL #2]    ;

HERE   B      HERE
MYDATA         DCD    0x45, 0x2489ACF5, 0x2489AC23
       END
```

Solution:

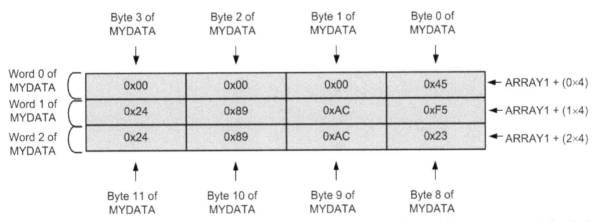

After running the LDR R4, [ARRAY1, INDEX, LSL #2]] instruction, element 0 of array MYDATA is loaded to R4. Now R4=0x45.

Next, after running the LDR R5, [ARRAY1, INDEX, LSL #2] instruction, element 1 of array MYDATA is loaded to R5. Now R5 = 0x2489ACF5.

Next, after running the LDR R6, [ARRAY1, INDEX, LSL #2] instruction, element 2 of array of MYDATA is loaded to R6. So the content of R6 = 0x2489AC23.

Look-up table

One application of indexed addressing mode is for implementing look-up tables. The look-up table is an array of pre-calculated constants. It allows obtaining frequently used values with no complex arithmetic operations during run-time at the cost of the memory space for the table. This technique is often used in embedded systems with lower computing power and stringent real time demand. The constant data in the look-up table may be calculated when the program is written or they may be calculated during the initialization of the program. In the Examples 6-14 through 6-16, the look-up tables are stored in program memory space and accessed as an array using indexed addressing mode.

Example 6-14

Write a program to use the x value in R9 and leave the value of $x^2 + 2x + 3$ in R10. Assume R9 has the x value range of 0–9. Use a look-up table instead of a multiply instructions.

Solution:

```
        EXPORT  __main
        AREA LOOKUP_EXAMP6_14, READONLY, CODE
__main      PROC
        ADR   R2, LOOKUP        ; point to LOOKUP
        LDRB  R10, [R2, R9]     ; R10 = entry of lookup table index by R9
HERE    B     HERE              ; stay here forever
        ENDP

LOOKUP DCB  3, 6, 11, 18, 27, 38, 51, 66, 83, 102
        END
```

Example 6-15

Write a program to use the x value in R9 and get the factorial of x in R10. Assume R9 has the x value range of 0–10. Use a look-up table instead of a multiply instruction.

Solution:

```
        EXPORT  __main
        AREA LOOKUP_EXAMP6_15, READONLY, CODE
__main PROC
        MOV   R9, #5
        ADR   R2, LOOKUP             ; point to LOOKUP
        LDR   R10, [R2, R9, LSL #2]  ; R10 = entry of lookup table index by R9
HERE    B     HERE                   ; stay here forever
        ENDP
LOOKUP DCD  1, 1, 2, 6, 24, 120, 720, 5040, 40320, 362880, 3628800
        END
```

Example 6-16

Write a program that calculates 10 to the power of R2 and stores the result in R3. Assume R2 has the x value range of 0–6. Use a look-up table instead of a multiply instruction.

Solution:

```
        EXPORT  __main
        AREA LOOKUP_EXAMP_6_16, READONLY, CODE
__main          PROC
        ADR     R1, LOOKUP              ; point to LOOKUP
        LDR     R3, [R1, R2, LSL #2]    ; R3 = entry of lookup table index by R2
HERE    B       HERE                    ; stay here forever
        ENDP
LOOKUP  DCD     1, 10, 100, 1000, 10000, 100000, 1000000
        END
```

Review Questions
1. Indexed addressing mode in Arm uses (register, memory) as pointer to data location.
2. List the three types of Indexed addressing mode in Arm
3. True or false. In the preindexed addressing mode the value of register does not change after the instruction is executed.
4. What is the difference between the preindexed and preindexed with write back?
5. What symbol do we use to indicate the preinexed with write back?

Section 6.3: ADR, LDR, and PC Relative Addressing

In indexed addressing modes, any registers including the PC (R15) register can be used as the pointer register. For example, the following instruction reads the contents of memory location PC+4:

```
LDR    R0, [PC, #4]
```

In this way, the data which has a known distance from the current executing line can be accessed. As discussed in Chapter 4, the PC register points 4 bytes ahead of executing instruction. As a result, "LDR R0, [PC, #4]" accesses a memory location whose address is 4+4 bytes ahead of the current instruction. Generally speaking, the address of the memory location which is being accessed using "LDR R0, [PC, offset]" can be found using this formula: the address of current instruction + 4 + offset. For instance, if "LDR R0, [PC, #4]" is located in address 0x10 the effective address is: 0x10 + 4 + 4 = 0x18.

Calculating the offset from current PC is a tedious job that needs be done every time new instructions are inserted or deleted. There are two pseudo-instructions using PC relative addressing mode, ADR and LDR with "=" to make programming easier.

The ADR Pseudo-instruction

The ADR pseudo-instruction uses the PC relative addressing mode to load a register with an address. It has the syntax of

```
        ADR    Rn, Label
```

The assembler calculates the offset from the current PC value to the line where Label is and translates the pseudo-instruction into:

```
        ADD    Rn, PC, #offset
```

For example, see the following program:

```
        AREA   LOOKUP_EXAMPLE, READONLY, CODE
__main
        ADR    R2, OUR_FIXED_DATA       ; R2 points to OUR_FIXED_DATA
        LDRB   R0, [R2]                 ; load R0 with the contents
                                        ; of memory pointed to by R2
        ADD    R1, R1, R0               ; add R0 to R1
HERE    B      HERE                     ; stay here forever
OUR_FIXED_DATA
        DCB    0x55, 0x33, 1, 2, 3, 4, 5, 6
        END
```

See Figure 6-10. At compile time, the ADR is replaced with A201 which is the machine code for "ADD R2, PC, #0x04". Since the instruction is at address 0x0800012C, the instruction accesses location 0x0800012C + 4 + 0x04 = 0x08000134. As shown in the Figure, where 0x08000134 is the address of OUR_FIXED_DATA.

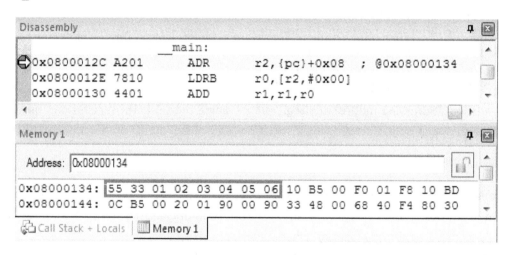

Figure 6-10: Memory Dump for ADR Instruction

Implementing the LDR Pseudo-instruction

Arm instructions are 12-bit or 32-bit long. It is impossible to incorporate a 32-bit immediate data in a 32-bit instruction. To load a register with a 32-bit immediate data, the Arm assembler stores the value as a constant data in program memory and accesses it using the LDR instruction and the PC relative addressing mode. Figure 6-11 shows the implementation of Program 6-1. For example, 0x12345678 is stored in memory locations 0x08000140–0x08000143, and the LDR directive is replaced with LDR R0, [PC, #8]. The LDR R0,=0x1234567 is located at address 0x08000134. Now we have 0x08000134+4+8= 0x08000140.

176

```
        EXPORT   __main
        AREA   PROG6_1, READONLY, CODE
__main
        LDR    R0, =0x12345678
        LDR    R1, =0x86427531
        ADD    R2, R0, R1
H1      B      H1
        END
```

Figure 6-11: Memory Dump for LDR Instruction

The memory region that the assembler reserved to store the constant data for LDR pseudo-instruction is called the "Literal pool." Literal pool is normally located at the end of the current section. (Section is terminated either by END or by another AREA directive.) The LDR instruction with immediate offset allows a range of -4095 to 4095. It is a good programming practice not to write a program section longer than 1000 instructions. Just in case you have a need to have a long section that the distance from the LDR instruction to the end of the section is beyond the range, Arm assembler allows you to designate a location within the section for an additional literal pool using LTORG directive. Remember, you should not designate a location for literal pool where the program execution may encounter and attempt to execute the constant data as instructions.

Review Questions

1. Which register is used as the pointer in PC relative addressing mode?
2. Which directive is more optimized ADR or LDR? Why?

Section 6.4: Arm Bit-Addressable Memory Region

Arm memory/peripheral is byte-addressable, that means the smallest size of memory access by the CPU is a single byte (8-bit). This presents an issue. In order to modify a single bit in the memory or peripheral, the whole byte where the bit resides is read, the bit is modified using AND, OR, or exclusive-OR operation, then the whole byte is written back. This is a procedure commonly referred to as the Read-Modify-Write (RMW) operation. One problem with RMW is that it incurs three steps and generally three separate instructions. In a multi-tasking environment, two RMW operations to the same byte may occur simultaneously, one interrupts the other. In that case, the second write will wipe out the modification of the first write.

177

There are software techniques to mitigate the issue of RMW but Arm introduced the "bit-banding" option for Cortex-M in hardware. It is generally available in M3 and M4 controllers though the manufacturers have the option to decide whether they implement it or not in the controllers.

Bit-banding is a feature that creates an alias word address for each bit of the selected memory and peripheral regions. Writing to the bit-banded alias address will change only the corresponding bit in the memory or peripheral without affecting all other bits of the same byte. Reading from the bit-banded alias address will return only the value of the addressed bit. Although internally writing to bit-banded memory or peripheral is still implemented in a read-modify-write in hardware, it is done with a single write instruction and therefore an "atomic" operation that will not be interrupted by the other instruction.

Since bit-banded alias addresses are word-size addresses, they are read and written in word size. Writing a word to a bit-banded alias address will transfer Bit n of the word to the selected bit. All other bits in the word have no effect. Reading from a bit-banded alias address will return the bit value in Bit n of the word. All other bits will be 0.

Bit-addressable (bit-banded) memory region

Since bit-banding assigns each bit with a word address and each word has 32 bits, bit-banding requires 32 times the address space than the regular memory addressing. Of the 4GB memory space of the Arm, only few small regions of memory or peripheral are bit-addressable, or the bit-banded regions. Recall bit-banding is created to mitigate the issues of Read-Modify-Write, so none of the read-only memory is bit-banded. Only the RAM and peripheral regions might be bit-banded.

The bit-banded RAM and peripheral locations vary among the family members and manufacturers. The Arm Cortex-M generic manual defines the address regions of bit-banding as 0x20000000 to 0x200FFFFF for SRAM and 0x40000000 to 0x400FFFFF for peripherals. We will use these address regions for the discussion in the rest of this section. Notice they are located at the lowest 1 MB address space of SRAM and peripherals. It must be also noted that the bit-banded (bit-addressable) regions are the only region that can be accessed in both bit and byte/halfword/word formats while the other area of memory must be accessed in byte/halfword/word size.

For the Arm Cortex-M, the bit-banded SRAM has addresses of 0x20000000 to 0x200FFFFF. This 1M bytes bit-addressable region is given 32M-byte bit-banded alias addresses of 0x22000000 to 0x23FFFFFF. The higher addresses are called alias address because they are addressing the exact same memory as the lower direct addressed SRAM, only each word address represents a single bit in the lower address. Because each bit occupies a word (4-byte) address in the bit-banded alias address region, to find out the alias address of a bit, the following formula is used:

$$\text{Bit alias address} = \text{Bit alias base address} + \text{Byte offset} \times 32 + \text{Bit number} \times 4$$

For example, to calculate the bit alias address of bit 3 of 0x20000004

Bit alias base address = 0x22000000
Byte offset = 0x20000004 − 0x20000000 = 4
Bit number = 3

Bit alias address = 0x22000000 + 4 * 32 + 3 * 4 = 0x22000000 + 128 + 12 = 0x22000000 + 0x8C
= 0x2200008C

Therefore, the bit addresses 0x22000000 to 0x2200001F are for the first byte of SRAM location 0x20000000, and 0x22000020 to 0x2200003F are the bit addresses of the second byte of SRAM location 0x20000001, and so on. See Figure 6-12.

SRAM Byte addresses	SRAM Bit addresses (We use these addresses to access the individual bits)							
	D7	D6	D5	D4	D3	D2	D1	D0
200FFFFF	23FFFFFC	F8	F4	F0	EC	E8	E4	23FFFFE0
200FFFFE	23FFFFDC	D8	D4	D0	CC	C8	C4	23FFFFC0
200FFFFD	23FFFFBC	B8	B4	B0	AC	A8	A4	23FFFFA0
200FFFFC	23FFFF9C	98	94	90	8C	88	84	23FFFF80
200FFFFB	23FFFF7C	78	74	70	6C	68	64	23FFFF60
200FFFFA	23FFFF5C	x8	x4	x0	xC	x8	x4	23FFFF40
200XXXXX	2XXXXXXC	X8	X4	X0	XC	X8	X4	2XXXXXX0
20000008	2200011C	118	114		...		104	22000100
20000007	220000FC	F8	F4	F0	EC	E8	E4	220000E0
20000006	220000DC	D8	D4	D0	CC	C8	C4	220000C0
20000005	220000BC	B8	B4	B0	AC	A8	A4	220000A0
20000004	2200009C	98	94	90	8C	88	84	22000080
20000003	2200007C	78	74	70	6C	68	64	22000060
20000002	2200005C	58	54	50	4C	48	44	20000040
20000001	2200003C	38	34	30	2C	28	24	22000020
20000000	2200001C	18	14	10	0C	08	04	22000000

Figure 6-12: SRAM bit-addressable region and their alias addresses

Since each byte of SRAM has 8 bits we need an address for each bit. This means we need at least 8M address locations to access 8M bits, one address for each bit. However, to make the addresses word-aligned the Arm provides 4-byte alias address for each bit. For example, 0x22000000 to 0x2200001F is assigned to a single byte location of 0x20000000. That means we have 0x22000000 to 0x23FFFFFF (total of 32M locations, as alias addresses) for 1M bytes of address.

Bit map for SRAM

From Figure 6-12 once again notice the following facts:

1. The bit address 0x22000000 is assigned to D0 of SRAM location of 0x20000000.
2. The bit address 0x22000004 is assigned to D1 of SRAM location of 0x20000000.
3. The bit address 0x22000008 is assigned to D2 of SRAM location of 0x20000000.
4. The bit address 0x2200000C is assigned to D3 of SRAM location of 0x20000000.
5. The bit address 0x22000010 is assigned to D4 of SRAM location of 0x20000000.
6. The bit address 0x22000014 is assigned to D5 of SRAM location of 0x20000000.
7. The bit address 0x22000018 is assigned to D6 of SRAM location of 0x20000000.
8. The bit address 0x2200001C is assigned to D7 of SRAM location of 0x20000000.

Notice that SRAM locations 0x20000000 – 0x200FFFFF are both byte-addressable and bit-addressable. The only difference is when we access it in byte (or halfword or word) we use direct addresses 0x20000000 to 0x200FFFFF, but when they are accessed in bit, they are accessed via their alias addresses of 0x22000000 to 0x23FFFFFF. The reason they are called aliases is because it is the same physical memory but accessed by two different addresses. It is like a same person but different names (aliases) See Examples 6-17 through 6-19.

Example 6-17

The generic Arm chip has the following address assignments. Calculate the space and the amount of memory given to each region.
(a)   Address range of 0x20000000–200FFFFF for SRAM bit-addressable region
(b)   Address range of 0x22000000–23FFFFFF for alias addresses of bit-addressable SRAM

Solution:

(a)   200FFFFF – 20000000 = FFFFF bytes. Converting FFFFF to decimal, we get 1,048,575 + 1 = 1,048,576, which is equal to 1M bytes.
(b)   23FFFFFF – 22000000 = 1FFFFFF bytes. Converting 1FFFFFF to decimal, we get 33,554,431 + 1 = 33,554,432, which is equal to 32M bytes.

Example 6-18

Write a program to set HIGH the D6 of the SRAM location 0x20000001 using a) byte address and b) the bit alias address.

Solution:
a)

```
        LDR    R1, =0x20000001    ; load the address of the byte
        LDRB   R2, [R1]           ; get the byte
        ORR    R2, R2, #2_01000000    ; make D6 bit high
                          ; (binary representation in Keil for 0b01000000)
        STRB   R2, [R1]           ; write it back
```

b)   From Figure 6-12 we have address 0x22000038 as the bit address of D6 of SRAM location 0x20000001.

```
        LDR    R1, =0x22000038    ; load the alias address of the bit
        MOV    R2, #1             ; R2 = 1
        STR    R2, [R1]           ; Write one to D6
```

Example 6-19

Write a program to set LOW the D0 bit of the SRAM location 0x20000005 using a) byte address and b) the bit alias address.

Solution:

a)

```
LDR    R1, =0x20000005    ; load the address of byte
LDRB   R2, [R1]           ; get the byte
AND    R2, R2, #2_11111110   ; make D0 bit low
STRB   R2, [R1]           ; write it back
```

b)   From Figure 6-12 we have address 0x220000A0 as the bit address of D0 of SRAM location 0x20000005.

```
LDR R2, =0x220000A0       ; load the alias address of the bit
MOV R0, 0                 ; R0 = 0
STR R0, [R2]              ; write zero to D0
```

Peripheral I/O port bit-addressable region

The general purpose I/O (GPIO) and peripherals such as ADC, DAC, RTC, and serial COM port are widely used in the embedded system design. In many Arm-based trainer boards we see the connection of LEDs, switches, and LCD to the GPIO pins of the Arm chip. In such trainers the vendor provides the details of I/O port and peripheral connections to the Arm chip in addition to their address map. As we discussed earlier, the Arm Cortex-M3 and M4 have set aside 1M bytes of address space to be used bit-banding (bit-addressable) I/O and peripherals. The address space assigned to bit-banded peripherals and GPIO is 0x40000000 to 0x400FFFFF with bit-banded alias addresses of 0x42000000 to 0x43FFFFFF. Examine your trainer board data sheet for the bit-banded addresses implemented on the Arm chip.

Bit map for I/O peripherals

From Figure 6-13 once again notice the following facts.

1. The bit address 0x42000000 is assigned to D0 of peripherals location of 0x40000000.
2. The bit address 0x42000004 is assigned to D1 of peripherals location of 0x40000000.
3. The bit address 0x42000008 is assigned to D2 of peripherals location of 0x40000000.
4. The bit address 0x4200000C is assigned to D3 of peripherals location of 0x40000000.
5. The bit address 0x42000010 is assigned to D4 of peripherals location of 0x40000000.
6. The bit address 0x42000014 is assigned to D5 of peripherals location of 0x40000000.
7. The bit address 0x42000018 is assigned to D6 of peripherals location of 0x40000000.
8. The bit address 0x4200001C is assigned to D7 of peripherals location of 0x40000000.

When accessing a peripheral port in a single-bit manner, we must use the address aliases of 0x42000000 – 0x43FFFFFF.

Peripherals Byte addresses	Peripherals Bit addresses (We use these addresses to access the individual bits)							
	D7	D6	D5	D4	D3	D2	D1	D0
400FFFFF	43FFFFFC	F8	F4	F0	EC	E8	E4	43FFFFE0
400FFFFE	43FFFFDC	D8	D4	D0	CC	C8	C4	43FFFFC0
400FFFFD	43FFFFBC	B8	B4	B0	AC	A8	A4	43FFFFA0
400FFFFC	43FFFF9C	98	94	90	8C	88	84	43FFFF80
400FFFFB	43FFFF7C	78	74	70	6C	68	64	43FFFF60
400FFFFA	43FFFF5C	x8	x4	x0	xC	x8	x4	43FFFF40
400XXXXX	4XXXXXXC	X8	X4	X0	XC	X8	X4	4XXXXXX0
40000008	4200011C	118	114		. . .		104	42000100
40000007	420000FC	F8	F4	F0	EC	E8	E4	420000E0
40000006	420000DC	D8	D4	D0	CC	C8	C4	420000C0
40000005	420000BC	B8	B4	B0	AC	A8	A4	420000A0
40000004	4200009C	98	94	90	8C	88	84	42000080
40000003	4200007C	78	74	70	6C	68	64	42000060
40000002	4200005C	58	54	50	4C	48	44	42000040
40000001	4200003C	38	34	30	2C	28	24	42000020
40000000	4200001C	18	14	10	0C	08	04	42000000

Figure 6-13: Peripherals bit-addressable region and their alias addresses.

Review Questions

1. True or false. All bytes of SRAM in Arm are bit-addressable.
2. True or false. All bits of the I/O peripherals in Arm are bit-addressable.
3. True or false. All ROM locations of the Arm are bit-addressable.
4. Of the 4G bytes of memory in the Arm, how many bytes are bit-addressable? List them.
5. How would you check to see whether bit D0 of location 0x20000002 is high or low?
6. Find out to which byte each of the following bits belongs. Give the address of the RAM byte in hex.

   (a) 0x23000030   (b) 0x23000040   (c) 0x23000048
   (d) 0x4200003C   (e) 0x43FFFFFC

Problems

Section 6.1: Arm Memory Map and Memory Access

1. What is the bus bandwidth unit?
2. Give the variables that affect the bus bandwidth.
3. True or false. One way to increase the bus bandwidth is to widen the data bus.
4. True or false. An increase in the number of address bus pins results in a higher bus bandwidth for the system.
5. Calculate the memory bus bandwidth for the following systems.
   (a) Arm of 100 MHz bus speed and 0 WS
   (b) Arm of 80 MHz bus speed and 1 WS

182

6. Indicate which of the following addresses is word aligned.

    (a) 0x1200004A   (b) 0x52000068   (c) 0x66000082
    (d) 0x23FFFF86   (e) 0x23FFFFF0   (f) 0x4200004F
    (g) 0x18000014   (h) 0x43FFFFF3   (i) 0x44FFFF05

7. Show how data is placed after execution of the following code using (a) little endian and (b) big endian.

```
LDR    R2, =0xFA98E322
LDR    R1, =0x20000100
STR    [R1], R2
```

8. True or false. In Arm, instructions are always word aligned.
9. True or false. In a word aligned address the lower digit of the address is 0, 4, 8, or C.
10. Show how many memory cycles does it take to fetch the following data into register

```
LDR    R1, =0x20000004
LDR    R2, [R1]
```

11. Show how many memory cycles does it take to fetch the following data into register

```
LDR    R1, =0x20000102
LDR    R2, [R1]
```

12. Show how many memory cycles does it take to fetch the following data into register

```
LDR    R1, =0x20000103
LDR    R2, [R1]
```

13. Show how many memory cycles does it take to fetch the following data into register

```
LDR    R1, =0x20000006
LDRH   R2, [R1]
```

14. Show how many memory cycles does it take to fetch the following data into register

```
LDR    R1, =0x20000C10
LDRB   R2, [R1]
```

Section 6.2: Advanced Indexed Addressing Mode
15. True or false. Writeback is by default enabled in pre-indexed addressing mode.
16. Indicate the addressing mode in each of the following instructions
    (a) LDR R1, [R5], R2, LSL #2   (b) STR R2, [R1, R0]
    (c) STR R2, [R1, R0, LSL #2]!   (d) STR R9, [R1], R0
17. Which addressing mode uses the register as pointer to data location?
18. True or false. In the preindexed addressing mode with write back the value of register does not change after the instruction is executed.
19. How many Indexed addressing modes do we have in Arm? Name them.

20. In which indexed addressing mode the value of register does not change after the instruction is executed.

21. True or false. In the preindexed addressing mode only a fixed value can be used as offset.

22. True or false. In the preindexed addressing mode both fixed value and a register can be used as offset.

Section 6.3: ADR, LDR, and PC Relative Addressing

23. Assuming that the instruction "LDR R2, [PC, #8] is located in address 0x300, calculate the address of the memory location which is accessed.

24. Using PC relative addressing mode, write an LDR instruction that accesses a memory location which is 0x20 bytes ahead of itself.

25. Why ADR is called pseudo-instruction?

Section 6.4: Arm Bit-Addressable Memory Region

26. Give the bit-addressable SRAM region address for generic Arm.

27. What bit addresses are assigned to byte address of 0x20000004?

28. What bit addresses are assigned to byte address of 0x20000010?

29. What bit addresses are assigned to byte address of 0x200FFFFF?

30. What bit addresses are assigned to byte address of 0x20000020?

31. What bit addresses are assigned to byte address of 0x40000008?

32. What bit addresses are assigned to byte address of 0x4000000C?

33. What bit addresses are assigned to byte address of 0x40000020?

34. The following are bit addresses. Indicate where each one belongs.

(a) 0x2200004C	(b) 0x22000068	(c) 0x22000080
(d) 0x23FFFF80	(e) 0x23FFFF00	(f) 0x4200004C
(g) 0x42000014	(h) 0x43FFFFF0	(i) 0x43FFFF00

35. Of the 4G bytes of memory locations in the Arm, how many of them are also assigned a bit address as well? Indicate which bytes those are.

36. True or false. The bit-addressable region cannot be accessed in byte.

37. True or false. The bit-addressable region cannot be accessed in word.

38. Write a program to see whether the D7 bit of RAM location 0x20000020 is high. If so, send a 1 to D1 of RAM location 0x20000000.

39. Write a program to see whether the D7 bit of I/O location 0x40000000 is low. If so, send a 0 to the D0 of location 0x400FFFFF.

Answers to Review Questions

Section 6.1

1. Compilers ensure that codes are word aligned.

2. little endian

3. 1/66 MHz = 15.15 ns is the bus clock period. Since the bus cycle time of zero wait states is 2 clocks, we have 2 × 15.15 = 30.3 ns

4. 1/100 MHz = 10 ns is the bus clock period. 50 ns - 10 ns = 40 ns. The Number of WS is 40 ns / 10 ns = 4.

5. False, most of the Arm devices use little endian as default.

Section 6.2

1. Register

2. Preinseded, postindexed and preindexed with write back.

3. True

4. In the preindexed write back the calculated value is written back to the pointing register. That is not the case for preindexed mode.

5. !

Section 6.3

1. PC (R15)

2. ADR, To implement the LDR directive the value is stored in memory; as a result, it uses more memory while the ADR uses no memory.

Section 6.4

1. False

2. False

3. False

4. 2MBytes; locations 0x20000000 to 0x200FFFFF of SRAM and 0x40000000 to 0x400FFFFF of GPIO

5.

```
LDR    R0,  =0x22000040
LDR    R1,  [R0]
CMP    R1,  #0
BNE    L1
    ...
L1
```

6.

(a)   0x23000030 - 0x22000000 = 0x1000030; 0x1000030 / 0x20 = 0x80001; thus, it is in location 0x20000000 + 0x80001 = 0x20080001

(0x1000030 % 32) / 4 = (48 % 32) / 4 = 16 / 4 = 4; it is D4 of 0x20080001.

(b)   0x1000040 / 0x20 = 0x80002; it is in location 0x20080002

(0x1000040 % 0x20) / 4 = 0; it is D0 of location 0x20080002

(c)   0x1000048 / 0x20 = 80002; it is in location 0x20080002

(0x1000048 % 0x20) / 4 = 2; it is D2 of location 0x20080002

(d)   0x4200003C - 0x42000000 = 0x03; 0x03C / 0x20 = 0x01

(0x3C % 0x20) / 4 = 0x1C / 4 = 7; it is D7 of 0x40000001

(e)   0x43FFFFFC − 0x42000000 = 0x1FFFFFC; 0x1FFFFFC / 0x20 = 0xFFFFF

(0x1FFFFFC % 0x20) / 4 = 0x1C / 4 = 7; D7 of 0x400FFFFF

Appendix A: ARM Cortex-M3 Instruction Description

Section A.1: List of ARM Cortex-M3 Instructions

ADC	Add with Carry
ADD	Add
ADR	Load PC-Relative Address
AND	Logical AND
ASR	Arithmetic Shift right
B	Branch (unconditional jump)
Bxx	Branch Conditional
BFC	Bit Field Clear
BFI	Bit Field Insert
BIC	Bit Clear
BKPT	Breakpoint
BL	Branch with Link (this is Call instruction)
BLX	Branch Indirect with Link
BX	Branch Indirect (BX LR is used for Return)
CBNZ	Compare and Branch on Non-Zero
CBZ	Compare and Branch on Zero
CDP	Coprocessor Data processing
CLREX	Clear Exclusive
CLZ	Count Leading Zero
CMN	Compare Negative
CMP	Compare
CPSID	Change processor ID and Disable Interrupt
CPSIE	Change Processor State and Enable Interrupt
DMB	Data Memory Barrier
DSB	Data Synchronization Barrier
EOR	Exclusive OR
ISB	Instruction Synchronization Barrier
IT	If-Then Condition Block

LDC	Load Coprocessor
LDM	Load Multiple registers
LDMDB	Load Multiple registers and Decrement Before each access
LDMEA	Load Multiple registers from Empty Ascending
LDMFD	Load Multiple registers Full Descending
LDMIA	Load Multiple registers and Increment after each Access
LDR	Load Register
LDR Rx, =Value	Load Register with 32-bit value
LDRB	Load Register Byte
LDRH	Load Register Halfword
LDRSB	Load Register signed Byte
LDRSH	Load Register Signed Halfword
LDRT	Load Register with Translation
LSL	Logical Shift Left
LSR	Logical Shift Right
MCR	Move to Coprocessor from ARM Register
MLA	Multiply Accumulate
MLS	Multiply and Subtract
MOV	Move (ARM7)
MOV	Move (ARM Cortex)
MOVT	Move Top
MOVW	Move 16-bit constant
MRC	Move to ARM Register from Coprocessor
MRS	Move to general Register from Special register
MSR	Move to Special register from general Register
MUL	Unsigned Multiplication
MVN	Move Negative
NOP	No Operation
ORN	Logical OR Not
ORR	Logical OR
POP	POP register from Stack
PUSH	PUSH register onto stack

RBIT	Reverse Bits
REV	Reverse byte order in a word
RV16	Reverse byte order in 16-bit
REVSH	Reverse byte order in bottom halfword and sign extend
ROR	Rotate Right
RRX	Rotate Right with extend
RSB	Reverse Subtract
SBC	Subtract with Carry (Borrow)
SBFX	Sign Bit Field extract
SDIV	Signed Divide
SEV	Send Event
SMLAL	Signed Multiply Accumulate Long
SMULL	Signed Multiply Long
SSAT	Sign Saturate
STM	Store Multiple
STMDB	Store Multiple register and Decrement Before
STMEA	Store Multiple register Empty Ascending
STMIA	Store Multiple register Empty Ascending
STMFD	Store Multiple register Full Descending
STR	Store Register
STRB	Store Register Byte
STRD	Store Register Double (two words)
STRH	Store Register Halfword
STRT	Store Register
SUB	Subtract
SUBS	Subtract
SVC	supervisor Call (Software Interrupt)
SXTB	Sign Extend byte
SXTH	Sign Extend Halfword
TBB	Table Branch Byte
TBH	Table Branch halfword
TEQ	Test Equivalence

TST	Test
UBFX	Unsigned Bit filed extract
UDIV	Unsigned Divide
UMLAL	Unsigned Multiply with Accumulate
UMULL	Unsigned Multiply Long
UXBT	Zero extend a byte
UXTH	Zero extend halfword
WFE	Wait for event
WFI	Wait for interrupt

Section A.2: ARM Instruction Description

ADC   Add with Carry
Flags: Unaffected.

Format: ADC Rd, Rn, Op2   ; Rd = Rn + Op2 + C

Function: If C = 1 prior to this instruction, then after execution of this instruction, Op2 is added to Rn plus 1 and the result is placed in Rd. If C = 0, Op2 is added to Rn plus 0. Used widely in multiword additions. After the execution the flags are not updated. The ADCS instruction updates the flags.

Example 1:
```
    LDR   R0, =0xFFFFFFFB          ;   R0=0xFFFFFFFB
    LDR   R1, =0xFFFFFFFF          ;   R1=0xFFFFFFFF
    MOV   R2, #3                   ;  R2=3
    MOV   R3, #4                   ;  R3=4
    ADDS  R4, R0, R1               ;  R4=R0+R1,  C=1
    ADC   R5, R2, R3               ;  R5=R2+R3+C=R2+R3+1
```

ADD   ADD
Flags: Unaffected

Format: ADD Rd, Rn, Op2   ; Rd = Rn + Op2

Function: Adds source operands together and places the result in destination. This will not update the flags. To update the flags, we must use ADDS.

Example 1:
```
    LDR   R0, =0xFFFFFFFF          ; R0=0xFFFFFFFB
    MOV   R1, #0x5                 ; R1=0x5
    ADD   R2, R0, R1
      ; R2=R0+R1=0xFFFFFFFB+0x5=00000000
      ; flags unchanged
```

Example 2:
```
LDR   R0, =0xFFFFFFFF            ; R0=0xFFFFFFFF
ADD   R2, R0, #0xF1
  ; R2=R0+0xF1=R1=0xFFFFFFFF+0xF1=000000F0
  ; flags unchanged
```

ADR   Load PC-Relative Address

Flags: Unaffected:

Format: ADR Rd, label   ; Rd= address of label

Function: This allows loading into Rd register an address relative to the current PC (program counter). The label target address must be within the -4,095 to +4,096 bytes from the address in PC register. That is no farther than 1024 instructions in either direction of backward or forward.

Example:
```
     ADR   R3, MyMessage
HERE     B  HERE
MyMessage  DCB  "Hello"
```

AND   Logical AND

Flags: Unaffected

Format: AND Rd, Rn, Op2   ; Rd= Rn ANDed Op2

Function: Performs logical AND on the operands, bit by bit, storing the result in the destination. This will not update the flags. To update the flags, we must use ANDS. Notice that C flag is updated during calculation of Op2 when LSR or LSL are used.

Inputs		Output
X	Y	X AND Y
0	0	0
0	1	0
1	0	0
1	1	1

Example 1:
```
MOV   R0, #0x39   ; R0=0x39
MOV   R1, #0x0F   ; R1=0x0F
AND   R2, R1, R0  ; R2=09
        ; 39  0011 1001
        ; 0F  0000 1111
        ; --  ---------
        ; 09  0000 1001  Flags unchanged
```

Example 2:
```
MOV   R0, #0x37   ; R0=0x37
AND   R1, R0, #0x0F     ; R1 = R0 ANDed 0x0F = 07
        ; 37  0011 0111
        ; 0F  0000 1111
        ; --  ---------
```

```
            ; 07 0000 0111  Flags unchanged
```

ASR   Arithmetic Shift right

Flags: Unaffected. Except C

Format: ASR Rd, Rm, Rn

Function: As each bit of Rm register is shifted right, the LSB is removed and the empty bits filled with the sign bit (MSB). The number of bits to be shifted right is given by Rn and the result is placed in Rd register. The flags are unchanged. To update the flags, use ASRS instruction.

Example 1:
```
   LDR   R2, =0xFFFFFF82
   ASR   R0, R2, #6  ; R0=R2 is shifted right 6 times
         ; now, R0 = 0xFFFFFFFE
```

Example 2:
```
   LDR   R0, =0x2000FF18
   MOV   R1,  #12
   ASR   R2, R0, R1  ; R2=R0 is shifted right R1 number of times.
         ; now, R2 = 0x0002000F
```

Example 3:
```
   LDR   R0, =0x0000FF18
   MOV   R1,  #16
   ASR   R2, R0, R1  ; R2=R0 is shifted right R1 number of times
         ; now, R2 = 0x00000000
```
ASR arithmetic shift is used for signed number shifting. ASR essentially divides Rm by a power of 2 for each bit shift.

B   Branch (unconditional jump)

Flags: Unchanged.

Format: B target   ; jump to target address

Function: This instruction is used to transfer control unconditionally to a new address. The difference between B and BL is that the BL instruction saves the address of the next instruction to LR (the link register, R14). For ARM7, the target address is calculated by (a) shifting the 24-bit signed (2's comp) offset left two bits, (b) sign-extend the result to 32-bit, and (c) add it to contents of PC (program counter). This means the target address could be within the −32M bytes to +32M bytes of address space from the current program counter. For ARM Cortex M3. the target address must be within −16MB to +16 MB address space from current instruction.

Bxx   Branch Conditional

Flags: Unaffected.

Format: Bxx target ; jump to target upon condition

Function: Used to jump to a target address if certain conditions are met. In ARM7, the target address cannot be more than −32MB to +32MB bytes away. For ARM Cortex M3. the target address must be within −16MB to +16 MB address space from current instruction. The conditions are indicated by the flag register. The conditions that determine whether the jump takes place can be categorized into three groups:

1. flag values,
2. the comparison of unsigned numbers, and
3. the comparison of signed numbers.

Each is explained next.

1. "B condition" where the condition refers to flag values. The status of each bit of the flag register has been decided by execution of instructions prior to the jump. The following "B condition" instructions check if a certain flag bit is raised or not.

Instruction		Condition
BCS	Branch if Carry Set	jump if C=1
BCC	Branch if Carry Clear	jump if C=0
BEQ	Branch if Equal	jump if Z=1
BNE	Branch if Not Equal	jump if Z=0
BMI	Branch if Minus/Negative	jump if N=1
BPL	Branch if Plus/Positive	jump if N=0
BVS	Branch if Overflow	jump if V=1
BVC	Branch if No overflow	jump if V=0

2. "B condition" where the condition refers to the comparison of unsigned numbers. After a compare (CMP Rn, Op2) instruction is executed, C and Z indicate the result of the comparison, as follows:

	C	Z
Rn > Op2	1	0
Rn = Op2	1	1
Rn < Op2	0	0

Since the operands compared are viewed as unsigned numbers, the following "B condition" instructions are used.

Instruction		Condition
BHI	Branch if Higher	jump if C=1 and Z=0
BEQ	Branch if Equal	jump if C=1 and Z=1
BLS	Branch if Lower or same	jump if C=0 or Z=1

In reality, the "CMP Rn, Op2" is a subtract instruction (Rn-Op2). After the subtraction the result is discarded and flags are changed according to the result. Notice in ARM the subtract affects the C flag setting differently from the x86 and other CPUs. See the SUB instruction.

3. "B condition" where the condition refers to the comparison of signed numbers. In the case of the signed number comparison, although the same instruction, "CMP Rn, Op2", is used, the flags used to check the result are as follows:

Rn > Op2	V=N or Z=0
Rn = Op2	Z=1
Rn < Op2	V inverse of N

Consequently, the "B condition" instructions used are different. They are as follows:

Instruction		
BGE	Branch Greater or Equal	jump if N=1 and V=1 or N=0 and V=0 (V=N)
BLT	Branch Less than	jump if N=1 and V=0 or N=0 and V=1 (N not equal to V)
BGT	Branch Greater than	jump if Z=0 and either N=1 and V=1 or N=0 and V=0 (N=V)
BLE	Branch Less or Equal	jump if Z=1 or N=1 and V=0. Or N=0 and V=1 (Z=1 or N not equal to V)
BEQ	Branch if Equal	jump if Z = 1

All "B condition" instructions are short jumps, meaning that the target address cannot be more than -32M bytes backward or +32M bytes forward from the PC of the instruction following the jump. In ARM Cortex M3 it is 16MB in each direction. What happens if a programmer needs to use a "B condition" to go to a target address beyond the -32MB to +32MB range? The solution is to use the "BX condition, Rm" since Rm can be 32-bit address and covers the entire 4GB address space of the ARM. This is shown next.

```
    LDR   R4,  =MYTARGET
    ADDS R1, R2, R3
    BXEQ R4 ; branch to address held by R4 if Z=1
MYTRGT  SUBS R7, #4
    NOP
    NOP
    . . . .
```

	C	Z	N	V
Rn > Op2	0	0	0	N
Rn = Op2	0	1	0	N
Rn < Op2	1	0	1	Inverse of N

BFC   Bit Field Clear

Flags: Unaffected.

Format: BFC Rd, #LSB, #Width

Function: Clears selected bits of Rd. The start location of the Rd bit is indicated by #LSB and must be in the range of 0–31. How many bits should be cleared is indicated by #Width and must be in the range of 1–32.

Example 1:
```
   LDR   R1,  =0xFFFFFFFF    ; R1=0xFFFFFFFF
   BFC   R1,  #2, #14        ; now R1=0xFFFF0003
```

Example 2:
```
   LDR   R2,  =0x999999999   ; R2=0x99999999
   BFC   R2,  #8, #24        ; now R2=0x00000099
```

BFI   Bit Field Insert
Flags: Unaffected.

Format: BFI Rd, Rn, #LSB, #Width

Function: Selected bits of Rn are copied to Rd. The start location of the Rd bit is indicated by #LSB and must be in the range of 0 – 31. How many bits should be copied is indicated by #Width and must be in the range of 1–32. The start bit location of Rn is always bit 0 (D0).

Example:
```
   LDR   R1,  =0xABCDABCD    ; R1=0xABCDABCD
   LDR   R2,  =0x12345678    ; R2=0x12345678
   BFI   R1,  R2, #4, #8     ; now R1=0xABCDA78D
```

BIC   Bit Clear
Flags: Unaffected.

Format: BIC Rd, Rn, Op2 ; Rd=Rn ANDed with NOT of Op2

Function: Selected bits of Rn are cleared and placed in Rd. The Op2 provides the bits selection. If the selected bits in Op2 are high, then corresponding bits in Rn are cleared and the result is placed in Rd. If the selected bits in Op2 are low the corresponding bits in Rn are left unchanged and the result is placed in Rd. In reality, the BIC performs the AND operation on the bits of Rn with the complement of the bits in Op2. The BIC will not update the flags. To update the flags, we must use BICS.

Inputs		Output
X	Y	X AND (NOT Y)
0	0	0
0	1	0
1	0	1
1	1	0

Example:
```
   LDR   R1,  =0xFFFFFF00    ; R1=0xFFFFFF00
   LDR   R2,  =0x99999999    ; R2=0x9999999
```

```
BIC   R3, R2, R1           ; now R3=0x00000099
```

BKPT   Breakpoint

Flags: Unaffected.

Format: BKPT #imme_value

Function: used by compiler to insert breakpoint into programs. Upon execution of the BKPT instruction the program enters the Debug mode. See your ARM compiler for more information

BL   Branch with Link (this is Call instruction)

Flags: Unchanged.

Format: BL Subroutine_Addr   ; transfer control to a subroutine

Function: Transfers control to a subroutine. This instruction saves the address of the instruction after the BL in R14 (link register). At the end of the subroutine the control to the instruction after the BL is achieved by copying the LR (R14) register to PC. In ARM7, the target address cannot be more than – 32MB to +32MB bytes away. For ARM Cortex M3. the target address must be within –16MB to +16 MB address space from current instruction.

Example:
```
  LDR   R7, =20000000
  BL DELAY    ; Call subroutine MY_DELAY
  ADD   R3, #4     ; address of this instruction is saved in R14
  . . .
  . . .
DELAY SUBS  R7, #4
  NOP
  NOP
  MOV  PC, R14     ; Return, could have used "BX LR" instruction
```

BLX   Branch Indirect with Link

Flags: Unaffected.

Format: BLX Rm   ; transfer control to a subroutine whose

                            ; address is given by Rm

Function: Transfers control to a subroutine whose address is given by the Rm register. This instruction saves the address of the instruction after the BL in R14 (link register). At the end of the subroutine the control to the instruction after the BL is achieved by copying the LR (R14) register to PC. One can use "BX LR" as return instruction. Notice the difference between this instruction and "BL Target_Addr" instruction. In the "BL Target_Addr" instruction the target address of the subroutine is given right there. However, in the "BLX Rm" instruction, the target address of the subroutine is held by register Rm.

Example:
```
  ADR   R2, DELAY
```

```
   BLX   R2    ; Call subroutine pointed to by R2
   ADD   R3, #4   ; address of this instruction is saved in R14
   ...
   ...
DELAY SUBS  R1, #4
   NOP
   NOP
   BX LR    ; return
```

BX   Branch Indirect (BX LR is used for Return)

Flags: Unchanged.

Format: BX Rm   ; BX LR is used for Return from a subroutine

Function: The most widely usage of this instruction is in the form of "BX LR" for the purpose of return instruction at the end of subroutine.

Example:
```
   LDR   R1, =20000000
   BL DELAY    ; Call subroutine MY_DELAY
   ADD   R3, #4   ; address of this instr. is saved in R14
   ......
DELAY SUBS  R1, #4
   NOP
   NOP
   BX    LR    ; return to caller
```

CBNZ   Compare and Branch on Non-Zero

Flags: Unchanged.

Format: CBNZ Rn, Target

Function: Transfers control to the target location if Rn is not equal to zero. The Rn must be in the range of R0–R7 and target address cannot be farther than 130 bytes away from the instruction. This instruction compares the Rn with zero and jumps only if Rn is not zero. The comparison has no effect on flags. This can be used for loops in which the body of the loop is no more than 20 instructions.

Example 1:
```
   MOV   R1, #10 ; R1=10
L1 NOP
   NOP
   NOP
   SUB  R1, R1, #1   ; R1=R1-1
   CBNZ  R1, L1
```

CBZ   Compare and Branch on Zero

Flags: Unaffected.

Format: CBZ Rn, Target

Function: Transfers control to the target location if Rn is zero. The Rn must be in the range of R0–R7 and target address cannot be farther than 130 bytes away from the instruction. This instruction compares the Rn with zero and jumps only if Rn is zero. The comparison has no effect on flags. This can be used to test a register value after reading a port.

Example 1:
```
  LDR  R0, =MYPORT_ADR   ; R0 = MYPORT address
HERE LDR  R2, [R0]        ; read from MYPORT
  CBZ  R2, HERE           ; keep reading MYPORT until it is zero
```

CDP   Coprocessor Data processing
See ARM Cortex-M Manual.

CLREX   Clear Exclusive
See ARM Cortex-M Manual.

CLZ   Count Leading Zero
Flags: Unchanged.

Format: CLZ Rd, Rn

Function: Scans the Rn register contents from most significant bit (D31) toward least significant bit (D0) until it find the first HIGH. The number of binary zero bits before it encounters the first binary HIGH is placed in Rd.

Example:
```
  LDR  R3, =0x01FFFFFF
  CLZ  R1, R3       ; R1=7 since there are 7 zeros before the first binary 1
```

CMN   Compare Negative
Flags: Affected: V, N, Z, C.

Format: CMN Rn, Op2   ; sets flags as if "Rn + Op2"

                        ; Notice, the Rn -(-Op2)=Rn+Op2

Function: Compares Rn register value with the negative of Op2 value. This is done by Rn - (negative of Op2) which is Rn - (-Op2) = Rn + Op2. The Rn and Op2 operands are not altered. In other words, the CMN adds the Op2 to Rn (Rn+Op2) and sets the flags accordingly. This is the same as ADDS instruction except the operands are unchanged and the result is discarded. See Bxx instruction for possible cases of comparison.

CMP   Compare
Flags: Affected: V, N, Z, C.

Format: CMP Rn, Op2   ; sets flags as if "Rn-Op2"

Function: Compares two operands. The operands are not altered. Performs comparison by subtracting the Op2 operand from the Rn and updates flags as if SUBS were performed. As we can see in SUBS, the CMP perform the operation of Rn + 2's comp of Op2 and sets the flags according to the result. See Bxx instruction for possible cases of comparison.

CPSID   Change processor ID and Disable Interrupt
Flags: Unaffected

Format: CPSID iflag   ; iflag is i in PRIMASK or f in FAULTMASK

Function: Used for disabling the interrupt flags in PRIMASK or FAULTMASK registers. See ARM Cortex manual.

CPSIE   Change Processor State and Enable Interrupt
Flags: Unaffected

Format: CPSIE iflag   ; iflag is i in PRIMASK or f in FAULTMASK

Function: Used for enabling the interrupt flags in PRIMSK or FAULTMASK registers. See ARM Cortex manual.

DMB   Data Memory Barrier
Flags: Unaffected

Format: DMB

Function: It makes sure that all the explicit memory accesses prior to DMB instruction are completed before the explicit memory accesses after the DMB. See ARM Cortex manual.

DSB   Data Synchronization Barrier
Flags: Unaffected

Format: DSB

Function: It makes sure that all the explicit memory accesses prior to DSB instruction are completed before the DSB instruction is executed. See ARM Cortex manual.

EOR   Exclusive OR
Flags: Unaffected

Format: EOR Rd, Rn, Op2

Function: Performs logical Ex-OR on the Rn and Op2 operands, bit by bit, storing the result in the Rd. This will not update the flags. Use EORS instruction to updates the flags.

	Inputs	Output
X	Y	X EOR Y
0	0	0
0	1	1
1	0	1
1	1	0

Example 1:
```
MOV  R0, #0xAA   ; R0=0xAA
EOR  R2, R0, #0xFF      ; now, R2=0x55
         ; AA  1010 1010
         ; FF  1111 1111
         ; --  ---------
         ; 55  0101 0101  flags unchanged
```

Example 2:
```
LDR  R0, =0xAAAAAAAA    ; R0=0xAAAAAAAA
LDR  R1, =0x55555555    ; R1=0x55555555
EOR  R2, R1, R0         ; R2=0xFFFFFFFF
         ; AA   1010 1010
         ; 55   0101 0101
         ; --   ---------
         ; FF   1111 1111    flags unchanged
```
The "EOR Rd, Rx, Rx" can be used to clear Rd.

Example 3:
```
MOV  R1, #0x55
EOR  R2, R1, R1 ; R2=0
         ; 55  0101 0101
         ; 55  0101 0101
         ; --  ---------
         ; 00  0000 0000  flags unchanged
```
To complement the bits of Rn, EX-OR it with 0xFF.

Example 4:
```
LDR  R0, =0xAAAAAAAA    ; R0=0xAAAAAAAA
LDR  R1, =0xFFFFFFFF    ; R1=0xFFFFFFFF
EOR  R2, R1, R0         ; R2=0x55555555
         ; AA   1010 1010
         ; FF   1111 1111
         ; --   ---------
         ; 55   0101 0101    flags unchanged
```

ISB   Instruction Synchronization Barrier

Flags: Unaffected.

Format: ISB

Function: It flushes the pipeline to make sure the instructions executed right after the ISB instruction are fetched fresh from the cache or memory.

IT   If-Then Condition Block

Flags: Unaffected

Format: See ARM manual

Function: It allows the execution of up to four instructions after the IT to be conditional.

LDC   Load Coprocessor

See the ARM Manual

LDM   Load Multiple registers

Flags: Unaffected.

Format: LDM Rn, {Rx, Ry, ...}

Function: Loads into registers from consecutive memory locations. The starting address of memory location is given by Rn register. The destination registers separated by comma and placed in braces. In the ARM Cortex, the stack is descending meaning that as information is pushed onto stack the stack pointer is decremented. This IA (Increment the address after each Access) is the default for loading (Poping). This instruction is widely used for Poping (loading) multiple words from descending stack into CPU registers.

Example:

```
; Assume the following memory locations with the contents:
; 12000=(46)
; 12001=(10)
; 12002=(38)
; 12003=(82)
; 12004=(56)
; 12005=(50)
; 12006=(58)
; 12007=(15)
; 12008=(63)
; 12009=(60)
; 1200A=(68)
; 1200B=(39)
; 1200C=(79)
; 1200D=(70)
; 1200E=(75)
; 1200F=(92)

LDR   R7, =0x12000
LDM   R7, {R0, R2, R4}
; now, R0=0x82381046, R2=0x15585056, ...
; the contents of memory locations 0x12000-0x12003 are
; moved to register R0, and the contents of memory
; locations 0x12004-0x12007 are moved to register
; R2, and so on. Therefore we have R0=0x82381046,
; R2=0x15585056, and R4=0x39686063.
```

LDMDB Load Multiple registers and Decrement Before each access

Flags: Unaffected.

Format: LDMDB Rn, {Rx, Ry, ...}

Function: This is the same as LDMEA (load multiple registers from Empty Ascending) used for cases in which the stack is ascending. See LDMEA instruction.

LDMEA Load Multiple registers from Empty Ascending
Flags: Unaffected.

Format: LDMEA Rn, {Rx, Ry, ...}

Function: Loads into registers from consecutive memory locations. The starting address of memory location is given by Rn register. The destination registers separated by comma and placed in braces. In the ARM Cortex, the default for stack is descending meaning that as information are pushed onto stack the stack pointer is decremented. The IA (Increment the address after each Access) is the default. If we change the default of descending stack to ascending stack, then we have to use the EA (Empty Ascending). The ascending stack means as information are pushed onto stack the stack pointer is incremented. The LDMEA is used for Popping (loading) multiple words from ascending stack into CPU registers.

LDMFD Load Multiple registers Full Descending
Flags: Unaffected.

Format: LDMFD Rn, {Rx, Ry, ...}

Function: This is the same as LDM and LDMIA.

LDMIA Load Multiple registers and Increment after each Access
Flags: Unaffected.

Format: LDM Rn, {Rx, Ry, ...}

Function: This is the same as the LDM instructions. In the ARM Cortex, the stack is descending meaning that as information are pushed onto stack the stack pointer is decremented. This IA (Increment the address after each Access) is the default. We use this for Popping (loading) multiple words from descending stack into CPU registers.

LDR   Load Register
Flags: Unaffected.

Format: LDR Rd, [Rx]   ; load into Rd a word from memory location pointed to be Rx

Function: Loads into destination register the contents of four memory locations. The [Rx] points to address of memory location. This is widely used to load 32-bit data from memory into Rd register of the ARM since in the "MOV Rd, #immediate_value" the immediate value cannot be larger than 0xFF.

Example:

```
; Assume the following memory locations with the contents:
; 12000=(46)
; 12001=(10)
; 12002=(38)
; 12003=(82)
LDR R0, =0x12000
LDR R1, [R0]
; now, R1=82381046.
```

LDR Rx, =Value   Load Register with 32-bit value

Flags: Unaffected.

Format: LDR Rd, =32_bit_value   ; load Rd with 32-bit value

Function: Loads into destination register a 32-bit immediate value. This is widely used to load 32-bit immediate value into Rd register of the ARM since in the "MOV Rd, #immediate_value" the immediate value cannot be larger than 0xFF.

Example:

```
LDR   R0, =0x1200000     ; R0=0x1200000
LDR   R1, =0x2FFFF        ; R1=0x2FFFF
LDR   R0, =0xFFFFFFFF     ; R0=0xFFFFFFFF
LDR   R1, =200000000      ; R1=200000000
```

LDRB   Load Register Byte

Flags: Unaffected.

Format: LDRB Rd, [Rx]   ; load into Rd a byte from memory location pointed to be Rx

Function: Loads into destination register the contents of a single memory location indicated by Rx.

Example:

```
; Assume the following memory locations with the contents:
; 12000=(46)
; 12001=(10)
; 12002=(38)
; 12003=(82)
LDR   R0, =0x12000
LDRB R1, [R0]
; now, R0=00000046
```

LDRH   Load Register Halfword

Flags: Unaffected.

Format: LDRH Rd, [Rx]   ; load into Rd a 2-byte from memory location pointed to be Rx

Function: Loads into destination register the contents of the two consecutive memory locations (halfword) indicated by Rx.

Example:

```
; Assume the following memory locations with the contents:
```

202

```
; 12000=(46)
; 12001=(10)
; 12002=(38)
; 12003=(82)
LDR  R0, =0x12000
LDRH R1, [R0]
; now, R0=00001046
```

LDRSB   Load Register signed Byte

Flags: Unaffected.

Format: LDRSB Rd, [Rx]

Function: Loads into Rd register a byte from memory location pointed to by Rx and sign-extends the byte to 32-bit word. That means the sign (D7) of the byte is copied to all the upper 24 bits of the Rd register.

Example 1:
```
; Assume the following memory locations with the contents:
; 12000=(85)
; 12001=(10)
; 12002=(38)
; 12003=(82)
LDR  R0, =0x12000
LDRB R1, [R0]    ; now  R1=FFFFFF85 because MSB of 85 is 1
```

Example 2:
```
; Assume the following memory locations with the contents:
; 12000=(15)
; 12001=(20)
; 12002=(3F)
; 12003=(82)
LDR  R0, =0x12000
LDRB R1, [R0]    ; now, R1=00000015 because MSB of 15 is 0
```

LDRSH   Load Register Signed Halfword

Flags: Unaffected.

Format: LDRSH Rd, [Rx]

Function: Loads into Rd register a half-word (2-byte) from memory location pointed to by Rx and sign-extends it to 32-bit word. That means the sign (D15) of the 16-bit operand is copied to all the upper 16 bits of the Rd register.

Example 1:
```
; Assume the following memory locations with the contents:
; 12000=(46)
; 12001=(F3)
; 12002=(38)
; 12003=(82)
LDR  R0, =0x12000
LDRB R1, [R0]    ; now, R0=FFFFF346 because MSB of F3 is 1
```

Example 2:
```
; Assume the following memory locations with the contents:
; 12000=(4F)
; 12001=(23)
; 12002=(18)
; 12003=(B2)
LDR  R0, =0x12000
LDRB R1, [R0]    ; now, R1=0000234F because MSB of 23 is 0
```

LDRT   Load Register with Translation
Flags: Unaffected

Format: LDRT Rd, [Rx]

Function: Loads into Rd register a byte from memory location pointed to by Rx and zero-extends the byte to 32-bit word. That means a zero is copied to all the upper 24 bits of the Rd register. Used for unprivileged memory access.

Example:
```
; Assume the following memory locations with the contents:
; 12000=(46)
; 12001=(10)
; 12002=(38)
; 12003=(82)
LDR  R0, =0x12000
LDRB R1, [R0]    ; now, R1=00000046
```

LSL   Logical Shift Left
Flags: Unaffected.

Format: LSL Rd, Rm, Rn

Function: As each bit of Rm register is shifted left, the MSB is removed and the empty bits are filled with zeros. The number of bits to be shifted left is given by Rn and the result is placed in Rd register. The LSL does not update the flags.

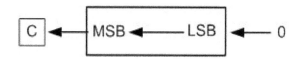

Example 1:
```
LDR  R2, =0x00000010
LSL  R0, R2, #8  ; R0=R2 is shifted left 8 times
         ; now, R0= 0x00001000, flags not changed
```

Example 2:
```
LDR  R0, =0x00000018
MOV  R1, #12
LSL  R2, R0, R1  ; R2=R0 is shifted left R1 number of times
         ; now, R2= 0x000018000, flags not changed
```

Example 3:
```
LDR   R0,  =0x0000FF18
MOV   R1,  #16
LSL   R2,  R0, R1  ; R2=R0 is shifted left R1 number of times
          ; now, R2= 0xFF180000, flags not changed
```
The logical shift left used for unsigned number shifting. LSL essentially multiplies Rm by a power of 2 for each bit shift.

LSR   Logical Shift Right

Flags: Unaffected.

Format: LSR Rd, Rm, Rn

Function: As each bit of Rm register is shifted right, the LSB is removed and the empty bits are filled with zeros. The number of bits to be shifted left is given by Rn and the result is placed in Rd register. The LSR does not update the flags.

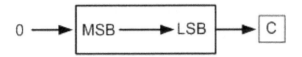

Example 1:
```
LDR   R2,  =0x00001000
LSR   R0,  R2, #8  ; R0=R2 is shifted right 8 times
          ; now, R0= 0x00000010, C=0
```

Example 2:
```
LDR   R0,  =0x000018000
MOV   R1,  #12
LSR   R2,  R0, R1  ; R2=R0 is shifted right R1 number of times
          ; now, R2= 0x00000018, C=0
```

Example 3:
```
LDR   R0,  =0x7F180000
MOV   R1,  #16
LSR   R2,  R0, R1  ; R2=R0 is shifted right R1 number of times
          ; now, R2=0x00007F18, C=0
```
The logical shift right used for shifting unsigned numbers. LSR essentially divides Rm by a power of 2 for each bit shift.

MCR   Move to Coprocessor from ARM Register
See ARM Manual.

MLA   Multiply Accumulate
Flags: Unaffected

Format: MLA Rd, Rs1, Rs2, Rs3 ; Rd= (Rs1 × Rs2) + Rs3

Function: Multiplies an unsigned word held by Rs1 by a unsigned word in Rs2 and the result is added to Rs3 and placed in Rd.

Example:
```
MOV   R0, #0x20   ; R0=0x20
MOV   R1, #0x50   ; R1=0x50
MOV   R2, #0x10   ; R2=0x10
MLA   R4, R0, R1, R2     ; now R4= (0x20 × 0x50)+10= 0xA10
```

MLS   Multiply and Subtract
Flags: Unaffected

Format: MLS Rd, Rm, Rs, Rn ; Rd= Rn -(Rs × Rm)

Function: Multiplies an unsigned word held by Rm by an unsigned word in Rs and the result is subtracted from Rn and placed in Rd.

Example:
```
MOV   R0, #0x20   ; R0=0x20
MOV   R1, #0x50   ; R1=0x50
LDR   R2, =0x1000 ; R2=0x1000
MLS   R4, R0, R1, R2     ; now R4= 0x1000-(0x20×0x50)=0x600
```

MOV   Move   (ARM7)
Flags: Unaffected.

Format: MOV Rd, #imm_value   ; Rd=imm_Value < 0x200

Function: Load the Rd register with an immediate value. The immediate value cannot be larger than 0xFF (0–255). After the execution the flags are not updated. The MOVS instruction updates the flags.

Example 1:
```
MOV   R0, #0x25   ; R0=0x25
MOV   R1, #0x5F   ; R1=0x5F
```
        To load the ARM register with value larger than 0xFF we must use the "LDR Rd, = 32_bit_data." For example, we can use LDR R2, =0xFFFFFFFF.

Example 2:
```
        LDR   R0, =0x2000000          ; R0=0x2000000
```

MOVT   Move Top
Flags: Unaffected.

Format: MOVT Rd, #imm_value ; imm_value < 0x10000

Function: Loads the upper 16-bit of Rd register with an immediate value. The immediate value cannot be larger than 0xFFFF (0–65535). The lower 16-bit of the Rd register remains unchanged.

Example:
```
LDR   R0, =0x25579934     ; R0=0x25579934
MOVT R0, #0xAAAA          ; R0=0xAAAA9934
```

MOVW   Move 16-bit constant

Flags: Unaffected.

Format: MOVW Rd, #imm_value   ; imm_value < 0x10000

Function: Load the Rd register with an immediate value. The immediate value cannot be larger than 0xFFFF (0–65535).

Example:
```
MOVW R1, #0x5555 ; R1=0x5555
```
To load the ARM register with value larger than 0xFFFF we must use the "LDR Rd, = 32_bit_data." For example, we can use LDR R2, =0xFFFFFFFF.

MRC   Move to ARM Register from Coprocessor
See ARM manual

MRS   Move to general Register from Special register

Flags: Unaffected.

Format: MRS Rd, special_reg   ; copy special_reg to Rd

Function: Copies the contents of a special function register to a general-purpose register. This instruction along with the MSR is widely used to modify the special function registers such as CONTROL, PRIMASK, and ISPR. This is the only way we can access the special function registers.

Example:
```
MRS  R1, CONTROL ; R1=CONTROL
AND  R1, #0x00   ; mask the lower 8 bits
MSR  CONTROL, R1
```

MSR   Move to Special register from general Register

Flags: Unaffected.

Format: MSR special_reg, Rn   ; copy special_reg to Rn

Function: Copies the contents of a general-purpose register to special function register. This instruction along with the MRS is widely used to modify the contents of special function registers such as CONTROL, PRIMASK, and ISPR. This is the only way we can access the special function registers.

Example:
```
MRS  R1, CONTROL ; R1=CONTROL
AND  R1, #0x00   ; mask the lower 8 bits
MSR  CONTROL, R1 ; mask the lower 8 bits of CONTROL reg.
```

MUL   Unsigned Multiplication

Flags: Affected: N, Z, Unaffected: C, V

Format: MUL Rd, Rn, Rm   ; Rd = Rn × Rm

Function: Multiplies a word in register Rn by a word in register Rm and places the result in Rd.

Example 1:
```
MOV   R0, #100    ; R0=100
MOV   R1, #200    ; R1=200
MUL   R3, R0, R1  ; R3 = R0 x R1 = 100 x 200 =20000
```

Example 2:
```
LDR   R0, =10000   ; R0=10000
LDR   R1, =20000   ; R1=20000
MUL   R3, R0, R1   ; R3 = R0 x R1= 10000 x 20000 = 200000000
```

MVN   Move Negative

Flags: Unaffected.

Format: MVN Rd, Op2   ; Rd = 1's comp. of Op2

Function: Places in Rd the negation (the 1's complement) of Op2. Each bit of Op2 is inverted (logical NOT) and placed in Rd while flags remain unchanged.

Example 1:
```
MOV   R0, #0xAA   ; R0=0xAA
MVN   R2, R0   ; now, R2=0xFFFFFF55
```

Example 2:
```
LDR   R0, =0xAAAAAAAA   ; R0=0xAAAAAAAA
MVN   R1, R0      ; R1=0x55555555
```

Example 3:
```
MVN   R0, #0x0F   ; R0=0xFFFFFFF0
```

Example 4:
```
MVN   R2, #0x0    ; R0=0xFFFFFFFF widely used to load Rx with all 1s
```

NOP   No Operation

Flags: Unaffected.

Format: NOP

Function: Performs no operation. Sometimes used for timing delays to waste clock cycles. Updates PC (program counter) to point to next instruction following NOP. In some ARM CPUs, the pipeline removes the NOP before it reaches the execution stage.

ORN   Logical OR Not

Flags: Unaffected.

Format: ORN Rd, Rn, Op2   ; Rd = Rn ORed with 1's comp of Op2

Function: Performs the OR operation on the bits of Rn with the complement of the bits in Op2. The ORN will not update the flags. To update the flags, we must use ORNS.

Inputs		Output
A	B	A OR (NOT B)
0	0	1
0	1	0
1	0	1
1	1	1

Example 1:
```
LDR   R1, =0xFFFFFF00    ; R1=0xFFFFFF00
LDR   R2, =0x99999999    ; R2=0x9999999
ORN   R3, R2, R1         ; now R3=0x999999FF
```

Example 2:
```
MOV   R1, #0             ; R1=0
LDR   R0, =0xFFFFFFFF         ; R0=0xFFFFFFFF
ORN   R2, R1, R0         ; now, R2=0x0
```

ORR   Logical OR

Flags: Unaffected

Format: ORR Rd, Rn, Op2   ; Rd= Rn ORed Op2

Function: Performs logical OR on the bits of Rn and Op2, and places the result in Rd. Often used to turn a bit on. ORR will not update the flags.

Example 1:
```
MOV  R0, #0xAA    ; R0=0xAA
ORR  R2, R0, #0x55       ; now, R2=0xFF
```

Example 2:
```
LDR   R0, =0x00010203    ; R0=00010203
LDR   R1, =0x30303030
ORR   R2, R0, R1         ; R2=0x30313233
```

Example 3:
```
LDR   R0, =0x55555555    ; R0=0x55555555
LDR   R1, =0xAAAAAAAA    ; R0=0xAAAAAAAA
ORR   R2, R1, R0         ; R1=0xFFFFFFFF
```

POP   POP register from Stack

Flags: Unaffected.

Format: POP {reg_list}   ; reg_reg = words off top of stack

Function: Copies the words pointed to by the stack pointer to the registers indicated by the reg_list and increments the SP by 4, 8, 12, 16, ... depending on the number of registers in the reg_list.

Example:
```
POP   {R1}      ; POP the top word of stack to R1
POP   {R1, R4, R7}       ; POP the top 3 words of stack to R1, R4, R7
POP   {R2-R6}       ; POP the top 5 words of stack to R2-R6
```

```
    POP   {R0, R5}    ; POP the top 2 words of stack to R0 and R5
    POP   {R0-R7}     ; POP the top 8 words of stack to R0-R7
```
The POP instruction is synonyms for LDMIA.

PUSH   PUSH register onto stack
Flags: Unaffected.

Format: PUSH {reg_list}   ; PUSH reg_list onto stack

Function: Copies the contents of registers stated in reg_list onto the stack and decrements SP by 4, 8, 12, 16, ... depending on the number of registers in reg_list.

```
Example:
    PUSH {R1}      ; PUSH the R1 onto top of stack
    PUSH {R1, R4, R7}       ; PUSH R1, R4, R7 onto top of stack
    PUSH {R2-R6}    ; PUSH the R2, R3, R4, R5, R6 onto top of stack
    PUSH {R0, R5}   ; PUSH the R0 and R5 onto top of stack
    PUSH {R0-R7}    ; PUSH the R0 through R7 onto top of stack
```
The PUSH instruction is synonyms for STMDB.

RBIT   Reverse Bits
Flags: Unaffected.

Format: RBIT Rd, Rn   ; Reverse the bit order of Rn and place in Rd

Function: Reverses the bit position order of the 32-bit value in Rn register and place the result in Rd.

```
Example:
    MOV  R1, #0x5F
    RBIT R2, R1      ; now, R2=0xF5000000
```

REV   Reverse byte order in a word
Flags: Unaffected

Format: REV Rd, Rn   ; Reverse the byte of Rn and place it in Rd

Function: Reverses the byte position order of the 32-bit value in Rn register and places the result in Rd. This can be used to convert from little endian to big endian or from big endian to little endian.

```
Example:
    LDR  R1, =0x12345678
    REV  R2, R1     ; now, R2=0x78564312
```

RV16   Reverse byte order in 16-bit
Flags: Unaffected

Format: REV16 Rd, Rn   ; Reverse the bits if Rn and place it in Rd

Function: Reverses the 16-bit position order of the 32-bit value in Rn register and places the result in Rd. This can be used to convert 16-bit little endian to big endian or from 16-bit big endian to little endian.

Example:
```
LDR   R1, =0x559922FF
RV16  R2, R1      ; now, R2=0x22FF5599
```

REVSH Reverse byte order in bottom halfword and sign extend
Flags: Unaffected

Format: REVSH Rd, Rn ; Rd=Reverse the byte and sign extend Rn

Function: Reverses the 16-bit position order of Rn register and after sign extending to 32-bit it is placed in Rd. This can be used to convert a signed 16-bit little endian to 32-bit signed big endian or from signed 16-bit big endian to 32-bit signed little endian.

Example:
```
LDR    R1, =0x559922FF
REVSH R2, R1               ; now, R2=0x22FF5599
```

ROR   Rotate Right
Flags: Unaffected.

Format: ROR Rd, Rm, Rn ; Rd=rotate Rm right Rn bit positions

Function: As each bit of Rm register shifts from left to right, they exit from the right end (LSB) and enter from left end (MSB). The number of bits to be rotated right is given by Rn and the result is placed in Rd register. The ROR does not update the flags.

Example 1:
```
LDR   R2, =0x00000010
ROR   R0, R2, #8  ; R0=R2 is rotated right 8 times
        ; now, R0 = 0x10000000, C=0
```

Example 2:
```
LDR   R0, =0x00000018
MOV   R1, #12
ROR   R2, R0, R1  ; R2=R0 is rotated right R1 number of times
        ; now, R2 = 0x01800000, C=0
```

Example 3:
```
LDR   R0, =0x0000FF18
MOV   R1, #16
ROR   R2, R0, R1  ; R2=R0 is rotated right R1 number of times
```

```
                 ; Now, R2 = 0xFF180000, C=0
```

RRX   Rotate Right with extend

Flags: Unaffected.

Format: RRX Rd, Rm   ; Rd=rotate Rm right 1-bit position

Function: Each bit of Rm register is shifted from left to right one bit. The RRX does not update the flags.

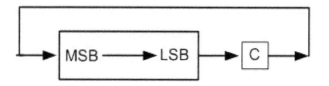

Example:
```
    LDR   R2, =0x00000002
    RRX   R0, R2  ; R0=R2 is shifted right one bit
           ; now, R0=0x00000001
```

RSB   Reverse Subtract

Flags: Unaffected

Format: RSB Rd, Rn, Op2   ; Rd = Op2 - Rn

Function: Subtracts the Rn from the Op2 and puts the result in the Rd. The RSB has no effect on flags. The steps for subtraction performed by the internal hardware of the CPU are as follows:

1. Takes the 2's complement of the Rn
2. Adds this to the Op2
3. Places the result in Rd

   The Op2 and Rn operands remain unchanged by this instruction.

Example:
```
    LDR   R0, =0x55555555    ; R0=0x55555555
    LDR   R1, =0x99999999    ; R1=0x99999999
    RSB   R2, R0, R1  ; R2=R1-R0
     ; For "RSB R2, R0, R1" we have:
     ; R2=R1-R0=0x99999999 - 0x55555555 =
     ; R2=0x99999999 + 2's comp of 0x55555555
     ; R2=0x99999999 + 0xAAAAAAAB = 0x44444444
     ;   0x99999999
     ; - 0x55555555
     ;   ----------------
     ;   0x44444444
```

SBC   Subtract with Carry (Borrow)

Flags: Unaffected

Format: SBC Rd, Rn, Op2   ; Rd = Rn − Op2 − (1− C)

Function: Subtracts the Op2 operand from the Rn, placing the result in Rd. If C = 0, it subtracts 1 from the result; otherwise, it operates like SUB. The SBC has no effect on flags. This is used widely for multiword (64-bit) subtraction.

Example:
```
LDR  R0, =0x55555555   ; R0=0x55555555
LDR  R1, =0x99999999   ; R1=0x99999999
SUBS R2, R0, R1  ; R2=R0 - R1
MOV  R3, #0x09   ; R3=0x09
SBC  R4, R3,#03  ; R4=R3 - 0x3
     ; For SUBS we have:
     ; R2=R1 - R0 = 0x55555555 - 0x99999999 =
     ; R2=0x55555555 + 2's comp of 0x99999999
     ; R2=0x55555555 + 0x66666667 = 0xBBBBBBBC   C=0
     ; For SBC we have:
     ; R4=R3-0x3=0x09 - 0x3 -(1 - C) = 9 - 3 - 1
     ; R4= 0x9 +2'comp. of -4 = 0x9 + 0xFFFFFFFC = 0x05
     ;    0x0000000955555555
     ; - 0x0000000399999999
```

SBFX   Sign Bit Field extract
Flags: Unaffected

Format: SBFX Rd, Rn, #LSB, #Width

Function: Extracts the bit field from the Rn register and then after sign extending it is placed in Rd. The #LSB indicates which bit and #Width indicates how many bits.

Example 1:
```
LDR  R0, =0x00000543   ; R0=0x00000543
SBFX R2, R0, #8, #4    ; now, R2=0x00000005
```

Example 2:
```
LDR  R0, =0x00000C43   ; R0=0x00000C43
SBFX  R2, R0, #4, #8   ; now, R2=0xFFFFFFC4
```

SDIV   Signed Divide
Flags: Unaffected

Format: SDIV Rd, Rn, Rm   ; Rd= Rn/Rm

Function: Divides a signed integer word in Rn by another signed integer word in Rm. The quotient result is placed in Rd. If value in Rn register is not divisible by the value in Rm register, the result is rounded to zero and placed in Rd. Divide by zero causes interrupt type 3.

Example:
```
LDR  R0, =-20000 ; R0=-20000
LDR  R1, =-1000  ; R1=-1000
SDIV R2, R0, R1  ; now, R2 = -2000/-1000= 2
```

SEV   Send Event

Flags: Affected.

Format: SEV

Function: Sends signal to all the processors in the multiprocessors system. See the ARM Cortex manual.

SMLAL   Signed Multiply Accumulate Long

Flags: Unaffected

Format: SMLAL Rdlo, Rdhi, Rn, Rm ; Rdhi:Rdlo=(Rm × Rn) + (Rdhi:Rdlo)

Function: Multiplies signed words in Rn and Rm register, adds the 64-bit result to Rdhi:Rdlo register, and saves the final result in Rdhi:Rdlo. The Rdlo (low) and Rdhi(high) are the lower word and higher word of a 64-bit value.

Example 1:

```
LDR   R0, =0
LDR   R1, =0x23
LDR   R2, =-5000
LDR   R3, =-4000
SMLAL  R0, R1, R2, R3  ; now, R3:R2= (R3:R2)+ (R1 × R0)
        ; = 0x2300000000 + (-5000 × -4000)
        ; = 0x2300000000 + 20000000
        ; = 0x23000000 + 0x1312D00 = 0x2301312D00
        ; => R0 = 0x1312D00 and R1 = 0x23
```

SMULL   Signed Multiply Long

Flags: Unaffected

Format: SMULL Rdlo, Rdhi, Rn, Rm ; Rdhi:Rdlo = Rm × Rn

Function: Multiplies signed words in Rn and Rm register, and saves the result in Rdhi:Rdlo. The Rdl (low) and Rdh(high) are the lower word and higher word of a 64-bit value.

Example:

```
LDR   R0, =-20000 ; R0=-20000 (signed 2's comp)
LDR   R1, =-1000000      ; R0=-100000 (signed 2's comp)
SMLAL R2, R3, R0, R1     ; now, R3:R2= R1 × R0 = -20000 × -1000000 =
        ; 20000000000 =0x4A817C800 => R3 = 0x4 and
        ; R2 = 0xA817C800
```

SSAT   Sign Saturate

Flags: Unaffected.

Format: SSAT Rd, #n, Rm, shift#

Function: Used for saturation operation. See ARM Cortex manual.

214

STM   Store Multiple

Flags: Unaffected.

Format: STM Rn, {Rx, Ry, ...}

Function: Stores registers Rx, Ry, ... into consecutive memory locations. The starting address of memory location is given by Rn register. The source registers are separated by comma and placed in braces. In the ARM Cortex, the default stack is descending meaning that as information are pushed onto stack the stack pointer is decremented. This IA (Increment the address After each access) is the default. This instruction is widely used for Pushing (storing) multiple registers into ascending stack.

Example:
```
LDR   R7, =0x12000
LDR   R0, =0x82381046    ; R0=0x82381046
LDR   R2, =0x15585056    ; R2=0x15585056
LDR   R4, =0x39686063    ; R4=0x39686063
STM   R7, {R0, R2, R4}            ; now, R2=0x15585056, ..
; The contents of registers R0, R2, and R4 are stored into
; consecutive memory locations starting at an address given by R7.
; The R0 contents are stored into memory locations 0x12000-0x12003,
; the R2 contents are stored into memory locations 0x12004 through
; 0x12007, and so on. This is shown below.
; 12000=(46)
; 12001=(10)
; 12002=(38)
; 12003=(82)
; 12004=(56)
; 12005=(50)
; 12006=(58)
; 12007=(15)
; 12008=(63)
; 12009=(60)
; 1200A=(68)
; 1200B=(39)
```

STMDB Store Multiple register and Decrement Before

Flags: Unaffected.

Format: STMDB Rn, {Rx, Ry, ...}

Function: Stores registers Rx, Ry, ... into consecutive memory locations. The starting address of memory location is given by Rn register. The source registers are separated by comma and placed in braces. In the ARM Cortex, the default stack is descending meaning that as information are pushed onto stack the stack pointer is decremented. Since IA (Increment the address After each access) is the default we need to use DB (Decrement the address Before each access) is to overwrite the default. This instruction is widely used for Pushing (storing) multiple registers into Descending stack.

Example:
```
LDR   R7, =0x12000
LDR   R0, =0x39686063    ; R0=0x39686063
LDR   R2, =0x15585056    ; R2=0x15585056
```

```
LDR  R4, =0x82381046    ; R4=0x82381046
STMDB R7, {R0, R2, R4}
; The contents of registers R0, R2, and R4 are stored into
; consecutive memory locations starting at an address given by R7.
; The R0 contents are stored into memory locations 0x11FFF-0x11FFC,
; the R2 contents are stored into memory locations 0x11FFB
; through 0x11FF8, and so on. This is shown below.
; 11FF4=(46)
; 11FF5=(10)
; 11FF6=(38)
; 11FF7=(82)
; 11FF8=(56)
; 11FF9=(50)
; 11FFA=(58)
; 11FFB=(15)
; 11FFC=(63)
; 11FFD=(60)
; 11FFE=(68)
; 11FFF=(39)
```

STMEA Store Multiple register Empty Ascending

Flags: Unaffected.

Format: STMEA Rn, {Rx, Ry, ...}

Function: This is same as STM.

STMIA Store Multiple register Empty Ascending

Flags: Unaffected.

Format: STMIA Rn, {Rx, Ry, ...}

Function: This is same as STM.

STMFD   Store Multiple register Full Descending

Flags: Unaffected.

Format: STMFD Rn, {Rx, Ry, ...}

Function: This is another name for STMDB. The FD is for pushing onto Full Descending stacks

STR   Store Register

Flags: Unaffected.

Format: STR Rd, [Rx]   ; Store Rd into memory location pointed to be Rx

Function: Stores Rd register into four consecutive memory locations. The [Rx] points to starting address of memory location. This is widely used to store 32-bit register into memory locations.

Example:
```
LDR  R1, =0x82381046    ; R1=0x82381046
LDR  R0, =0x12000       ; R0=0x12000
```

216

```
      STR   R1, [R0]                ; now,
                     ; 12000=(46)
                     ; 12001=(10)
                     ; 12002=(38)
                     ; 12003=(82)
```

STRB   Store Register Byte

Flags: Unaffected.

Format: STRB Rd, [Rn]

Function: Stores the lowest byte of the Rd register into a single memory location indicated by Rn.

Example:
```
   LDR   R1, =0x82381046    ; R1=0x82381046
   LDR   R0, =0x12000              ; R0=0x12000
   STRB R1, [R0]                   ; now, 12000=(46)
```

STRD   Store Register Double (two words)

Flags: Unaffected.

Format: STRD Rd, [Rn]

Function: Stores two registers of Rd and Rd+1 into 8 consecutive memory locations indicated by Rn. Rd can be R0, R2, R4, R6, R8, R10, or R12.

Example:
```
   LDR   R2, =0x12000
   LDR   R0, =0x82381046    ; R0=0x82381046
   LDR   R1, =0x15585056    ; R1=0x15585056
   STRD R0, R1, [R2] ; store R0 and R1 into memory locations starting
           ; at an address given by R2. Now, we have:
   ; 12000=(46)
   ; 12001=(10)
   ; 12002=(38)
   ; 12003=(82)
   ; 12004=(56)
   ; 12005=(50)
   ; 12006=(58)
   ; 12007=(15)
```

STRH   Store Register Halfword

Flags: Unaffected.

Format: STRH Rd, [Rn]

Function: Stores the lower 2 bytes of the Rd register into two consecutive memory locations indicated by Rn.

Example:
```
   LDR   R1, =0x82381046    ; R1=0x82381046
   LDR   R0, =0x12000       ; R0=0x12000
```

217

```
   STRB  R1, [R0]                 ; now, 12000=(46), and  12001=(10)
```

STRT   Store Register
Flags: Unaffected

Format: STRT Rx, [Rn]

Function: Stores Rx register into memory location pointed to by Rx. This is the same as STR but is used for unprivileged memory access. See ARM Cortex manual.

Example:
```
   LDR  R1, =0x82381046    ; R1=0x82381046
   LDR  R0, =0x12000       ; R0=0x12000
   STRT R1, [R0]
            ; now, 12000=(0x82381046)
```

SUB   Subtract
Flags: Unaffected

Format: SUB Rd, Rn, Op2   ; Rd = Rn – Op2

Function: Subtracts the Op2 from the Rn and puts the result in the Rd. Has no effect on flags. The steps for subtraction performed by the internal hardware of the CPU are as follows:

1. Takes the 2's complement of the Op2
2. Adds this to the Rn
3. Place the result in the Rd

The Rd and Op2 operands remain unchanged by this instruction.

Example:
```
   LDR  R0, =0x55555555    ; R0=0x55555555
   LDR  R1, =0x99999999    ; R1=0x99999999
   SUB  R2, R1, R0         ; R2=R1-R0
         ; For "SUB R2, R1, R0" we have:
         ; R2=R1-R0=0x99999999 - 0x55555555 =
         ; R2=0x99999999 + 2's comp of 0x55555555
         ; R2=0x99999999 + 0xAAAAAAAB = 0x44444444
         ;    0x99999999
         ; -  0x55555555
         ;    --------------
         ;    0x44444444
```

SVC   supervisor Call (Software Interrupt)
Flags: Unaffected.

Format: SVC #imm_value

Function: It is used by application software to get services from operating systems (OS). This is like the SWI (software interrupt) instruction in ARM7.

218

SXTB   Sign Extend byte
Flags: Unaffected.

Format: SXTB Rd, Rm

Function: Converts a signed byte in Rm into a signed word by copying the sign bit (D7) of Rm into all the bits of Rd. Used widely to convert a signed byte in Rm to a signed word to avoid the overflow problem in signed number arithmetic.

Example:
```
  MOV  R1, #0xFB   ; R1=0xFB which is 2's complement of -5
  SXTB R0, R1  ; now, R0=0xFFFFFFFB
          ; R1= 0000 0000 0000 0000 0000 0000 1111 1011
          ; now R0=0xFFFFFFFB
          ; R0 = 1111 1111 1111 1111 1111 1111 1111 1011
```

SXTH   Sign Extend Halfword
Flags: Unaffected.

Format: SXTH Rd, Rm

Function: Converts a signed halfword in Rm into a signed word by copying the sign bit (D15) of Rm into all the bits of Rd. Used widely to convert a signed halfword (16-bit) in Rm to a signed word.

Example:
```
  ; assume R1=0xFFFB (which is -5)
  SXTH  R0, R1 ; now, R0=0xFFFFFFFB
  ; R1 = 0000 0000 0000 0000 1111 1111 1111 1011
  ; R0 = 1111 1111 1111 1111 1111 1111 1111 1011
```

TBB   Table Branch Byte
Flags: Unaffected.

Format: TBB [Rn, Rm]

Function: Branches forward using table of single byte offset using PC-relative addressing mode. Rn has starting address of the table and Rm is an index into the table. See ARM Cortex M3 manual.

TBH   Table Branch halfword
Flags: Unaffected.

Format: TBH [Rn, Rm, LSL #1]

Function: Branches forward using table of halfword offset using PC-relative addressing mode. Rn has starting address of the table and Rm is an index into the table. The "LSL # 1" shifts left the address once to make it halfword aligned address. See ARM Cortex M3 manual.

TEQ   Test Equivalence
Flags: Affected: N and Z

Format: TEQ Rn, Op2   ; performs Rn Ex-OR Op2

Function: Performs a bitwise logical Ex-OR on Rn and Op2, setting flags but leaving the contents of both Rn and Op2 unchanged. While the EORS instruction changes the contents of the destination and the flag bits, the TEQ instruction changes only the flag bits. This is widely used to see if two registers are equal.

Example 1:
```
    TEQ  R1, R2  ; check to see if R1=R2. If so Z=1. R1 and R2
             ; remain unchanged
```

Example 2:
```
    TEQ  R2, #0x01   ; check to see if D0 of R2 is 1, if so Z=1. R2
             ; remains unchanged
```

Example 3:
```
    TEQ  R1, #0xFF   ; check to see if D7_D0 of R1 are 1s,
             ; if so Z=1. R1 remains unchanged
```

TST   Test

Flags: Affected: N and Z

Format: TST Rn, Op2   ; performs Rn AND Op2

Function: Performs a bitwise logical AND on Rn and Op2, setting flags but leaving the contents of both Rn and Op2 unchanged. While the ANDS instruction changes the contents of the destination and the flag bits, the TST instruction changes only the flag bits. To test whether a bit of Rn is 0 or 1, use the TST instruction with an Op2 constant that has that bit set to 1 and all other bits cleared to 0.

Example 1:
```
    TST  R1, #0x01   ; check to see if D0 of R1 is zero, if so Z=1.
             ; R1 remain unchanged
```

Example 2:
```
    TST  R1, #0xFF   ; check to see if any bits of R1 is zero, if so
             ; Z=1. R1 remain unchanged
```

UBFX   Unsigned Bit field extract
Flags: Unaffected.

Format: UBFX Rd, Rn, #LSB, #Width

Function: Extracts the bit field from the Rn register and then zero extends it and places in Rd. The #LSB indicates from which bit and #Width indicates how many bits.

Example 1:
```
    LDR  R0, =0x00077555   ; R0=0x00077555
    UBFX R2, R0, #8, #4    ; now, R2=0x00000005
```

Example 2:
```
LDR   R0, =0x12345678   ; R0=0x12345678
UBFX R2, R0, #8, #12    ; now, R2=0x00000456
```

UDIV   Unsigned Divide

Flags: Unaffected

Format: UDIV Rd, Rn, Rm   ; Rd= Rn/Rm

Function: Divides an unsigned integer word in Rn by another unsigned integer word in Rm. The quotient result is placed in Rd. If value in Rn register is not divisible by the value in Rm register, the result is rounded to zero and placed in Rd. Divide by zero causes exception interrupt.

Example 1:
```
LDR   R0, =100    ; R0=100
LDR   R1, =2000
UDIV R2, R1, R0  ; now, R2=R1/R0=2000/100=20
```

Example 2:
```
LDR   R0, =20000  ; R0=20000
UDIV R2, R0, #100        ; now, R2=2000/100=20
```

UMLAL Unsigned Multiply with Accumulate

Flags: Unaffected

Format: UMLAL RdLo, RdHi, Rn, Rm ; RdHi:RdLo=(Rm × Rn) + (RdHi:RdLo)

Function: Multiplies unsigned words in Rn and Rm register, adds the 64-bit result to RdHi:RdLo registers, and saves the final result in RdHi:RdLo. The RdLo (low) and RdHi(high) are the unsigned lower word and higher word of the 64-bit value.

Example:
```
LDR   R0, =20000 ; R0=20000
LDR   R1, =1000
LDR   R2, =5000
LDR   R3, =4000
UMLAL R2, R3, R0, R1     ; now, R3:R2= R1 × R0 + R3:R2
```

UMULL Unsigned Multiply Long

Flags: Unaffected

Format: UMULL RdLo, RdHi, Rn, Rm ; RdHi:RdLo = Rm × Rn

Function: Multiplies unsigned words in Rn and Rm registers, and saves the result in RdHi:RdLo. The RdLo (low) and RdHi(high) are the lower word and higher word of a 64-bit value.

Example:
```
LDR   R0, =20000 ; R0=20000
LDR   R1, =10000 ; R1=10000
LDR   R2, =50000 ; R2=50000
```

```
LDR   R3, =40000   ; R3=40000
UMULL R2, R3, R0, R1      ; now, R3:R2= R1 × R0
```

UXBT   Zero extend a byte

Flags: Unaffected

Format: UXBT Rd, Rm

Function: Zero extends a byte in Rm and places in Rd. Used widely to convert a byte in Rm to word for signed number operations.

Example:
```
MOV   R1, #0xFB   ; R1=0xFB
UXBT  R0, R1  ; now, R0=0x00000000FB
      ; R1= 0000 0000 0000 0000 0000 0000 1111 1011
      ; now R0=0x000000FB
      ; R0 = 0000 00000 0000 0000 0000 0000 1111 1011
```

UXTH   Unsigned zero extend halfword

Flags: Unaffected

Format: UXTH Rd, Rm

Function: Zero extends a halfword in Rm and places in Rd. It extracts bits 0-15 and fills bits 16-31 with zeros.

Example:
```
         ; assume R1=0x1234FFFB
UXTH  R0, R1  ; now, R0=0x00000FFFB
```

WFE   Wait for event

Flags: Unaffected

Format: WFE

Function: Used by power management. See ARM Cortex M3 manual.

WFI   Wait for interrupt

Flags: Unaffected

Format: WFI

Function: Suspends execution until one of the following events occurs:

1. a non-masked interrupt occurs and is taken,
2. an interrupt masked by PRIMASK becomes pending,
3. a Debug Entry request.

See ARM Cortex manual.

Appendix B: ARM Assembler Directives

Section B.1: List of ARM Assembler Directives

ALIGN

AREA

DCB directive (define constant byte)

DCD directive (define constant word)

DCW directive (define constant half-word)

ENDP or ENDFUNC

ENTRY

EQU (Equate)

EXPORT or GLOBAL

EXTRN (External)

FUNCTION or PROC

INCLUDE

RN (equate)

Section B.2: Description of ARM Assembler Directives

Directives, or as they are sometimes called, pseudo-ops or pseudo-instructions, are used by the assembler to translate Assembly language programs into machine language. Unlike the microprocessor's instructions, directives do not generate any opcode; therefore, no memory locations are occupied by directives in the final hex version of the assembly program. To summarize, directives give directions to the assembler program to tell it how to generate the machine code; instructions are assembled into machine code to give instructions to the CPU at execution time. The following are descriptions of the some of the most widely used directives for the ARM assembler. They are given in alphabetical order for ease of reference.

ALIGN
Format:

```
ALIGN   n  ; n is any power of 2 from 2⁰ to 2³¹
```

This is used to make sure data is aligned in 32-bit word or 16-bit half word memory address. If n is not specified, ALIGN sets the current location to the next word (four byte) boundary. The following uses ALIGN to make the data word and half word aligned:

```
ALIGN   4    ; The next instruction is word (4 bytes) aligned
ALIGN        ; The next instruction is word (4 bytes) aligned
ALIGN   2    ; The next instruction is half word (2 bytes) aligned
```

Notice that, this ALIGN directive should not be confused with the ALIGN attribute of the AREA directive.

AREA
Format:

```
AREA    sectionname      attribute, attribute, ...
```

The AREA directive tells the assembler to define a new section of memory. The memory can be code or data and can have attributes such as ReadOnly, ReadWrite, and so on. This is widely used to define one or more blocks of indivisible memory for code or data to be used by the linker. Every assembly language program has at least one AREA.

The following line defines a new area named MY_ASM_PROG1 which has CODE and READONLY attributes:

```
AREA MY_ASM_PROG1      CODE, READONLY
```

Among widely used attributes are CODE, DATA, READONLY, READWRITE, COMMON, and ALIGN. The following describes these widely used attributes.

CODE is an attribute given to an area of memory used for executable machine instruction. Since it is used for code section of the program it is by default READONLY memory. In ARM Assembly language we use this area to write our instructions.

DATA is an attribute given to an area of memory used for data and no instruction (machine instructions) can be placed in this area. Since it is used for data section of the program it is by default a READWRITE memory. In ARM Assembly language we use this area to set aside SRAM memory for scratch pad and stack.

READWRITE is an attribute given to an area of memory which can be read from and written to. Since it is READWRITE section of the program it is by default for DATA. In ARM Assembly language we use this area to set aside SRAM memory for scratch pad and stack.

READONLY is an attribute given to an area of memory which can only be read from. Since it is READONLY section of the program it is by default for CODE. In ARM Assembly language we use this area to write our instructions for machine code execution.

COMMON is an attribute given to an area of DATA memory section which can be used commonly by several program codes. We do not initialize the COMMON section of the memory since it is used by compiler exclusively. The compiler initializes the COMMON memory area with all zeros.

ALIGN is another attribute given to an area of memory to indicate how memory should be allocated according to the addresses. When the ALIGN is used for CODE and READONLY it aligned in 4-bytes address boundary by default since the ARM instructions are all 32-bit (4-bytes) word. The ALIGN attribute of AREA has a number after like ALIGN=3 which indicates the information should be placed in memory with addresses of 2^3, that is 0x50000, 0x50008, 0x50010, 0x50020, and so on. This ALIGN attribute of the AREA should not be confused with the ALIGN directive.

DCB directive (define constant byte)
Format:

```
label   DCB   n        ; n between -128 to 256 , byte or string
```
      The DCB directive allocates a byte size memory and initializes the values for reading only.

```
MYVALUE DCB   5              ; MYVALUE = 5
MYMSAGE DCB   "HELLO WORLD"; string
```

DCD directive (define constant word)
Format:

```
label     DCD   n
```
      The DCD directive allocates a word size memory and initializes the values for reading only. The data is 32 bit aligned.

```
MYDATA   DCD   0x200000, 0xF30F5, 5000000, 0xFFFF9CD7
```

DCW directive (define constant half-word)
Format:

```
label     DCB   n
```
      The DCW directive allocates a half-word size memory and initializes the values for reading only.

```
MYDATA   DCW   0x20, 0xF230, 5000, 0x9CD7
```

END
      The END directive tells the assembler that it has reached the end of the program (not the end of the source file). All the text beyond the END directive is ignored by the assembler.

ENDP or ENDFUNC
      The ENDFUNC or ENDP directive informs the assembler that it has reached the end of a function. ENDFUNC and ENDP are the same. See FUNCTION or PROC directives.

ENTRY
      The ENTRY directive shows the entry point of a program to the assembler. Each program must have one entry point. *The newer versions of ARM Linker have alternative methods of specifying the program entry point that overwrite this directive.*

EQU (Equate)
      To assign a fixed value to a name, one uses the EQU directive. The assembler will replace each occurrence of the name with the value assigned to it.

```
DATA1 EQU   0x39      ; the way to define hex value
PORTB EQU   0xF0018000      ; SFR Port B address
SUM1  EQU   0x40000120      ; assign RAM location to SUM1
```
      Unlike data directives such as DCB, DCD, and so on, EQU does not assign any memory storage; therefore, it can be defined at any time and at any place, and can even be used within the code segment.

EXPORT or GLOBAL

To inform the assembler that a name or symbol will be referenced by other modules (in other files), it is marked by the EXPORT or GLOBAL directives. If a module is referencing a name outside itself, that name must be declared as EXTRN (or IMPORT). Correspondingly, in the module where the variable is defined, that variable must be declared as EXPORT or GLOBAL in order to allow it to be referenced by other modules. See the EXTRN directive for examples of the use of both EXTRN and EXPORT.

EXTRN (External)

The EXTRN directive is used to indicate that certain variables and names used in a module are defined by another module. In the absence of the EXTRN directive, the assembler would search for the definition and give an error when it couldn't find it. The format of this directive is:

```
EXTRN    name
```

The following example shows how the EXPORT and EXTERN directives are used:

```
; from the main program:
EXTRN MY_FUNC
...
BL MY_FUNC
...
; ---------------------------------------
; MY_FUNC is located in a different file:
AREA  OUR_EXAMPLE,CODE,READONLY
EXTRN    DATA1
EXPORT    MY_FUNC
MY_FUNC FUNCTION
...
LDR   R1,=DATA1
...
ENDFUNC
```

Notice that the EXTRN directive is used in the main procedure to show that MY_FUNC is defined in another module. This is needed because MY_FUNC is not defined in that module. Correspondingly, MY_FUNC is defined as GLOABAL in the module where it is defined. EXTRN is used in the MY_FUNC module to declare that operand DATA1 has been defined in another module. Correspondingly, DATA1 is declared as GLOBAL in the calling module.

FUNCTION or PROC

Often, a group of Assembly language instructions will be combined into a procedure so that it can be called by another module. The FUNCTION and ENDFUNC directives are used to indicate the beginning and end of the procedure. *Some versions of Keil uVision debugger require the code to be enclosed in PROC/ENDP pair to be single stepped.* See the following example:

```
MY_FUNC FUNCTION
   ...
   ...
   ENDFUNC
```

INCLUDE

When there is a group of macros written and saved in a separate file, the INCLUDE directive can be used to bring them into another file.

RN (Register Naming)

This is used to define a name for a register. The RN directive does not set aside a separate storage for the name, but associates a register with that name. The following code shows how we use RN:

```
VAL1  RN R1 ; define VAL1 as a name for R1
VAL2  RN R2 ; define VAL2 as a name for R2
SUM   RN R3 ; define SUM as a name for R3

   AREA   PROG_2_1, CODE, READONLY
   ENTRY
   MOV   VAL1, #0x25        ; R1 = 0x25
   MOV   VAL2, #0x34        ; R2 = 0x34
   ADD   SUM, VAL1, VAL2    ; add R2 to R1 and place it in R3
HERE  B  HERE
   END
```

Appendix C: Macros

What is a macro and how is it used?

There are applications in Assembly language programming where a group of instructions performs a task that is used repeatedly. For example, you might need to add three registers together. So it does not make sense to rewrite them every time they are needed. Therefore, to reduce the time that it takes to write these codes and reduce the possibility of errors, the concept of macros was born. Macros allow the programmer to write the task (set of codes to perform a specific job) once only and to invoke it whenever it is needed, wherever it is needed.

MACRO definition

Every macro definition must have three parts, as follows:

```
       MACRO
[$label]        macroName parameter1, parameter2, ..., parameterN
  ...   ...
  ...   ...
       MEND
```

The MACRO directive indicates the beginning of the macro definition and the MEND directive signals the end. What goes in between the MACRO and MEND directives is called the body of the macro. The name must be unique and must follow Assembly language naming conventions. The parameters are names, or parameters, or even registers that are mentioned in the body of the macro. After the macro has been written, it can be invoked (or called) by its name, and appropriate values are substituted for parameters. For example, you might want to have an instruction that adds three registers. The following is a macro for the purpose:

```
       MACRO
ADD3VAL     $DEST, $ARG1, $ARG2, $ARG3
ADD         $DEST, $ARG1, $ARG2
ADD         $DEST, $DEST, $ARG3
       MEND
```

The above code is the macro definition. Note that parameters $DEST, $ARG1, $ARG2, and $ARG3 are mentioned in the body of the macro. To distinguish parameters, they must start with $. In the following example, the macro is invoked by its name with the user's actual data:

```
AREA OURCODE, READONLY, CODE
MOV    R1, #5
MOV    R2, #2
ADD3VAL     R0, R1, R2, #5
```

The instruction "ADD3VAL R0, R1, R2, #5" invokes the macro.

The assembler expands the macro by providing the following code in the .LST file:

```
3 00000008 E0810002          ADD    R0, R1, R2
4 0000000C E2800005          ADD    R0, R0, #5
```

Default Values for parameters

We can define default values for parameters as shown below:

228

```
    MACRO
ADD3VAL      $DEST, $ARG1=R3, $ARG2, $ARG3=#5
ADD      $DEST, $ARG1, $ARG2
ADD      $DEST, $DEST, $ARG3
MEND
```

To use the default value, we put a '|' instead of the parameter while invoking the macro:

```
ADD3VAL      R0, R1, R2, |
```

The above code uses the default value of $ARG3 which is set to #5.

Using labels in macros

In the discussion of macros so far, examples have been chosen that do not have a label or name in the body of the macro. This is because if a macro is expanded more than once in a program and there is a label in the label field of the body of the macro, the same label would be generated more than once and an assembler error would be generated. To address the problem, we can give a unique label to the macro when we invoke it, as shown below:

```
    MACRO
$lbl    OUR_MACRO
    CMP R1,#5
    BEQ $lbl
    MOV R1, #1
$lbl
    MEND

    AREA    OURCODE, READONLY, CODE
    ENTRY
    MOV R1, #3
label1  OUR_MACRO
    MOV R1, #5
label2  OUR_MACRO
HERE    B    HERE
```

The assembler expands the macro by providing the following code in the .LST file:

```
20 00000000                   AREA OURCODE, READONLY, CODE
21
22 00000000 E3A01003          MOV  R1, #3
23 00000004          label1   OUR_MACRO
 3 00000004 E3510005          CMP  R1, #5
 4 00000008 0A000000          BEQ  label1
 5 0000000C E3A01001          MOV  R1, #1
 6 00000010          label1
24 00000010 E3A01005          MOV  R1, #5
25 00000014          label2   OUR_MACRO
 3 00000014 E3510005          CMP  R1, #5
 4 00000018 0A000000          BEQ label2
 5 0000001C E3A01001          MOV R1, #1
 6 00000020          label2
26 00000020 EAFFFFFE
                    HERE    B    HERE
```

In cases that there is more than one label in a macro the lines can be labeled as shown below:

```
    MACRO
$lbl      OUR_MACRO
```

```
    CMP  R1, #5
    BEQ  $lbl.equal
    MOV  R1, #1
    B $lbl.next
$lbl.equal
    MOV  R1, #2
$lbl.next
    MEND


    AREA  OURCODE, READONLY, CODE

    MOV  R1, #3
label1  OUR_MACRO
    MOV  R1, #5
label2  OUR_MACRO
HERE  B  HERE
```

The assembler expands the macro by providing the following code in the .LST file:

```
13 00000000                      AREA OURCODE, READONLY, CODE
14
15 00000000 E3A01003        MOV R1, #3
16 00000004         label1  OUR_MACRO
 3 00000004 E3510005          CMP R1, #5
 4 00000008 0A000001          BEQ label1equal
 5 0000000C E3A01001          MOV R1, #1
 6 00000010 EA000000          B   label1next
 7 00000014         label1equal
 8 00000014 E3A01002          MOV R1, #2
 9 00000018         label1next
17 00000018 E3A01005        MOV R1, #5
18 0000001C         label2  OUR_MACRO
 3 0000001C E3510005          CMP R1, #5
 4 00000020 0A000001          BEQ label2equal
 5 00000024 E3A01001          MOV R1, #1
 6 00000028 EA000000          B   label2next
 7 0000002C         label2equal
 8 0000002C E3A01002          MOV R1, #2
 9 00000030         label2next
19 00000030 EAFFFFFE
                      HERE    B    HERE
```

Conditional macros

We can pass condition into macros, as well:

```
    MACRO
$lbl  OurMacro$cond
    CMP  R1, #5
    B$cond    $lbl.equal
    MOV  R1, #1
$lbl.equal
    MEND


    AREA  OURCODE, READONLY, CODE

    MOV  R1, #3
label1  OurMacroEQ  ; in the macro check equality
    MOV  R1, #3
```

```
label2  OurMacroLO  ; in the macro check if is lower
HERE    B HERE
```

The assembler expands the macro by providing the following code in the .LST file:

```
10 00000000                    AREA OURCODE, READONLY, CODE
11
12 00000000 E3A01003          MOV   R1, #3
13 00000004          label1   OurMacroEQ
 3 00000004 E3510005          CMP   R1, #5
 4 00000008 0A000000          BEQ   label1equal
 5 0000000C E3A01001          MOV   R1, #1
 6 00000010          label1equal
14 00000010 E3A01003          MOV   R1, #3
15 00000014          label2   OurMacroLO
 3 00000014 E3510005          CMP   R1, #5
 4 00000018 3A000000          BLO   label2equal
 5 0000001C E3A01001          MOV   R1, #1
 6 00000020          label2equal
16 00000020 EAFFFFFE
                       HERE          B     HERE
```

Notice that the first B$cond is substituted with BEQ while the second B$cond is substituted with BLO since the conditions EQ and LO are used respectively.

INCLUDE directive

Assume that there are several macros that are used in every program. Must they be rewritten every time? The answer is no if the concept of the INCLUDE directive is known. The INCLUDE directive allows a programmer to write macros and save them in a file, and later bring them into any file. For example, assuming that some widely used macros were written and then saved under the filename "MYMACRO1.S", the INCLUDE directive can be used to bring this file into any ".asm" file and then the program can call upon any of the macros as many times as needed. In the following example the ADD3VAL macro is defined in the MyMACRO.s file and it is used in the example.asm file.

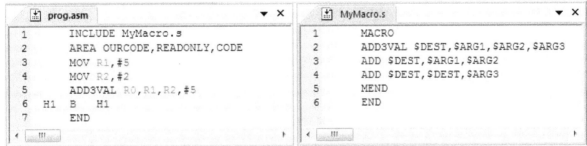

Figure C. 1: Defining a Macro in an Include File

Macros vs. subroutines

Macros and subroutines are useful in writing assembly programs, but each has limitations. Macros increase code size every time they are invoked. For example, if you call a 10-instruction macro 10 times, the code size is increased by 100 instructions; whereas, if you call the same subroutine 10 times, the code size is only that of the subroutine instructions. On the other hand, a function call takes 3 clocks and the return instruction takes 3 clocks to get executed. So, using functions adds around 6 clock cycles. The subroutines might use stack space as well when called, while the macros do not.

231

Appendix D: Passing Arguments into Functions

There are different ways to pass arguments (parameters) to functions. Some of them are:

- through registers
- through memory using references
- using stack

D.1: Passing arguments through registers

In the following program the BIGGER function gets two values through R0 and R1. After comparing R0 and R1, it returns the bigger value through R0.

Program D-1

```
        EXPORT  __main
        AREA    OUR_PROG, CODE, READONLY
__main
        MOV     R0, #5       ; R0 = 5
        MOV     R1, #7       ; R1 = 7
        BL      BIGGER       ; BIGGER(5, 7)
HERE    B       HERE    ; stay here


        ; ========================================
        ; BIGGER returns the bigger value
        ; Parameters:
        ;     R0 and R1: the values to be compared
        ; Returns:
        ;     R0: containing the bigger value
        ; ========================================
BIGGER
        CMP     R0, R1
        BHI     L1           ; if R0 > R1 go to L1
        MOV     R0, R1       ; R0 = R1
L1      BX      LR           ; return
        END
```

This is a fast way of passing arguments to the function.

D.2: Passing through memory using references

We can store the data in memory and pass its address through a register. In the following program the STR_LENGTH function gets the address of a zero-ended string through R0 and returns the length of the string through R1.

Program D-2

```
        EXPORT  __main
        AREA    OUR_PROG, CODE, READONLY
```

```
        __main
             ADR    R0, OUR_STR  ; R0 = addr. of OUR_STR
             BL     STR_LENGTH   ; STR_LENGTH(&OUR_STR)
        HERE B      HERE   ; stay here

        OUR_STR DCB "HELLO!"
             ALIGN 4
             ; ======================================
             ; STR_LENGTH returns the length of string
             ; Parameters:
             ;     R0: address of the string
             ; Returns:
             ;     R0: the length of string
             ; ======================================
        STR_LENGTH
        MOV    R1, R0                ; move string pointer to R1
             MOV    R0, #0            ; use R0 as string length counter
        L_BEGIN
             LDRB   R2, [R1]          ; fetch a character from string
             CMP    R2, #0
             BXEQ   LR             ; return if character is null (end of string)
             ADD    R1, R1, #1    ; point to next character in string
             ADD    R0, R0, #1     ; increment the counter
             B      L_BEGIN

             END
```

D.3: Passing arguments through stack

Passing through the stack is a flexible way of passing arguments. To do so, the arguments are pushed onto the stack just before calling the function and popped off after returning. In Program D-3, the BIGGER function gets two arguments through the stack and returns the bigger value in R0.

Program D-3

```
        EXPORT __main
        AREA   OUR_PROG, CODE, READONLY
__main
        MOV    R0, #5
        PUSH   {R0}         ; push Arg1
        MOV    R0, #7
        PUSH   {R0}         ; push Arg2

        BL     BIGGER       ; BIGGER(5, 7)
        ADD    SP, SP, #8   ; adjust the stack pointer to remove the arguments

HERE    B      HERE         ; stay here

        ; ======================================
```

```
; BIGGER returns the bigger value
; Parameters:
;     values to be compared on stack
; Returns:
;     R0: the bigger value
; ======================================
BIGGER
        LDR    R0, [SP, #8]       ; R0 = arg1
        LDR    R1, [SP, #4]       ; R1 = arg2

        CMP    R0, R1
        MOVLO  R0, R1             ; if R0 < R1 move R1 into R0
L1      BX     LR                 ; return

        END
```

This method of passing arguments is used in x86 computers because they have very few general purpose registers. In ARM CPU, the arguments are passed in the first four registers if there are four or fewer arguments. If there are more than four arguments, the first four are passed in the first four registers and the rest are passed on the stack.

It is important to remember that after returning from the call, the caller must clear the arguments on the stack.

D.4: AAPCS (ARM Application Procedure Call Standard)

The AAPCS provides a standard for implementing the functions and the function calls so that the codes made by different compilers and different programmers can work with each other. Some of the rules of the standard are:

- The arguments must be sent through R0 to R3. Each register cannot hold more than one argument. If there more than four words are needed, the first four words are sent in R0 to R3, the rest are passed on the stack.

- The return value must be returned in R0 (and R1 if the return value is 64-bit).

- The functions can use R4 to R8, R10 and R11 for temporary storage (Thumb code can only use R4 to R7). But their values must be saved upon entering the function and restored before returning. To do so, we push the registers before using them and pop them before returning from the function.

- The stack must be used as Full Descending

In Program D-4 the above rules are considered.

```
      EXPORT  __main
      AREA   OUR_PROG, CODE, READONLY
__main

      MOV   R0, #20
      BL    DELAY ; DELAY(20)
HERE  B     HERE  ; stay here

      ; =======================================
      ; DELAY waits for a while
      ; Parameters:
      ;     R0: the amount of wait
      ; Returns:
      ;     none
      ; =======================================
DELAY
      CMP   R0, #0
      BXEQ  LR            ; return if zero

      PUSH  {R5}          ; save R5

      LDR   R5, =5000000      ; R5 = 5000000
L1    SUBS  R5, R5, #1  ; R5=R5-1
      BNE   L1            ; go to L1 if R5 is not zero

      POP   {R5}          ; restore R5
      BX    LR            ; return

      END
```

More information

For more information about AAPCS see the following article or search "AAPCS" on the Internet:

http://infocenter.arm.com/help/topic/com.arm.doc.ihi0042e/IHI0042E_aapcs.pdf

Dec	Hex	Ch	Dec	Hex	Ch	Dec	Hex	Ch	Dec	Hex	Ch
0	00		32	20		64	40	@	96	60	`
1	01	☺	33	21	!	65	41	A	97	61	a
2	02	☻	34	22	"	66	42	B	98	62	b
3	03	♥	35	23	#	67	43	C	99	63	c
4	04	♦	36	24	$	68	44	D	100	64	d
5	05	♣	37	25	%	69	45	E	101	65	e
6	06	♠	38	26	&	70	46	F	102	66	f
7	07	•	39	27	'	71	47	G	103	67	g
8	08	◘	40	28	(	72	48	H	104	68	h
9	09	○	41	29	)	73	49	I	105	69	i
10	0A	◙	42	2A	*	74	4A	J	106	6A	j
11	0B	♂	43	2B	+	75	4B	K	107	6B	k
12	0C	♀	44	2C	,	76	4C	L	108	6C	l
13	0D	♪	45	2D	−	77	4D	M	109	6D	m
14	0E	♫	46	2E	.	78	4E	N	110	6E	n
15	0F	☼	47	2F	/	79	4F	O	111	6F	o
16	10	►	48	30	0	80	50	P	112	70	p
17	11	◄	49	31	1	81	51	Q	113	71	q
18	12	↕	50	32	2	82	52	R	114	72	r
19	13	‼	51	33	3	83	53	S	115	73	s
20	14	¶	52	34	4	84	54	T	116	74	t
21	15	§	53	35	5	85	55	U	117	75	u
22	16	▬	54	36	6	86	56	V	118	76	v
23	17	↨	55	37	7	87	57	W	119	77	w
24	18	↑	56	38	8	88	58	X	120	78	x
25	19	↓	57	39	9	89	59	Y	121	79	y
26	1A	→	58	3A	:	90	5A	Z	122	7A	z
27	1B	←	59	3B	;	91	5B	[	123	7B	{
28	1C	∟	60	3C	<	92	5C	\	124	7C	|
29	1D	↔	61	3D	=	93	5D	]	125	7D	}
30	1E	▲	62	3E	>	94	5E	^	126	7E	~
31	1F	▼	63	3F	?	95	5F	_	127	7F	⌂

www.ingramcontent.com/pod-product-compliance
Lightning Source LLC
LaVergne TN
LVHW060139070326
832902LV00018B/2853